Learning Game AI Programming with Lua

Leverage the power of Lua programming to create game AI that focuses on motion, animation, and tactics

David Young

[PACKT] open source ✳
PUBLISHING   community experience distilled

BIRMINGHAM - MUMBAI

Learning Game AI Programming with Lua

First published: November 2014

Production reference: 1241114

Published by Packt Publishing Ltd.
Livery Place
35 Livery Street
Birmingham B3 2PB, UK.

ISBN 978-1-78328-133-6

www.packtpub.com

Cover image by Aniket Sawant (aniket_sawant_photography@hotmail.com)

Credits

Author
David Young

Reviewers
Mitch Allen
Stanislav Costiuc
Predrag Končar
Bayard Randel
Ross Rothenstine
Jayant C Varma

Commissioning Editor
Aarthi Kumaraswamy

Acquisition Editor
Nikhil Karkal

Content Development Editor
Mohammed Fahad

Technical Editor
Veronica Fernandes

Copy Editor
Stuti Srivastava

Project Coordinator
Danuta Jones

Proofreaders
Paul Hindle
Julie Jackson
Clyde Jenkins

Indexer
Rekha Nair

Production Coordinator
Kyle Albuquerque

Cover Work
Kyle Albuquerque

About the Author

David Young is a professional software engineer who works within the game industry. He started his career at NASA's Deep Space Network and later moved to NASA's Jet Propulsion Laboratory for the Curiosity rover mission. After leaving NASA, he worked on the platform that powers Riot Game's *League of Legends*. David is pursuing a PhD at the University of Southern California, focusing on graphics research in the field of real-time hair rendering and simulation.

I would like to thank my wife; without her support, this book would not have been possible.

About the Reviewers

Mitch Allen publishes video games for iOS and Android using Corona SDK and Unity3D. You can find links to his apps at `http://mitchallen.com`. You can also follow him on Twitter at `@mitchallen`.

He has worked on web and mobile projects for Lotus, IBM, the New York Times, Caterpillar Inc., Dragon Systems, Dictaphone, Nuance Communications, Yahoo!, Intuit Inc., and a number of startups.

He specializes in software development, automated testing, website performance testing, SDK testing, API testing, and technical writing.

He has served as a technical reviewer for *Corona SDK Mobile Game Development Beginner's Guide*, *Packt Publishing*.

Predrag Končar is a game developer and multimedia researcher. His primary areas of interest are games and combining technology and art. He is also into image and audio processing and interactive design and likes to spend his free time painting. In the last 12 years, he has worked as a technical and creative director for many online projects, published over 40 online games, participated in the production of several iOS apps, and worked with Packt Publishing as a technical reviewer on *Corona SDK Mobile Game Development Beginner's Guide* and *Corona SDK Application Design*. He has a strong background in Unity, C#, ActionScript, Lua, MEL script, Maya, and Python. He is a member of MENSA and ACM SIGGRAPH.

Bayard Randel is a software engineer at Canonical and is working on the Ubuntu Linux infrastructure. He lives in Dunedin, New Zealand. His technical interests include software education with Lua, web development, distributed systems, and functional programming.

Jayant C Varma is an Australian author, developer, trainer, and consultant with a special focus on mobile development and the use of mobile applications in businesses. He is the author of *Learn Lua for iOS Game Development* and is in the process of authoring another book for Packt Publishing on Xcode 6, apart from a few other books with other publishers. He is the principal consultant at OZ Apps, which is a company he founded. It specializes in mobile business solutions and development-related services.

Jayant has been in the IT Industry for quite a while and has seen things change from 8-bit computers and apps on cassette tapes to present-day mobile devices and app stores. He has always been drawn toward new technologies. He has worked in different domains during his career—which have seen him travel to different countries—including as the IT manager for BMW dealerships. He has also helped them set up wireless diagnostics in their workshop and contactless key readers at service receptions, and he has also automated the front office (including sales automation, ordering, prospecting, CRM, and so on in the early 2000s). He has also worked as a lecturer at the James Cook University and a trainer for the Apple University Consortium (AUC) and Australian Computer Society (ACS), among others, actively conducting trainings and workshops. He has created several mobile and desktop applications for clients, which are available on the App Store.

He has been a reviewer on more than half a dozen books for Packt Publishing. He can be contacted via his website at http://www.oz-apps.com.

www.PacktPub.com

Support files, eBooks, discount offers, and more

For support files and downloads related to your book, please visit www.PacktPub.com.

Did you know that Packt offers eBook versions of every book published, with PDF and ePub files available? You can upgrade to the eBook version at www.PacktPub.com and as a print book customer, you are entitled to a discount on the eBook copy. Get in touch with us at service@packtpub.com for more details.

At www.PacktPub.com, you can also read a collection of free technical articles, sign up for a range of free newsletters and receive exclusive discounts and offers on Packt books and eBooks.

https://www2.packtpub.com/books/subscription/packtlib

Do you need instant solutions to your IT questions? PacktLib is Packt's online digital book library. Here, you can search, access, and read Packt's entire library of books.

Why subscribe?

- Fully searchable across every book published by Packt
- Copy and paste, print, and bookmark content
- On demand and accessible via a web browser

Free access for Packt account holders

If you have an account with Packt at www.PacktPub.com, you can use this to access PacktLib today and view 9 entirely free books. Simply use your login credentials for immediate access.

Table of Contents

Preface

Game AI is a combination of decision making and animation playback. Although classic or academic AI is focused solely on finding the right decision to make, game AI is responsible for acting on numerous decisions over time. Treating game AI independent from animation is a classic mistake that this book avoids by integrating animation and locomotion systems immediately into the AI systems. This subtle difference of decision making and execution changes many of the aspects that game AI programmers have to focus on.

The other large issue with game AI is regarding the specific needs and implementation strategies that are genre-specific. In order to prevent a watered-down approach, this book focuses on one specific genre, which is the first- and third-person action genre. Limiting the AI to this decision allows for an in-depth, tutorial-based approach of creating a full AI system. The overall goal of this book is to create an AI sandbox composed of professional level C and C++ open source libraries exposed to an AI system scripted in Lua.

What this book covers

Chapter 1, Getting Started with AI Sandbox, begins with learning the overview of how projects are set up as well as how the Lua script interacts with C++ code. Here, the beginnings of the AI sandbox are built from open source technologies, starting with a framework that integrates Lua, Ogre3D, OpenSteer, and Bullet Physics.

Chapter 2, Creating and Moving Agents, starts off with examples of the lowest layer of AI interaction with the world, local steering, and movement. Here, agent seeking, avoiding, and group movement are introduced into the sandbox through the use of the OpenSteer library.

Chapter 3, Character Animations, continues with the AI sandbox by exposing Ogre3D's animation playback and resource handling of Lua scripts. Low-level structures for controlling animation clips, animation state machines, and layered animations are integrated into the sandbox.

Chapter 4, Mind Body Control, combines animation handling with local steering and agent movement. Two different approaches toward mind and body interactions will be implemented. The first will focus on the latency between agent decisions and actions, while the second approach will focus on the perceived quality of the agent's actions.

Chapter 5, Navigation, builds up from local movement and moves on to long distance movement and planning. Navigation mesh generation provided by the Recast library will be integrated into the AI sandbox in order to allow A* pathfinding provided by the Detour library.

Chapter 6, Decision Making, adds intelligence to the choices the AI agents make. Different data structures and approaches to creating modular and reusable decision logic are covered through Lua scripts. Decision trees, finite state machines, and behavior trees are integrated into the sandbox.

Chapter 7, Knowledge Representation, adds the ability to store long-term and short-term information for individual agents. A centralized approach to storing and propagating agent knowledge about the world is exposed to Lua.

Chapter 8, Perception, exposes the services that are available to agents for them to query information about the world. Approaches toward visual- and communication-based information is integrated into the sandbox.

Chapter 9, Tactics, exposes a high-level spatial knowledge of the environment to the sandbox. Through a grid-based representation of the world, different knowledge sources are combined in order to give you an accurate tactical view of the environment for decision making.

What you need for this book

The AI sandbox solution and project files are built automatically through Premake, which is the utility program. Visual Studio 2008, 2010, 2012, and 2013 were tested for compatibility with each of the included demos. With the large number of dependencies the sandbox builds from the source, the project setup is only supported from Visual Studio.

The open source Lua IDE, which is Decoda, is used to write and debug Lua scripts within the sandbox. While other Lua script editors can be used, the sandbox natively exposes information that allows seamless Lua debugging within Decoda.

Who this book is for

This book is aimed at programmers who are looking to understand all the facets involved with the creation of the game AI. You should be comfortable with C or C++ and the Lua programming language. While no direct C or C++ knowledge is required, being able to fully debug into the sandbox allows for extending the existing functionality. A combination of both functional and object-oriented Lua will be used by the sandbox, and both approaches will be explained. Additional understanding of modern game engines will be useful but is not required.

Conventions

In this book, you will find a number of text styles that distinguish between different kinds of information. Here are some examples of these styles and an explanation of their meaning.

Code words in text, database table names, folder names, filenames, file extensions, pathnames, dummy URLs, user input, and Twitter handles are shown as follows: "The `LuaScriptUtilities` header defines the metatable name of the vector type."

A block of code is set as follows:

```
local function CallCallbacks(callbacks, stateName, looping)
    for index = 1, #callbacks do
        callbacks[index].callback(
            stateName, looping, callbacks[index].data);
    end
end
```

New terms and **important words** are shown in bold. Words that you see on the screen, for example, in menus or dialog boxes, appear in the text like this: "Open the **Settings** menu under the **Project** menu."

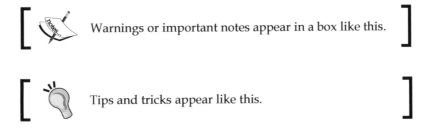

Warnings or important notes appear in a box like this.

Tips and tricks appear like this.

Reader feedback

Feedback from our readers is always welcome. Let us know what you think about this book—what you liked or disliked. Reader feedback is important for us as it helps us develop titles that you will really get the most out of.

To send us general feedback, simply e-mail feedback@packtpub.com, and mention the book's title in the subject of your message.

If there is a topic that you have expertise in and you are interested in either writing or contributing to a book, see our author guide at www.packtpub.com/authors.

Customer support

Now that you are the proud owner of a Packt book, we have a number of things to help you to get the most from your purchase.

Downloading the example code

You can download the example code files from your account at http://www.packtpub.com for all the Packt Publishing books you have purchased. If you purchased this book elsewhere, you can visit http://www.packtpub.com/support and register to have the files e-mailed directly to you.

Downloading the color images of this book

We also provide you with a PDF file that has color images of the screenshots/ diagrams used in this book. The color images will help you better understand the changes in the output. You can download this file from: https://www.packtpub.com/sites/default/files/downloads/1336OS_ColoredImages.pdf.

Errata

Although we have taken every care to ensure the accuracy of our content, mistakes do happen. If you find a mistake in one of our books—maybe a mistake in the text or the code—we would be grateful if you could report this to us. By doing so, you can save other readers from frustration and help us improve subsequent versions of this book. If you find any errata, please report them by visiting `http://www.packtpub.com/submit-errata`, selecting your book, clicking on the **Errata Submission Form** link, and entering the details of your errata. Once your errata are verified, your submission will be accepted and the errata will be uploaded to our website or added to any list of existing errata under the Errata section of that title.

To view the previously submitted errata, go to `https://www.packtpub.com/books/content/support` and enter the name of the book in the search field. The required information will appear under the **Errata** section.

Piracy

Piracy of copyrighted material on the Internet is an ongoing problem across all media. At Packt, we take the protection of our copyright and licenses very seriously. If you come across any illegal copies of our works in any form on the Internet, please provide us with the location address or website name immediately so that we can pursue a remedy.

Please contact us at `copyright@packtpub.com` with a link to the suspected pirated material.

We appreciate your help in protecting our authors and our ability to bring you valuable content.

Questions

If you have a problem with any aspect of this book, you can contact us at `questions@packtpub.com`, and we will do our best to address the problem.

1

Getting Started with AI Sandbox

In this chapter, we will cover the following topics:

- AI sandbox's project layout and compilation
- Using the Lua integrated development environment, Decoda
- Debugging Lua scripts and AI sandbox
- Passing and receiving data from C++ to Lua and vice versa
- C++ functions calling Lua functions
- Lua functions calling C++ functions
- Creating custom data types managed by C++ within Lua
- An overview of AI sandbox C++ classes

Introduction to AI sandbox

AI sandbox is a framework that is designed to do away with the tedious job of application management, resource handling, memory management, and Lua binding, so that you can focus immediately on creating AI in Lua. While the sandbox does the dirty work of a small game engine, none of the internals of the sandbox are hidden. The internal code base is well documented and explained here so that you can expand any additional functionality your AI might require.

The design behind the sandbox is a culmination of open source libraries preassembled in order to rapidly prototype and debug Lua's scripted AIs. While C++ code maintains and manages the data of AI, Lua scripts manage AI's decision-making logic. With a clear separation of data and logic, the logic represented in Lua scripts can be rapidly iterated on without worrying about corrupting or invalidating the current state of AI.

Understanding the sandbox

Before diving head-first into creating AI, this chapter goes over the internals and setup of the sandbox. While the AI scripting will all take place in Lua, it is important to understand how Lua interfaces with the sandbox and what responsibilities remain in C++ compared to Lua.

The project layout

The sandbox is laid out to easily support individual applications while sharing the same media resources between them. A key project, which is `demo_framework`, provides all the common code used throughout the book. The only difference between each individual chapter's C++ code is the setup of which Lua sandbox script to execute. Even though the entire sandbox framework is available from the beginning of the book, each chapter will introduce new functionality within the sandbox incrementally:

```
bin
    x32/debug
    x32/release
    x64/debug
    x64/release
build (generated folders)
    projects
    Learning Game AI Programming.sln
decoda
lib (generated folders)
    x32/debug
    x32/release
    x64/debug
    x64/release
media
    animations
    fonts
    materials
    models
    packs
    particle
    programs
    shaders
    textures
premake
    premake
    SandboxDemos
src
    chapter_1_movement (example)
```

```
        include
        script
        src
    ogre3d (example)
        include
        src
    ...
tools
    decoda
    premake
vs2008.bat
vs2010.bat
vs2012.bat
vs2013.bat
```

Downloading the example code

You can download the example code files for all Packt books you have purchased from your account at http://www.packtpub.com. If you purchased this book elsewhere, you can visit http://www.packtpub.com/support and register to have the files e-mailed directly to you.

Now we'll take a look at what each folder within the sandbox project contains:

- The bin folder will contain all built executables, based on which build configuration is selected in Visual Studio. Both 32-bit and 64-bit versions of the sandbox can be built side by side without the need to rebuild the solution.

While the sandbox can be built as both a 32-bit and 64-bit application, debugging Lua scripts is only supported in Decoda with 32-bit builds.

- The build folder contains Visual Studio's solution file. The build/projects folder contains each individual Visual Studio project along with the solution. It is safe to delete the build folder at any time and regenerate the solution and project files with the vs2008.bat, vs2010.bat, vs2012.bat, or vs2013.bat batch files. Any changes made directly to the Visual Studio solution should be avoided, as regenerating the solution file will remove all the local changes.

- The decoda folder contains the individual Decoda IDE project files that correspond to each chapter demo. These project files are not generated from build scripts.

- The lib folder is an intermediate output folder where static libraries are compiled. It is safe to delete this folder, as Visual Studio will build any missing libraries during the next build of the sandbox.

- The media folder contains all the shared assets used within the chapter demos. Assets used by the sandbox exist as both loose files and ZIP bundles.

- The premake folder contains the build script used to configure the sandbox's solution and project files. Any desired changes to the Visual Studio solution or projects should be made in the Premake script.

> The Premake script will detect any additional C++ or Lua files within the project's folder structure. When adding a new Lua script or C++ files, simply rerun the build scripts to update the Visual Studio solution.

- The src folder contains the source code for each open source library as well as the sandbox itself. Every project within the sandbox solution file will have a corresponding src folder, with separate folders for header files and source files. Chapter demos have an additional script folder that contains every Lua script for that particular chapter.

> Each open source library contains both a VERSION.txt and LICENSE.txt file, which states the version number of the open source library used as well as the license agreement that must be followed by all users.

- The tools folder contains the installer for the Decoda IDE as well as the Premake utility program that is used to create the Visual Studio solution.

The Premake build

Premake is a Lua-based build configuration tool. AI sandbox uses Premake in order to support multiple versions of Visual Studio without the need to maintain build configurations across solutions and build configurations.

Executing the vs2008.bat batch file will create a Visual Studio 2008 solution within the build folder. Correspondingly, the vs2010.bat and vs2012.bat batch files will create Visual Studio 2010 and Visual Studio 2012 solutions of AI sandbox.

Compiling the sandbox with Visual Studio 2008/2010/2012/2013

Building the sandbox requires only one dependency, which is the DirectX SDK. Make sure that your system has the DirectX SDK installed, or download the free SDK from Microsoft at `http://www.microsoft.com/en-us/download/details.aspx?id=6812`.

The sandbox solution file is located at `build/Learning Game AI Programming.sln` once one of the `vs2008.bat`, `vs2010.bat`, `vs2012.bat`, or `vs2013.bat` batch files have been executed. The initial build of the sandbox might take several minutes to build all of the libraries the sandbox uses, and further builds will be much faster.

Open source libraries

Lua 5.1.5 is used by the sandbox instead of the latest Lua 5.2.x library. The latest build of the Decoda IDE's debugger only supports up to 5.1.x of Lua. Newer versions of Lua can be substituted into the sandbox, but Lua's debugging support will no longer function.

At the time of writing this, Ogre3D 1.9.0 is the latest stable build of the Ogre3D graphics library. A minimal configuration of Ogre3D is used by the sandbox, which only requires the minimum library dependencies for image handling, font handling, ZIP compression, and DirectX graphics support.

The included dependencies required by Ogre3D are:

- FreeImage 3.15.4
- FreeType 2.4.12
- libjpeg 8d
- OpenJPEG 1.5.1
- libpng 1.5.13
- LibRaw 0.14.7
- LibTIFF 4.0.3
- OpenEXR 1.5.0
- Imbase 0.9.0
- zlib 1.2.8
- zzip 0.13.62

The sandbox was created with the DirectX SDK Version 9.29.1962, but any later version of DirectX SDK will work as well. Additional open source libraries providing debug graphics, input handling, physics, steering, and pathfinding are detailed as follows:

- **Ogre3D Procedural 0.2**: This is a procedural geometry library that provides easy creation of objects such as spheres, planes, cylinders, and capsules used for debug- and prototyping-level creation within the sandbox.

- **OIS 1.3**: This is a platform-agnostic library that is responsible for all the input handling and input device management used by the sandbox.

- **Bullet Physics 2.81-rev2613**: This is the physics engine library that drives the AI movement and collision detection within the sandbox.

- **OpenSteer revision 190**: This is a local steering library that is used to calculate steering forces of AI agents.

- **Recast 1.4**: This provides the sandbox with runtime navigation mesh generation.

- **Detour 1.4**: This provides A* pathfinding on top of generated navigation meshes.

Open source tools

Premake dev e7a41f90fb80 is a development build of Premake that is based on the Premake development branch. The sandbox's Premake configuration files utilize the latest features that are only present in the development branch of Premake.

Decoda 1.6 build 1034 provides seamless Lua debugging through an inspection of the sandbox's debug symbol files.

Lua IDE – Decoda

Decoda is a professional Lua **integrated development environment (IDE)** that was released as open source by Unknown Worlds Entertainment, makers of Natural Selection 2 (`http://unknownworlds.com/decoda/`).

Decoda takes a unique approach to Lua script debugging, which makes integrating with an application far superior to other Lua debuggers. Instead of using a networked-based approach where an internal Lua virtual machine must be configured to support debugging, Decoda uses the debug symbol files produced by Visual Studio in order to support Lua debugging. The key advantage of this approach is that it supports Lua debugging without requiring any changes to the original application. This key difference in Decoda allows for easy debug support in the sandbox's embedded Lua virtual machines.

Running AI sandbox inside Decoda

Begin by opening this chapter's Decoda project (`decoda/chapter_1_movement.deproj`). Each sandbox Decoda project is already set up to run the correct corresponding sandbox executable. To run the sandbox within Decoda, press *Ctrl + F5*, or click on the **Start Without Debugging** option from the **Debug** menu.

Setting up a new Decoda project

Setting up a new Decoda project only requires a few initial steps to point Decoda to the correct executable and debug symbols.

A new Decoda project can be configured with the following steps:

1. Open the **Settings** menu under the **Project** menu, as shown in the following screenshot:

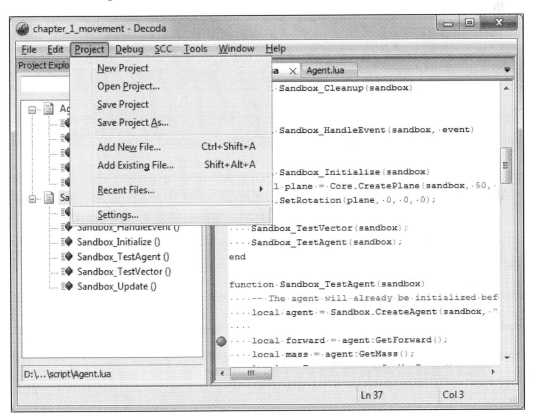

Accessing the Decoda project settings

2. Set the **Command** textbox to point to the new sandbox executable.

3. Set the **Working Directory** and **Symbols Directory** fields to the executable's directory.

 Decoda can only debug 32-bit applications where debug symbols are present. AI sandbox creates debug symbols in both Release and Debug build configurations.

The **Project Settings** screen can be seen as follows:

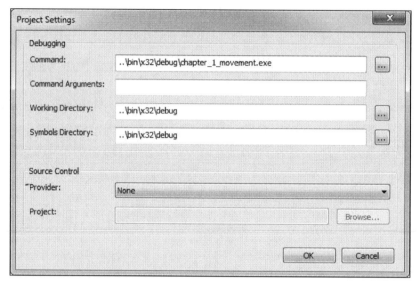

Setting the Decoda debug executable and working directory

Debugging Lua scripts

To begin debugging Lua scripts within the sandbox, press *F5* within Decoda. *F5* will launch the sandbox application and attach Decoda to the running process. Selecting **Break** from the **Debug** menu or setting a breakpoint over a running script will pause the sandbox for debugging.

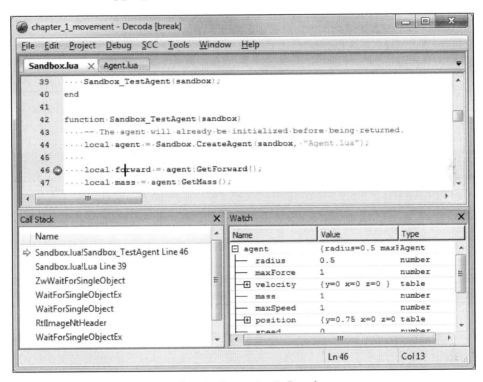

Debugging Lua scripts in Decoda

Decoda Watch window

If you're familiar with the Visual Studio Watch window, the Decoda Watch window is very similar. Type any variable within the Watch window to monitor that variable while debugging. Decoda also allows you to type in any arbitrary Lua statements within the Watch window. The Lua statement will be executed within the current scope of the debugger.

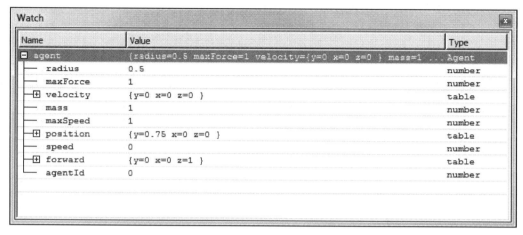

Viewing local Lua variables in the Decoda Watch window

Decoda Call Stack window

The stack window shows you the currently executing Lua call stack. Double-click on any line to jump to the caller. The Watch window will be automatically updated based on the current scope specified by the call stack.

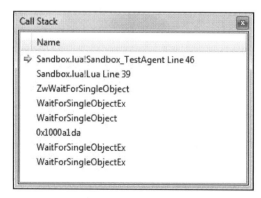

Analyzing the Lua call stack in the Decoda Call Stack window

The Decoda Virtual Machines window

The Virtual Machines window shows you each of the Lua virtual machines the sandbox is running. In this case, there is a separate virtual machine for the sandbox and a separate virtual machine for each of the running agents.

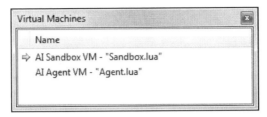

Debugging multiple Lua virtual machines within Decoda

Simultaneous Lua and C++ debugging

To simultaneously debug both the C++ sandbox and any running Lua scripts, there are a few approaches available.

Visual Studio – Attach to Process

If the sandbox was launched from Decoda, you can always attach it to the running process from Visual Studio through the **Debug** menu's **Attach to Process** option.

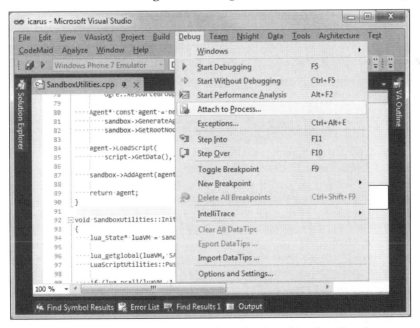

Simultaneously debug the C++ sandbox when launching from Decoda

Decoda – Attach to Process

Decoda can also attach itself to a running process through the **Debug** menu. If the sandbox is run through Visual Studio, you can attach Decoda at any time in the same fashion that Visual Studio attaches it to the sandbox.

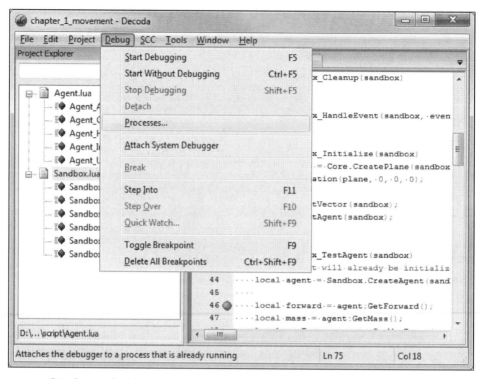

Simultaneously debug Lua scripts when launching the sandbox from Visual Studio

Decoda – Attach System Debugger

To automatically attach both Decoda and Visual Studio when the sandbox launches from Decoda, select the **Attach System Debugger** option from the **Debug** menu. Upon running the application from Decoda, Windows will prompt you to immediately attach a **Just-In-Time (JIT)** debugger.

 If your installed version of Visual Studio doesn't show up in the Just-In-Time debugger as a selectable option, enable JIT debugging for native applications from Visual Studio by navigating to **Tools | Options | Debugging | Just-In-Time**.

The following screenshot shows you the **Debug** option that we are accessing in order

to attach the system debugger:

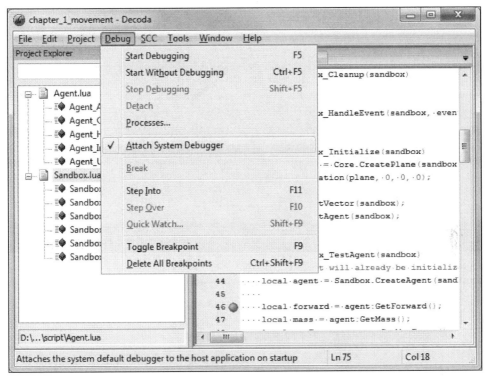

Automatically attach the Decoda debugger when launching the sandbox

Associating Lua scripts from code with Decoda

In order for Decoda to know which Lua file to associate the currently executing Lua script, the `luaL_loadbuffer` Lua API function must pass in the Lua filename as `chunkName` during the loading. The `luaL_loadbuffer` function is an auxiliary Lua helper function provided in `lauxlib.h`:

`lauxlib.h`

```
int luaL_loadbuffer(
    lua_State* luaVM, const char* buffer,
    size_t bufferSize, const char* chunkName);
```

The Lua virtual machine

The Lua virtual machine is represented by `lua_State struct`, which is defined in the `lstate.h` header file. Lua states are self-contained structures without the use for any global data, making them practical for threaded applications:

lstate.h

```
struct lua_State;
```

The sandbox runs multiple Lua virtual machines simultaneously. One main virtual machine is assigned to the sandbox itself, while each spawned agent runs its own separate virtual machine. The use of individual virtual machines comes to the sandbox at the cost of performance and memory but allows for iterating Lua scripts in real time on a per-agent basis.

The Lua stack

As Lua is a weakly typed language that supports functions that can receive an arbitrary amount of parameters as well as return an arbitrary number of return values, interfacing with C++ code is a bit tricky.

To get around the strong typing of C++, Lua uses a **First In First Out (FIFO)** stack to send and receive data from the Lua virtual machine. For example, when C++ wants to call a Lua function, the Lua function as well as the function parameters are pushed onto the stack and are then executed by the virtual machine. Any return values from the function are pushed back to the stack for the calling C++ code to handle.

The same process happens in reverse when the Lua code wants to call the C++ code. First, Lua pushes the C++ function onto the stack, followed by any parameters sent to the function. Once the code has finished executing, any return values are pushed back to the stack for the executing Lua script to handle.

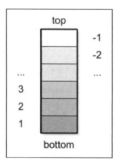

The Lua call stack indexing scheme

When interfacing with Lua, stack values can either be retrieved bottom-up, or top-down. The top element in the stack can be retrieved with an index of -1, while the bottom element of the stack can be retrieved with an index of 1. Additional elements can be retrieved by indexing -2, -3, 2, 3, and so on.

 Lua differs from most programming languages by index values beginning from 1 instead of 0.

Lua primitives

Lua has 8 basic primitives: nil, Boolean, number, string, function, userdata, thread, and table:

- **Nil**: Here, a value corresponds to a null value in C.
- **Boolean**: Here, values are equivalent to their C++ counterparts and represent either true or false.
- **Number**: This internally represent doubles that Lua uses to store integers, longs, floats, and doubles.
- **String**: This represents any sequence of characters.
- **Function**: Lua also considers functions as a primitive, which allows you to assign functions to variables.
- **Userdata**: This a special Lua type that maps a Lua variable to data managed by the C code.
- **Thread**: A thread primitive is used by Lua to implement coroutines.
- **Table**: This is an associative array that maps an index to a Lua primitive. A Lua table can be indexed by any Lua primitive.

Metatables

A metatable in Lua is a table primitive that allows custom functions to override common operations such as addition, subtraction, assignment, and so on. The sandbox uses metatables extensively in order to provide common functionality to the userdata that C++ manages.

To retrieve a metatable within Lua, use the getmetatable function on any object:

```
metatable getmetatable(object);
```

To set a metatable within Lua, use the `setmetatable` function that passes both the object to set and the metatable:

```
nil setmetatable(object, metatable);
```

 As the sandbox heavily uses metatables for userdata, you can always use `getmetatable` on the userdata to see which operations a specific userdata type supports.

Metamethods

A metamethod is a particular entry within a metatable that is called when an overriden operation is being requested by Lua. Typically, all Lua metamethods will begin with two underscores at the beginning of the function's name.

To add a metamethod to a metatable, assign a function to the metatable indexed by the metamethod's name. For example:

```
local metatable = getmetatable(table);
metatable.__add = function(left, right)
    return left.value + right.value;
end
setmetatable(table, metatable);
```

Userdata

Userdata is an arbitrary block of data whose lifetime is managed by Lua's garbage collector. Whenever a code creates userdata to push into Lua, a block of memory managed by Lua is requested from `lua_newuserdata`:

lua.h

```
void* lua_newuserdata(lua_State* luaVM, size_t userdataSize);
```

While the sandbox makes extensive use of userdata, the construction and destruction of the allocated memory is still handled within the sandbox. This allows for Lua scripts to be easily iterated without worrying about Lua's internal memory management. For instance, when an agent is exposed to Lua through userdata, the only memory that Lua manages for the agent is a pointer to the agent. Lua is free to garbage collect the pointer at any time and has no effect on the agent itself.

C/C++ calling Lua functions

The sandbox hooks into the Lua script through three predefined global Lua functions: `Sandbox_Initialize`, `Sandbox_Cleanup`, and `Sandbox_Update`. When the sandbox is first attached to the corresponding Lua script, the `Sandbox_Initialize` function is called. Each update tick of the sandbox will also invoke the `Sandbox_Update` function in the Lua script. When the sandbox is being destroyed or reloaded, the `Sandbox_Cleanup` function will have an opportunity to perform any script-side cleanup.

In order for C++ to call a Lua function, the function must be retrieved from Lua and pushed onto the stack. Function parameters are then pushed on top of the stack, followed by a call to `lua_pcall`, which executes the Lua function. The `lua_pcall` function specifies the number of arguments the Lua function receives, the number of expected return values, and specifies how to handle errors:

lua.h

```
int lua_pcall(
    lua_State* luaVM, int numberOfArguments,
    int numberOfResults, int errorFunction);
```

For example, the `Agent_Initialize` Lua script function is called in the `AgentUtilities` class in the following manner:

Agent.lua

```
function Agent_Initialize(agent)
    ...
end
```

First, the Lua function is retrieved from Lua by name and pushed onto the stack. Next, the agent itself is pushed as the only parameter to the `Agent_Initialize` function. Lastly, `lua_pcall` executes the function and checks whether it succeeded successfully; otherwise, an assertion is raised by the sandbox:

AgentUtilities.cpp

```
void AgentUtilities::Initialize(Agent* const agent)
{
    // Retrieves the lua virtual machine the agent script is
    // running on.    lua_State* luaVM = agent->GetLuaVM();

    lua_getglobal(luaVM, "Agent_Initialize");

    // Agent_Initialize accepts one parameter, an Agent.
```

```
    AgentUtilities::PushAgent(luaVM, agent);

    // Execute the Agent_Initialize function and check for
    // success.
    if (lua_pcall(luaVM, 1, 0, 0) != 0)
    {
        assert(false);
    }
}
```

Lua calling C/C++ functions

Exposing C++ functions to Lua takes place through a process called function binding. Any bound functions exposed to Lua become accessible either as a global function or as a function available through a package. Packages in Lua are similar to namespaces in C++ and are implemented as a global table within Lua.

Function binding

Any function exposed to Lua must fit the lua_CFunction declaration. A lua_CFunction declaration takes in the Lua virtual machine and returns the number of return values pushed onto the Lua stack:

lua.h

```
    typedef int (*lua_CFunction) (lua_State *L);
```

For example, the C++ GetRadius function exposed in the sandbox is declared in the LuaScriptBindings.h header file in the following manner:

LuaScriptBindings.h

```
    int Lua_Script_AgentGetRadius(lua_State* luaVM);
```

The actual function implementation is defined within the LuaScriptBindings.cpp file and contains the code for retrieving and pushing values back to the stack. The GetRadius function expects an agent pointer as the first and only parameter from Lua and returns the radius of the agent. The Lua_Script_AgentGetRadius function first checks the stack for the expected parameter count and then retrieves the userdata off the stack through a helper function within the AgentUtilities class. An additional helper function performs the actual work of calculating the agent's radius and pushes the value back onto the stack:

LuaScriptBindings.cpp

```
int Lua_Script_AgentGetRadius(lua_State* luaVM)
{
    if (lua_gettop(luaVM) == 1)
    {
        Agent* const agent = AgentUtilities::GetAgent(
            luaVM, 1);

        return AgentUtilities::PushRadius(luaVM, agent);
    }
    return 0;
}
```

To bind the function to Lua, we define a constant array that maps the function's name within Lua to the C function that should be called. The array of function mappings must always end with a null luaL_Reg type struct. Lua uses a null luaL_Reg type struct as a terminator when processing the function map:

AgentUtilities.cpp

```
const luaL_Reg AgentFunctions[] =
{
    { "GetRadius", Lua_Script_AgentGetRadius },
    { NULL, NULL }
};
```

The actual function binding to the Lua virtual machine takes place in the luaL_register helper function. The register function binds the table of function names to their corresponding C callback function. The package name is specified at this step and will be associated with each function within the mapping:

AgentUtilities.cpp

```
void AgentUtilities::BindVMFunctions(lua_State* const luaVM)
{
    luaL_register(luaVM, "Agent", AgentFunctions);
}
```

If NULL is passed in as the package name, Lua requires that a table be at the top of the Lua stack. Lua will add the C functions to the Lua table at the top of the stack.

Creating custom userdata

While the sandbox uses userdata to pass around agents and the sandbox itself, another use of userdata is to add basic primitives into the sandbox. These primitives are completely controlled by Lua's garbage collector.

The vector primitive added into the sandbox is a good example of using userdata that is completely controlled by Lua. As a vector is essentially a struct that only holds three values, it is a great choice for Lua to completely maintain the creation and destruction of the data. What this means to the C++ code interacting with Lua vectors is that code should never hold on to the memory address returned from Lua. Instead, the code should copy values retrieved from Lua and store them locally.

Looking at the vector data type

Elevating a vector into a basic Lua primitive means supporting all the expected operations users would like to perform on a vector variable in Lua. This means that vectors should support the addition, subtraction, multiplication, indexing, and any other basic operators supported by Lua.

To accomplish this, the vector data type uses metamethods to support basic arithmetic operators, as well as supporting the dot operator for the ".x", ".y", and ".z" style syntax:

LuaScriptUtilities.cpp

```
const luaL_Reg LuaVector3Metatable[] =
{
    { "__add", Lua_Script_Vector3Add },
    { "__div", Lua_Script_Vector3Divide },
    { "__eq", Lua_Script_Vector3Equal },
    { "__index", Lua_Script_Vector3Index },
    { "__mul", Lua_Script_Vector3Multiply },
    { "__newindex", Lua_Script_Vector3NewIndex },
    { "__sub", Lua_Script_Vector3Subtract },
    { "__tostring", Lua_Script_Vector3ToString },
    { "__towatch", Lua_Script_Vector3ToWatch },
    { "__unm", Lua_Script_Vector3Negation },
    { NULL, NULL }
};
```

LuaScriptUtilities.h

```
#define LUA_VECTOR3_METATABLE "Vector3Type"
```

To support this functionality from the code, we need to let Lua know what type of userdata it is working with when we allocate memory. The `LuaScriptUtilities` header defines the metatable name of the vector type:

LuaScriptUtilities.cpp

```
void LuaScriptUtilities::BindVMFunctions(lua_State* const luaVM)
{
    ...

    luaL_newmetatable(luaVM, LUA_VECTOR3_METATABLE);
    luaL_register(luaVM, NULL, LuaVector3Metatable);

    ...
}
```

When binding C++ functions to the Lua virtual machine, an additional step is added to support vectors. The `luaL_newmetatable` function creates a new metatable, associating the table with the vector userdata type. Immediately after the metatable is created and pushed onto the Lua stack, a call to `luaL_register` adds the metamethods listed in `LuaVector3Metatable` to the metatable:

LuaScriptUtilities.cpp

```
int LuaScriptUtilities::PushVector3(
    lua_State* const luaVM, const Ogre::Vector3& vector)
{
    const size_t vectorSize = sizeof(Ogre::Vector3);

    Ogre::Vector3* const scriptType =
        static_cast<Ogre::Vector3*>(
            lua_newuserdata(luaVM, vectorSize));

    *scriptType = vector;

    luaL_getmetatable(luaVM, LUA_VECTOR3_METATABLE);
    lua_setmetatable(luaVM, -2);
    return 1;
}
```

Whenever a vector is created in Lua, memory is allocated from `lua_newuserdata` and the vector metatable is retrieved from Lua and assigned to the userdata. This allows Lua to know what type of userdata it is dealing with and what functions are supported on the userdata.

The demo framework

The demo framework follows a very simple update, initialization, and cleanup design shared throughout many of the classes within the sandbox.

The following is a class overview of the `BaseApplication.h` header:

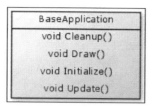

The BaseApplication abstract class overview

The `BaseApplication` class has the main responsibility to configure the application window, process input commands, as well as configure and interface with Ogre3D. The `Cleanup`, `Draw`, `Initialize`, and `Update` functions are stub functions with no implementation within the `BaseApplication` class itself. Classes that inherit from `BaseApplication` can overload any of these functions in order to plug in their own logic:

- In a derived class, the `Initialize` function is called once at the start of the application after Ogre has been initialized.

- The `Cleanup` function is called when the application requests to be shut down right before Ogre itself gets cleaned up.

- The `Draw` call is executed right before the **graphics processing unit (GPU)** renders the current application frame.

- The `Update` function is called immediately after the GPU has queued up all the rendering calls in order to process the current frame. This allows the GPU to work simultaneously as the CPU begins to prepare the next draw frame.

Ogre

Ogre3D handles the general update loop and window management of the sandbox. `BaseApplication` implements the `Ogre::FrameListener` interface in order to implement both the `Update` and `Draw` calls of the sandbox:

The following is a class overview of the `OgreFrameListener.h` header:

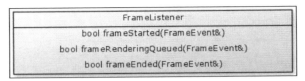

The Ogre3D FrameListener interface functions

The second interface, which is `Ogre::WindowEventListener`, enables the sandbox to receive specific callbacks to window events, such as the window movement, resizing, closing, closed, and window focus change:

The following is a class overview of the `OgreWindowEventListener.h` header:

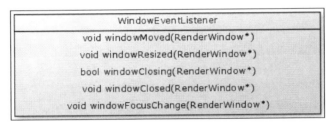

The Ogre3D WindowEventListener interface functions

 Both interfaces specify functions that are called from Ogre's main thread, so no race conditions exist to handle events.

Object-Oriented Input System

The **Object-Oriented Input System (OIS)** library is responsible for all the keyboard and mouse handling within the sandbox. The `BaseApplication` class implements both OIS interfaces in order to receive calls for key presses, mouse presses, and mouse movements. Once the `BaseApplication` class receives these events, it sends these events to the sandbox in turn.

The following is a class overview of the `OISKeyboard.h` header:

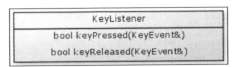

The Ogre3D KeyListener interface functions

The following is a class overview of the `OISMouse.h` header:

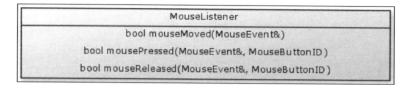

SandboxApplication

The main AI sandbox class, which is `SandboxApplication`, inherits from the `BaseApplication` class that implements the `Cleanup`, `Draw`, `Initialize`, and `Update` functions. The `CreateSandbox` function creates an instance of a sandbox and hooks up the Lua script specified by the filename parameter.

The following is a class overview of the `SandboxApplication.h` header:

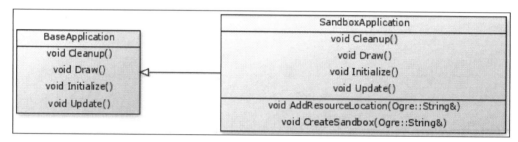

The SandboxApplication implementation of the BaseApplication abstract class

Sandbox

The sandbox class represents the sandbox data as well as handling calls into the Lua sandbox script. The creation of a sandbox requires an Ogre SceneNode instance to situate the sandbox in the world. The sandbox's SceneNode instance acts as the parent to any additional geometry SceneNodes used for rendering; this also includes the AI agents within the sandbox.

The following is a class overview of the `Sandbox.h` header:

Sandbox
Sandbox(Ogre::SceneNode*)
void AddAgent(Agent*)
void Cleanup()
void Initialize()
void LoadScript(char*, size_t, char*)
void Update(int)

The sandbox class overview

Agent

The agent class encapsulates the agent data and performs function calls to the corresponding Lua script assigned to the agent from the `LoadScript` function. A SceneNode is required to construct an agent instance to maintain an orient and position the agent within the world.

The following is a class overview of the `Agent.h` header:

Agent
Agent(unsigned int, Ogre::SceneNode*)
void Cleanup()
void Initialize()
void LoadScript(char*, size_t, char*)
void Update(int)

The agent class overview

Utility classes

AI sandbox heavily uses the utility pattern to separate logic and data. While both the sandbox and agent classes store their own relevant data, any manipulation of the data that interacts with the Lua virtual machine is handled through a utility class. This design separates the need for the agent and sandbox classes to know about the intricacies of interacting with the Lua stack. Instead, the Lua stack manipulation and data manipulation is left as the responsibility of a utility class.

For example, the `AgentUtilities` class handles all actions that are performed on an AI agent from Lua, while the `SandboxUtilities` class handles all actions that can be performed on the sandbox from Lua.

Any general purpose or miscellaneous interactions with the Lua virtual machine are handled by the `LuaScriptUtilities` class.

Lua binding

The `LuaScriptBindings.h` header file describes every C++ function that is exposed to the Lua virtual machine from the sandbox. You can always reference this file as the AI sandbox **application programming interface (API)**. Each function contains a description, function parameters, return values, and examples of how the function should be called from Lua.

Summary

So far, we went over the basic structure of AI sandbox and learned how code interacts with the Lua VM. Key concepts such as debugging Lua scripts and understanding the project layout will be fundamental when we move forward and start building new AI examples for your own sandbox.

In the next chapter, we'll cover how to create an AI representation within the sandbox and apply movement forces to the agent. Once we have a basic AI up and running, we'll build upon the foundation and add squad movement, collision avoidance, and path following.

2
Creating and Moving Agents

In this chapter, we will cover the following topics:

- Setting up your first sandbox executable
- Creating your first sandbox Lua scripts
- Understanding agent properties and their effects
- Basic Newtonian motion
- Agent-steering forces
- Creating seeking, pursuing, path following, and grouped agents

Now that we understand how AI sandbox is set up and some of the underlying system structure, we're going to dive head-first into creating a brand new sandbox demo. Throughout the rest of the book, the new Lua sandbox API will be introduced piece by piece, extending this demo with additional AI functionality, animation, graphics, and game play.

While the sandbox is doing a lot of heavy lifting in terms of graphics and physics, the core AI logic will be completely implemented in Lua, backed by data structures that are managed by the C++ code.

Creating a new sandbox project

First, to create a new sandbox executable, we need to declare a new Visual Studio demo project within the Premake build scripts. You can add a new sandbox project by opening the `SandboxDemos.lua` script and appending a new entry to the `SandboxDemos` table. In this case, you can name your `my_sandbox` demo or any other name you'd like. The project name will determine the name of the executable that is built:

SandboxDemos.lua:

```
SandboxDemos = {
    "chapter_1_introduction",
    ...
    "my_sandbox"
};
```

 All the heavy lifting of configuring a sandbox demo actually takes place in the `premake.lua` file by the `CreateDemoProject` function. The `premake.lua` script simply loops over all entries within the `SandboxDemos` table and creates the corresponding projects, setting up the source files, project dependencies, library includes, and so on.

Setting up the file structure

The next step is to set up the actual file structure for the C++ source files, C++ header files, and Lua script files for the demo. Create the corresponding directory structure based on the entry you added to the `SandboxDemos` table. Premake will automatically search for any `.h`, `.cpp`, and `.lua` files that reside within these folders and any subfolders, automatically adding them to the Visual Studio project during the solution regeneration:

```
src/my_sandbox/include
src/my_sandbox/src
src/my_sandbox/script
```

Extending the SandboxApplication class

Once your project has been set up, you need to create three blank files for Premake to discover.

Create the source and header files as follows:

```
src/my_sandbox/include/MySandbox.h
src/my_sandbox/src/MySandbox.cpp
src/my_sandbox/src/main.cpp
```

Now, it's time to regenerate the Visual Studio solution by executing `vs2008.bat`, `vs2010.bat`, `vs2012.bat`, or `vs2013.bat`. When you open the Visual Studio solution, you'll see your brand new `My_Sandbox` project!

Each of the sandbox demos is set up to extend the base `SandboxApplication` class and declare where to find the corresponding Lua script files for the executable.

Declaring your `MySandbox` class follows the same pattern and looks as follows:

`MySandbox.h`:

```
#include "demo_framework/include/SandboxApplication.h"

class MySandbox : public SandboxApplication {
public:
    MySandbox(void);

    virtual ~MySandbox(void);

    virtual void Initialize();
};
```

Inheriting from `SandboxApplication` gives you a base to start with. For now, we're only going to override the default behavior of `Initialize` in order to add the resource location for our Lua scripts.

> Inheriting from the `SandboxApplication` class also allows you to override other functions such as `Update` and `Cleanup`. Any special C++ code can be injected into the main application through these function hooks.
>
> You should always call the `SandboxApplication` class' original implementation of these functions if you override them, as they are responsible for cleaning, initializing, and updating the sandbox.

Creating the source file for the sandbox simply sets the resource location to find our sandbox Lua scripts and calls the parent class's initialization function.

`MySandbox.cpp`:

```
#include "my_sandbox/include/MySandbox.h"

MySandbox:: MySandbox ()
```

```
    : SandboxApplication("My Sandbox") {}

MySandbox::~ MySandbox () {}

void MySandbox::Initialize() {
    SandboxApplication::Initialize();

    // Relative location from the bin/x32/release/ or
    // bin/x32/debug folders
    AddResourceLocation("../../../src/my_sandbox/script");
}
```

Finally, you can add the small runner code to kick off your application from `main.cpp`:

`main.cpp`:

```
#include "my_sandbox/include/MySandbox.h"
#include "ogre3d/include/OgreException.h"

#define WIN32_LEAN_AND_MEAN
#include "windows.h"

int main() {
    MySandbox application;

    try {
        application.Run();
    }
    catch(Ogre::Exception& error) {
        MessageBox(
            NULL,
            error.getFullDescription().c_str(),
            "An exception has occurred!",
            MB_OK | MB_ICONERROR | MB_TASKMODAL);
    }
}
```

Running your sandbox for the first time

Now, compile your solution and run your sandbox. As no meshes, lights, and so on have been added to the sandbox yet, all you should see is a black screen. While this might seem small, a lot has happened already, and your SandboxApplication class is properly set up to let Lua take over.

Creating a new Decoda project

Once Visual Studio is out of the way, it's time to create a Decoda project. Open Decoda and create a blank new project. Save the project to the decoda folder, which will create the .deproj and .deuser files. Whenever we need to create a new Lua script file, we will create the file within Decoda and save the .lua file to the src/ my_sandbox/script folder:

```
decoda/my_sandbox.deproj
decoda/my_sandbox.deuser
```

Configuring Decoda's run executable

In order for Decoda to execute your sandbox, we need to configure the Decoda project with the following settings. You can access the project settings by navigating to **Project | Settings**. Typically, we'll have Decoda run the Release version of the sandbox executable for performance. Unless you need to debug the C++ sandbox code and Lua scripts at the same time, it's advisable to run the Release version of your executable.

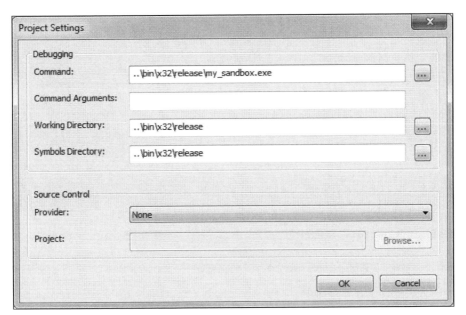

The configuration of new Decoda project debug settings

Note the relative path for the release executable. The path that Decoda will execute is based on the location of the `.deproj` file.

Remember that you have to build the Visual Studio solution before trying to debug with Decoda.

Creating a sandbox Lua script

With a basic sandbox application out of the way, we're going to create the basic Lua script that sets up the sandbox. First, create a new `Sandbox.lua` script within the script folder:

Create the Lua file as follows:

```
src/my_sandbox/script/Sandbox.lua
```

A sandbox Lua script must implement four global functions that the C++ code will call, and they are `Sandbox_Cleanup`, `Sandbox_HandleEvent`, `Sandbox_Initialize`, and `Sandbox_Update`:

`Sandbox.lua`:

```lua
function Sandbox_Cleanup(sandbox)
end

function Sandbox_HandleEvent(sandbox, event)
end

function Sandbox_Initialize(sandbox)
end

function Sandbox_Update(sandbox, deltaTimeInMillis)
end
```

With the basic hooks in place, modify your `SandboxApplication` class to create a sandbox based on your Lua script:

`MySandbox.cpp`:

```cpp
void MySandbox::Initialize() {
    SandboxApplication::Initialize();

    ...
    CreateSandbox("Sandbox.lua");
}
```

Don't forget to recompile your sandbox application whenever a change is made to any of the C++ files.

Creating a floor

Now that your sandbox is initialized and hooked into Lua, we can start adding some basic geometry and lighting. The sandbox package exposed to Lua provides a `CreatePlane` function that will create a plane mesh specified by a width and length. A corresponding physics half-space will also be created and added into the physics simulation.

 A physics half-space is a plane that expands infinitely in both the x and z directions.

Once a plane object has been created, we'll assign an Ogre material through the `Core.SetMaterial` function to give the plane a texture defined within `media/materials/base.material`.

 The sandbox is set up to handle standard diffuse, specular, and normal mapped material types. New materials can be added to the `media/materials/base.material` file.

In this case we'll assign the `Ground2` Ogre material to our newly created plane.

Sandbox.lua:

```
function Sandbox_Initialize(sandbox)
    local plane = Sandbox.CreatePlane(sandbox, 200, 200);
    Core.SetMaterial(plane, "Ground2");
end
```

If you run the sandbox at this point, you might expect to see the plane you created, but you'll see a black screen instead. Without any lighting in our sandbox, even though our plane had been created, we won't be able to see it yet.

Adding a light

Our plane isn't very exciting, as the sandbox has no lighting. The core package provides additional functions that create a directional light and assign diffuse and specular colors. The `Core.CreateDirectionalLight` function requires two parameters, the sandbox and a vector representing the direction of the light. Using a vector of `(1, -1, 1)` will create a light source that points diagonally in a downward direction.

`Sandbox.lua`:

```
function Sandbox_Initialize(sandbox)

    ...

    local directional = Core.CreateDirectionalLight(
        sandbox, Vector.new(1, -1, 1));

    --- Color is represented by a red, green, and blue vector.
    Core.SetLightDiffuse(
        directional, Vector.new(1.8, 1.4, 0.9));
    Core.SetLightSpecular(
        directional, Vector.new(1.8, 1.4, 0.9));
end
```

 Note that the color of the diffuse and specular light values defined by `Vector.new(red, green, blue)` are set to values above one. This allows you to change the amount of light emitted.

Now that we have a light source, you can run your sandbox and look at the beautiful plane you created. To orient the camera, simply hold the right mouse button and drag the mouse in the direction in which you would like to point the camera. To navigate through the sandbox, we can move the camera around the world using the *w*, *a*, *s*, and *d* keys. Holding the *Shift* key while pressing any of the *w*, *a*, *s*, and *d* keys will move the camera significantly faster.

Adding a skybox

Looking into infinite blackness isn't very exciting; `Sandbox.CreateSkyBox` allows us to create a skybox defined by the six textures specified in the Ogre material (`media/materials/skybox.material`). If you're unfamiliar with skyboxes, they are essentially six-sided boxes with a different texture on each face of the box. As the camera moves around the sandbox, the skybox moves accordingly in order to give the illusion of an actual sky.

The sandbox comes with multiple skybox materials. Take a peek at the `skybox.material` file in any text editor to see other available skybox textures and how to create your own brand new skybox material.

Our `Sandbox.CreateSkyBox` function takes in three parameters: the sandbox itself, the name of the Ogre material, as well as a rotation vector. The rotation vector is represented in degrees and allows us to add an initial offset to our skybox. In this case, we can rotate the initial skybox by 180 degrees to have the sky textures match the directional light we created previously:

`Sandbox.lua`:

```
function Sandbox_Initialize(sandbox)

    ...

    Sandbox.CreateSkyBox(
        sandbox,
        "ThickCloudsWaterSkyBox",
        Vector.new(0, 180, 0));
end
```

Running the sandbox now will show a cloudy sky and a lit environment.

A new sandbox with a skybox and ground plane

Adding meshes to the sandbox

An Ogre mesh is simply a visual piece of geometry within the sandbox without any physics representation. To add an Ogre mesh to the sandbox, simply call `Core.CreateMesh` and pass in the location and filename of an Ogre mesh file.

Setting the position and rotation of a mesh can be done through the `Core.SetPosition` and `Core.SetRotation` functions:

Sandbox.lua:

```
function Sandbox_Initialize(sandbox)

    ...

    local mesh = Core.CreateMesh(
        sandbox, "models/nobiax_modular/modular_block.mesh");
    Core.SetPosition(mesh, Vector.new(0, 1, 0));
    Core.SetRotation(mesh, Vector.new(0, 45, 0));
end
```

The rotation function expects a vector of angles expressed in degrees. For example, `Vector.new(0, 45, 0)` will rotate the mesh 45 degrees around the *y* axis.

Creating sandbox objects

If you want an Ogre mesh to be simulated with physics, you can create a sandbox object instead. `Sandbox.CreateObject` will automatically generate a convex hull for any Ogre mesh and allow the object to be simulated with physics.

> As generating a physics representation for an arbitrary mesh happens at runtime, complex meshes might increase the load times of your sandbox. Internally, bullet physics creates a simplified convex hull that approximates the Ogre mesh instead of being an identical one-to-one mapping. Keep this in mind, as the physics representation of any Ogre mesh will always be an approximation and never an exact replica of the original mesh.

We can now convert the block mesh we created earlier to a full-fledged physically simulated object.

Sandbox.lua:

```
function Sandbox_Initialize(sandbox)

    ...

    local object = Sandbox.CreateObject(
```

```
        sandbox, "models/nobiax_modular/modular_block.mesh");
    -- Set the mass of the block in kilograms.
    Core.SetMass(object, 15);
    Core.SetPosition(object, Vector.new(0, 1, 0));
    Core.SetRotation(object, Vector.new(0, 45, 0));
end
```

Shooting blocks

Now that we have some basic lighting, a physics plane, and the ability to create and simulate physics objects, it's time to start shooting things. Before we jump head-first into creating agents, we'll take a quick detour into accessing some of the physics aspects of sandbox objects, as well as interacting with input controls.

The `Sandbox_HandleEvent` function allows the sandbox to respond to mouse and keyboard inputs. The event parameter is a Lua table that stores the source of the event, whether the event was generated by a down or up key press, and what key caused the event. Mouse-movement events are similar, but contain the width and height location of the mouse cursor.

As we already know how to create a sandbox object, all we need to do to shoot objects is position the object at the camera's position and orientation and apply a physics impulse on the object.

In this case, we're going to create and shoot a block on a `space_key` press event. The camera's position and forward vector can be returned from the sandbox using the `Sandbox.GetCameraPosition` and `Sandox.GetCameraForward` functions. We'll assign the position and orientation to the block and apply a force to the block in the camera's forward direction. To add a bit of spin to the object, you can use the `Core.ApplyAngularImpulse` function to cause the block to start spinning as it flies through the air:

`Sandbox.lua`:

```
function Sandbox_HandleEvent(sandbox, event)
    if (event.source == "keyboard" and
        event.pressed and event.key == "space_key" ) then

        local block = Sandbox.CreateObject(
            sandbox,
            "models/nobiax_modular/modular_block.mesh");

        local cameraPosition =
            Sandbox.GetCameraPosition(sandbox);
        -- Normalized forward camera vector.
        local cameraForward =
```

```
        Sandbox.GetCameraForward(sandbox);
-- Offset the block's position in front of the camera.
local blockPosition =
    cameraPosition + cameraForward * 2;
local rotation = Sandbox.GetCameraOrientation(sandbox);

-- Mass of the block in kilograms.
Core.SetMass(block, 15);
Core.SetRotation(block, rotation);
Core.SetPosition(block, blockPosition);

-- Applies instantaneous force for only one update tick.
Core.ApplyImpulse(
    block, Vector.new(cameraForward * 15000));

-- Applies instantaneous angular force for one update
-- tick.  In this case blocks will always spin forwards
-- regardless where the camera is looking.
Core.ApplyAngularImpulse(
    block, Sandbox.GetCameraLeft(sandbox) * 10);
    end
end
```

If we run the sandbox now, we can move around, point the camera, and shoot blocks.

Shooting blocks in the sandbox

Creating an agent Lua script

To start creating an agent, we need to create another Lua script that implements the Agent_Cleanup, Agent_HandleEvent, Agent_Initialize, and Agent_Update functions:

Create the Lua file as follows:

```
src/my_sandbox/script/Agent.lua
```

Agent.lua:

```
function Agent_Cleanup(agent)
end

function Agent_HandleEvent(agent, event)
end

function Agent_Initialize(agent)
end

function Agent_Update(agent, deltaTimeInMillis)
end
```

Now that we have a basic agent script, we can create an instance of the agent within the sandbox. Modify the initialization of the sandbox in order to create your AI agent with the Sandbox.CreateAgent function.

 Remember that each AI agent runs within its own Lua **virtual machine (VM)**. Even though a separate VM is running the agent logic, you can still access and modify properties of an agent from the sandbox Lua script, as the C++ code manages agent data.

Modify the initialization of the sandbox in order to create your AI agent with the Sandbox.CreateAgent function.

Sandbox.lua:

```
function Sandbox_Initialize(sandbox)

    . . .

    Sandbox.CreateAgent(sandbox, "Agent.lua");
end
```

Creating a visual representation

Now that you have an agent running within the sandbox, we need to create a visual representation so that we can see the agent. This time, we use the `Core.CreateCapsule` function to procedurally generate a capsule mesh and attach the mesh to the agent itself. Passing the agent to `Core.CreateCapsule` will attach the Ogre mesh directly to the agent and automatically update the position and rotation of the capsule as the agent moves.

We only need to create a visual representation compared to a `Sandbox.CreateObject` object, as agents are already simulated within the physics simulation with a capsule representation:

Create the Lua file as follows:

```
src/my_sandbox/script/AgentUtilities.lua
```

AgentUtilities.lua:

```
function AgentUtilities_CreateAgentRepresentation(
    agent, height, radius)

    -- Capsule height and radius in meters.
    local capsule = Core.CreateCapsule(agent, height, radius);
    Core.SetMaterial(capsule, "Ground2");
end
```

Agent.lua:

```
function Agent_Initialize(agent)
    AgentUtilities_CreateAgentRepresentation(
        agent, agent:GetHeight(), agent:GetRadius());
end
```

Running the sandbox now will show our agent's visual representation, a capsule using the same Ogre `Ground2` material.

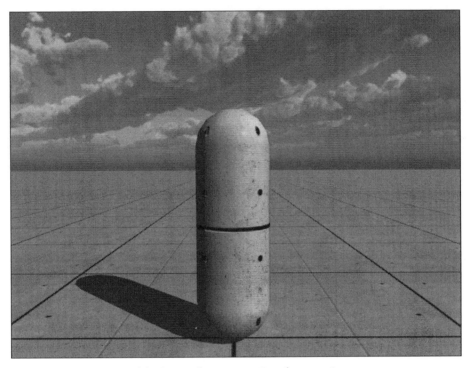

A basic capsule representation of our agents

Updating an agent position

To start moving an agent around directly, we can set the agent's position. As agents are simulated within the physics simulation, they will fall to the ground if they are positioned in the air or will be pushed to the top of the ground plane if placed below:

```
-- Position in meters.
local position = Vector.new(
    xCoordinate, yCoordinate, zCoordinate);
Agent.SetPosition(agent, position);
```

Updating an agent orientation

Changing the orientation of an agent is similar to setting a position vector, except that a forward vector must be provided. As the sandbox simulates humanoid agents, the physics simulation locks the orientation of the agent to force agents upright. When setting a forward vector of an agent, the sandbox assumes that the *y* axis is considered the up axis within the sandbox:

```
local forwardDirection = Vector.new(
    xDirection, 0, zDirection);
Agent.SetForward(agent, forwardDirection);
```

Agent properties

Now that we can create agents, we're going to take a step back and look at what properties are available to an agent and what they mean.

Orientation

Whenever you need to return the orientation of an agent, it's easiest to use the forward vector that usually represents the direction of movement of an agent. Both the left and up vectors of orientation are available as well. Whenever you need to change an agent's direction, simply set its forward vector.

The forward axis

To access and set the forward vector of our agents, we can use the built-in `GetForward` and `SetForward` helper functions.

```
local forwardVector = agent:GetForward();
Agent.SetForward(agent, forwardVector);
```

The left axis

We can also access the left orientation vector using the `GetLeft` helper function.

```
local leftVector = agent:GetLeft();
```

The up axis

Accessing the up orientation vector is similarly provided by a `GetUp` helper function.

```
local upVector = agent:GetUp();
```

Location

An agent's position is the center of the mass of its capsule representation within the physics simulation. If you need to determine the origin of an agent, simply return its position and subtract half its height from the y component of the position.

Position

To access and set the position of agents, we can use the GetPosition and SetPosition helper functions.

```
local positionVector = agent:GetPosition();
agent:SetPosition(positionVector);
```

Size

The size of the agent and their capsule representation is determined by the agent's height and radius. When changing these values, the physics simulation will also adjust and create a new representation for the agent based on the changes.

Height

Accessing the height of the agents can be done through the GetHeight and SetHeight helper functions.

```
local height = agent:GetHeight();
agent:SetHeight(height);
```

Radius

To access and modify the radius of an agent, we can use the GetRadius and SetRadius functions.

```
local radius = agent:GetRadius();
agent:SetRadius(radius);
```

Physics

Even though agents are simulated with physics, not all of the agent's physics parameters are enforced at the physics simulation level. The mass of an agent, for example, is the identical mass used within the physics simulation itself, while the MaxForce and MaxSpeed functions of an agent are only enforced by the agent. These two properties represent the maximum amount of force an agent can exert on itself and the max speed the agent can reach without any outside influences.

An intuitive example of why this separation is desirable when dealing with agent physics is gravity. When an agent accelerates to its max speed, we still want gravity to accelerate the agents downward in the case of falls. This acceleration can force agents to have a speed larger than their max speed property.

Mass

To access and modify the mass of our agents we can use the agent's GetMass and SetMass helper functions.

```
local mass = agent:GetMass();
agent:SetMass(mass);
```

The max force

The maximum force of our agents can be accessed and set using the GetMaxForce and SetMaxForce functions.

```
local maxForce = agent:GetMaxForce();
agent:SetMaxForce(maxForce);
```

The max speed

To set and access the max speed property of our agents, we can use the GetMaxSpeed and SetMaxSpeed functions.

```
local maxSpeed = agent:GetMaxSpeed();
agent:SetMaxSpeed(maxSpeed);
```

Speed

Setting and accessing the speed of our agents can be done through the `GetSpeed` and `SetSpeed` functions.

```
local speed = agent:GetSpeed();
agent:SetSpeed(speed);
```

Velocity

Similarly, to access and set the velocity of our agents, we can use the `GetVelocity` and `SetVelocity` functions.

```
local velocityVector = agent:GetVelocity();
agent:SetVelocity(velocityVector);
```

Knowledge

Agents themselves have a very basic set of knowledge so that external Lua scripts such as the sandbox script can direct agents with some amount of persistence. For example, when we create an agent that moves to a target position, we might want the sandbox to set this position instead of the agent having to determine its target.

Target

An agent's target is a vector position. Typically, agents will use the target as a position they want to reach or the known position of another agent.

```
local targetVector = agent:GetTarget();
agent:SetTarget(targetVector);
```

Target radius

A target radius is a number value that agents use to determine whether they are close enough to their target without having to be exactly at the target position. This fudge factor helps agents avoid circling a target position due to small numerical differences in their position and target position.

```
local targetRadius = agent:GetTargetRadius();
agent:SetTargetRadius(targetRadius );
```

Path

An agent's path is a series of vector points that the agent uses internally to determine where to move to during path following. Allowing agents to remember their path is a small optimization to avoid having to pass around the path itself during path following calculations. When assigning a path to the agent, we can pass an optional Boolean in order to let the agent know whether the path should loop.

```
local pathTable = agent:GetPath();
local hasPath = agent:HasPath();

local path = {
    Vector.new(0, 0, 0),
    Vector.new(10, 0, 10),
    Vector.new(0, 0, 10) };

agent:SetPath(path, cylic);
```

Agents' movement

As all agents within the sandbox are automatically simulated through the physics system, it's time to get acquainted with some basic Newtonian physics.

Mass

The mass of an agent comes into play when colliding with other objects and is based on how much the agent should accelerate based on the forces applied to the agent. All mass calculations within the sandbox occur in kilograms.

Speed

Speed defines how fast an agent is moving without considering the direction the agent is moving in. All speed values within the sandbox will be measured in meters per second and signify the magnitude of the velocity vector.

Velocity

Velocity, on the other hand, is both the speed and direction the agent is moving in. It is measured in meters per second and is represented as a vector.

Acceleration

Acceleration within the sandbox is always measured in meters per second squared and represents the change in the velocity of an agent.

Force

Force plays a large part when moving agents around and is measured in Newtons:

$$Newtons = kilograms * meters / second^2$$

Whenever a force is applied to an object, the object will either accelerate or decelerate based on the objects mass.

It is important to understand the values the sandbox works with to gain an intuitive understanding about values such as speed, distance, and mass.

Agent-steering forces

With some basic agent properties and a full-fledged physics system supporting the sandbox, we can begin moving agents realistically through forces. This type of movement system is best known as a steering-based locomotion system. Craig Reynolds' *Steering Behaviors For Autonomous Characters* (`http://www.red3d.com/cwr/papers/1999/gdc99steer.html`) is best known for describing this style of steering system for moving characters. Steering forces allow for an easy classification of different movement types and allow for an easy way to apply multiple forces to a character.

As the sandbox uses the OpenSteer library to steer calculations, this makes it painless for Lua to request steering forces. While the steering calculations are left to OpenSteer, the application of forces will reside within our Lua Scripts.

Seeking

Seeking is one of the core steering forces and calculates a force that moves the agent toward their target. OpenSteer combines both seeking- and arrival-steering forces together in order to allow agents to slow down slightly before reaching their target destination:

```
local seekForce = agent:ForceToPosition(destination);
```

Applying steering forces to an agent

Creating a seeking agent requires two major components. The first is the ability to apply force calculations to an agent while updating their forward direction, and the second is the ability to clamp an agent's horizontal speed to its `maxSpeed` property.

Whenever we apply force to an agent, we will apply the maximum amount of force. In essence, this causes agents to reach their maximum speed in the shortest time possible. Without applying the maximum amount of force, small forces can end up having no effect on the agent. This is important because steering forces aren't always comparable with each other in terms of strength.

First, we'll implement an `Agent_ApplyForce` function to handle applying steering forces to the physics system and update the agent's forward direction if there is a change in the direction of the agent's velocity:

AgentUtilities.lua:

```lua
function AgentUtilities_ApplyPhysicsSteeringForce (
    agent, steeringForce, deltaTimeInSeconds)

    -- Ignore very weak steering forces.
    if (Vector.LengthSquared(steeringForce) < 0.1) then
        return;
    end

    -- Agents with 0 mass are immovable.
    if (agent:GetMass() <= 0) then
        return;
    end

    -- Zero out any steering in the y direction
    steeringForce.y = 0;

    -- Maximize the steering force, essentially forces the agent
    -- to max acceleration.
    steeringForce =
        Vector.Normalize(steeringForce) * agent:GetMaxForce();

    -- Apply force to the physics representation.
    agent:ApplyForce(steeringForce);

    -- Newtons(kg*m/s^2) divided by mass(kg) results in
    -- acceleration(m/s^2).
```

```
    local acceleration = steeringForce / agent:GetMass();

    -- Velocity is measured in meters per second(m/s).
    local currentVelocity = agent:GetVelocity();

    -- Acceleration(m/s^2) multiplied by seconds results in
    -- velocity(m/s).
    local newVelocity =
        currentVelocity + (acceleration * deltaTimeInSeconds);

    -- Zero out any pitch changes to keep the Agent upright.
    -- NOTE: This implies that agents can immediately turn in any
    -- direction.
    newVelocity.y = 0;

    -- Point the agent in the direction of movement.
    agent:SetForward(newVelocity);
end
```

Before applying any steering force, we remove any steering force in the *y* axis. If our agents can fly, this would be undesirable, but as the primary type of agents the sandbox simulates are humanoid, humans can't move in the *y* axis unless they are jumping. Next, we normalize the steering force to a unit vector so that we can scale the steering force by the agent's maximum allowed force.

> Using a maximum force for all steering calculations isn't required, but it produces desirable results. Feel free to play with how forces are applied to agents in order to see different types of steering behavior.

Once our force is calculated, we simply apply the force through the agent's `ApplyForce` function. Now, we take our force and calculate the agent's change in acceleration. With acceleration, we can derive the change in velocity by multiplying acceleration by `deltaTimeInSeconds`. The change in velocity is added to the current velocity of the agent and the resulting vector is the agent's forward direction.

This is just one of many ways in which you can apply steering forces to agents, and it makes many assumptions about how our agents will look when changing directions and speeds. Later, we can refine steering even further to smooth out changes in the direction, for example.

> Remember that all time calculations take place in meters, seconds, and kilograms.

Clamping the horizontal speed of an agent

Next, we want to clamp the speed of our agent. If you think about the forces being applied to agents, acceleration changes will quickly cause the agent to move faster than their maximum speed allows.

When clamping the velocity, we only want to consider the agent's lateral velocity and ignore any speed attained through gravity. To calculate this, we first take the agent's speed and zero out all movement in the y axis. Next, we clamp the magnitude of the velocity with the agent's maximum speed.

Before assigning the velocity back to the agent, we set back the change in velocity in the y axis:

AgentUtilities.lua:

```
function AgentUtilities_ClampHorizontalSpeed(agent)
    local velocity = agent:GetVelocity();
    -- Store downward velocity to apply after clamping.
    local downwardVelocity = velocity.y;

    -- Ignore downward velocity since Agents never apply downward
    -- velocity themselves.
    velocity.y = 0;

    local maxSpeed = agent:GetMaxSpeed();
    local squaredSpeed = maxSpeed * maxSpeed;

    -- Using squared values avoids the cost of using the square
    -- root when calculating the magnitude of the velocity vector.
    if (Vector.LengthSquared(velocity) > squaredSpeed) then
      local newVelocity =
          Vector.Normalize(velocity) * maxSpeed;

        -- Reapply the original downward velocity after clamping.
        newVelocity.y = downwardVelocity;

        agent:SetVelocity(newVelocity);
    end
end
```

As we're clamping all of the horizontal speed of the agent in order to accurately calculate the agent's maximum speed, this has another significant trade-off. Any outside forces that affect the agent—for example, physics objects pushing the agent will have no effect on the actual velocity if the agent is already at their maximum speed.

Creating a seeking agent

With the application of forces and maximum speed out of the way, we can create a moving agent. Our seeking agent will calculate a seek force to their target position and will move to a new target position when the agent reaches the target radius of the target.

First, we calculate the seek steering force to the target destination and apply the force with the `Agent_ApplyPhysicsSteeringForce` function. Next, we call the `Agent_ClampHorizontalSpeed` function on the agent in order to remove any excess speed.

Additional debug information is drawn per frame in order to show you where the agent is moving toward and how large the target radius is around the target. If the agent moves within the target radius, a random target position is calculated and the agent starts seeking toward their new target destination all over again:

`Agent.lua`:

```lua
require "AgentUtilities";

function Agent_Initialize(agent)

    ...

    -- Assign a default target and acceptable target radius.
    agent:SetTarget(Vector.new(50, 0, 0));
    agent:SetTargetRadius(1.5);
end

function Agent_Update(agent, deltaTimeInMillis)
    local destination = agent:GetTarget();
    local deltaTimeInSeconds = deltaTimeInMillis / 1000;
    local seekForce = agent:ForceToPosition(destination);
    local targetRadius = agent:GetTargetRadius();
    local radius = agent:GetRadius();
    local position = agent:GetPosition();

    -- Apply seeking force.
    AgentUtilities_ApplyForce(
        agent, seekForce, deltaTimeInSeconds);
    AgentUtilities_ClampHorizontalSpeed(agent);

    local targetRadiusSquared =
        (targetRadius + radius) * (targetRadius + radius);

    -- Calculate the position where the Agent touches the ground.
    local adjustedPosition =
        agent:GetPosition() -
```

```
            Vector.new(0, agent:GetHeight()/2, 0);

    -- If the agent is within the target radius pick a new
    -- random position to move to.
    if (Vector.DistanceSquared(adjustedPosition, destination) <
        targetRadiusSquared) then

        -- New target is within the 100 meter squared movement
        -- space.
        local target = agent:GetTarget();
        target.x = math.random(-50, 50);
        target.z = math.random(-50, 50);

        agent:SetTarget(target);
    end

    -- Draw debug information for target and target radius.
    Core.DrawCircle(
        destination, targetRadius, Vector.new(1, 0, 0));
    Core.DrawLine(position, destination, Vector.new(0, 1, 0));

    -- Debug outline representing the space the Agent can move
    -- within.
    Core.DrawSquare(Vector.new(), 100, Vector.new(1, 0, 0));
end
```

Rename the Lua file as follows:

```
src/my_sandbox/script/Agent.lua to
src/my_sandbox/script/SeekingAgent.lua
```

An agent seeking toward a random position

Pursuit

Creating a pursuing agent is very similar to seeking, except that we predict the target position of another moving agent. Start by creating a new `PursuingAgent` Lua script and implement the basic `Agent_Cleanup`, `Agent_HandleEvent`, `Agent_Initialize`, and `Agent_Update` functions:

Create Lua file as follows:

```
src/my_sandbox/script/PursuingAgent.lua
```

As a pursuing agent needs to have an enemy to pursue, we create a persistent Lua variable *enemy* outside the scope of our `Initialize` and `Update` functions. During the initialization of the agent, we will request all agents that are currently within the sandbox and assign the first agent to be our enemy.

A minor change we make to the pursuing agent compared to the seeking agent is to use an agent's `PredictFuturePosition` function to calculate its future position. We pass in the number of seconds we want to predict in order to create the pursuing agent's target position.

We can even make our pursuing agents slower than their enemy while still being able to catch up to a future predicted position when the enemy agent changes directions:

PursuingAgent.lua:

```lua
require "AgentUtilities";

local enemy;

function Agent_Cleanup(agent)
end

function Agent_HandleEvent(agent, event)
end

function Agent_Initialize(agent)
    AgentUtilities_CreateAgentRepresentation(
        agent, agent:GetHeight(), agent:GetRadius());

    -- Assign an acceptable target radius.
    agent:SetTargetRadius(1.0);
    -- Randomly assign a position to the agent.
    agent:SetPosition(Vector.new(
        math.random(-50, 50),
        0,
```

```
            math.random(-50, 50)));

        local agents = Sandbox.GetAgents(agent:GetSandbox());

        -- Find the first valid agent and assign the agent as an
        -- enemy.
        for index = 1, #agents do
            if (agents[index] ~= agent) then
                enemy = agents[index];
                agent:SetTarget(enemy:GetPosition());
                break;
            end
        end

        -- Make the pursuing Agent slightly slower than the enemy.
        agent:SetMaxSpeed(enemy:GetMaxSpeed() * 0.8);
    end

    function Agent_Update(agent, deltaTimeInMillis)
        -- Calculate the future position of the enemy agent.
        agent:SetTarget(enemy:PredictFuturePosition(1));

        local destination = agent:GetTarget();
        local deltaTimeInSeconds = deltaTimeInMillis / 1000;
        local seekForce = agent:ForceToPosition(destination);
        local targetRadius = agent:GetTargetRadius();
        local position = agent:GetPosition();

        -- Apply seeking force to the predicted position.
        AgentUtilities_ApplyForce(
            agent, seekForce, deltaTimeInSeconds);
        AgentUtilities_ClampHorizontalSpeed(agent);

        -- Draw debug information for target and target radius.
        Core.DrawCircle(
            destination, targetRadius, Vector.new(1, 0, 0));
        Core.DrawLine(position, destination, Vector.new(0, 1, 0));
    end
```

As the pursuing agent needs an enemy, we create the agent in the sandbox after our seeking agent is already initialized:

Sandbox.lua:

```
    function Sandbox_Initialize(sandbox)

        ...

        Sandbox.CreateAgent(sandbox, "SeekingAgent.lua");
```

```
        Sandbox.CreateAgent(sandbox, "PursuingAgent.lua");
    end
```

Running the sandbox, we'll now have a pursing agent chasing after our seeking agent.

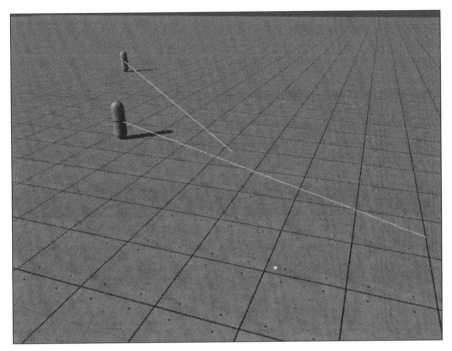

An agent intercepting another agent

Fleeing

Creating a fleeing steering behavior is nearly identical to a seeking steering behavior. The only difference is that the agent will move away from its target instead of moving toward the target. Requesting a fleeing force can be done through the `Agent.ForceToFleePosition` function:

```
local forceToFlee = agent:ForceToFleePosition(position);
```

Evasion

Evasion is a steering behavior that tries to make the agent flee from another agent. This behavior is the exact opposite of *pursue*. Instead of steering toward an enemy's future position, we flee from the enemy's future position:

```
local forceToEvade = agent:ForceToFleePosition(
    enemy:PredictFuturePosition(timeInSeconds));
```

Wandering

A wandering behavior essentially returns a tangent steering force to the agent's forward vector. Wandering is meant to add deviation to an agent's movement and is not to be used as a steering force by itself. Taking in a delta time in milliseconds allows wandering forces to change at a constant rate:

```
local forceToWander = agent:ForceToWander(deltaTimeInMillis);
```

The target speed

To adjust our agents' speed to match their desired target speed, we can use the `ForceToTargetSpeed` function to calculate a steering force that will cause our agents to speed up or slow down:

```
local forceToSpeed = agent:ForceToTargetSpeed(targetSpeed);
```

Path following

Having an agent path follow requires two different steering behaviors. The first steering force, which is `ForceToStayOnPath`, keeps the agent from straying off the path, and the second steering force, which is `ForceToFollowPath`, moves the agent along the path.

Creating a path following agent

Creating a path following agent is very similar to our seeking agent, which is `SeekingAgent.lua`. First, create a new Lua script for the `PathingAgent.lua` agent:

Create the Lua file as follows:

```
src/my_sandbox/script/PathingAgent.lua
```

This time, we will utilize a `DebugUtilities` function in order to draw out a path for us. `DebugUtilities` is a Lua script in `src/demo_framework/script/DebugUtilities.lua`. When we initialize our pathing agent, we'll assign it the path to be traveled. Paths are considered looping by default, so our agent will keep traveling in a large circle:

`PathingAgent.lua`:

```
require "AgentUtilities";
require "DebugUtilities";

function Agent_Initialize(agent)
```

```
    AgentUtilities_CreateAgentRepresentation(
        agent, agent:GetHeight(), agent:GetRadius());

    -- Randomly assign a position to the agent.
    agent:SetPosition(Vector.new(
        math.random(-50, 50),
        0,
        math.random(-50, 50)));
end

function Agent_Update(agent, deltaTimeInMillis)
    local deltaTimeInSeconds = deltaTimeInMillis / 1000;

    -- Force to continue moving along the path, can cause the
    -- agent to veer away from the path.
    local followForce = agent:ForceToFollowPath(1.25);

    -- Force to move to the closest point on the path.
    local stayForce = agent:ForceToStayOnPath(1);

    -- Slight deviation force to alleviate bumping other pathing
    -- agents.
    local wanderForce = agent:ForceToWander(deltaTimeInMillis);

    -- Sum steering forces using scalars.
    local totalForces =
        Vector.Normalize(followForce) +
        Vector.Normalize(stayForce) * 0.25 +
        Vector.Normalize(wanderForce) * 0.25;

    local targetSpeed = 3;

    -- Accelerate pathing agents to a minimum speed.
    if (agent:GetSpeed() < targetSpeed) then
        local speedForce = agent:ForceToTargetSpeed(targetSpeed);
        totalForces = totalForces + Vector.Normalize(speedForce);
    end

    -- Apply the summation of all forces.
    AgentUtilities_ApplyPhysicsSteeringForce(
        agent, totalForces, deltaTimeInSeconds);
    AgentUtilities_ClampHorizontalSpeed(agent);

    -- Draw the agent's path as a looping path.
    DebugUtilities_DrawPath(agent:GetPath(), true);
end
```

The `Agent_Update` function has a few new additions, which show you how to add two steering forces together. Both `ForceToFollowPath` and `ForceToStayOnPath` are added together with a lower weight associated with the `StayOnPath` force. An additional `ForceToTargetSpeed` function is also added to pathing agents in order to make sure that they don't fall below a minimum speed.

Creating pathing agents in the sandbox is identical to creating other agents, except that this time, we'll create 20 different agents with varying speeds—all following the same path. Once you run the sandbox, notice how agents will collide with each other and be unable to pass other agents. All we're missing is collision avoidance for a nice-looking path following:

`Sandbox.lua`:

```lua
    -- Default path to assign to path following agents.
local path = {
    Vector.new(0, 0, 0),
    Vector.new(30, 0, 0),
    Vector.new(30, 0, 50),
    Vector.new(-30, 0, 0),
    Vector.new(-30, 0, 20)};

function Sandbox_Initialize(sandbox)

    ...

    for i=1, 20 do
        local agent = Sandbox.CreateAgent(
            sandbox, "PathingAgent.lua");

        -- Assign the same path to every agent.
        agent:SetPath(path, true);

        -- Randomly vary speeds to allow agents to pass one
        -- another.
        local randomSpeed = math.random(
            agent:GetMaxSpeed() * 0.85,
            agent:GetMaxSpeed() * 1.15);

        agent:SetMaxSpeed(randomSpeed);
    end
end
```

Running the sandbox now, we can see 20 independent agents all following the same predefined path.

Multiple agents following a given path

Avoidance

Avoidance steering behavior involves avoiding collisions between moving agents, objects, and other moving agents. The collision avoidance calculated from `ForceToAvoidAgents` creates a steering force in the tangent direction of a potential agent as two agents move closer to one another. Predictive movements are used to determine whether two agents will collide within a given amount of time.

Obstacle avoidance, on the other hand, approximates sandbox objects using spheres and uses the agent's predictive movement to create a steering force tangent for the potential collision.

Collision avoidance

To calculate the force to avoid other agents, based on the minimum time, to collide with other agents, we can use the `ForceToAvoidAgents` function.

```
local avoidAgentForce =
    agent:ForceToAvoidAgents(minTimeToCollision);
```

Obstacle avoidance

A similar force to avoid other dynamic moving obstacles can be calculated using the `ForceToAvoidObjects` function.

```
local avoidObjectForce =
    agent:ForceToAvoidObjects(minTimeToCollision);
```

Avoiding blocks and agents

Modifying the `SeekingAgent.lua` script by adding the weighted sum of the `ForceToAvoidAgents` and `ForceToAvoidObjects` functions allows for the seeking agent to avoid potential collisions. When running the sandbox, try shooting boxes in the path of the agent and watch it navigate around the boxes:

SeekingAgent.lua

```
function Agent_Update(agent, deltaTimeInMillis)
    local destination = agent:GetTarget();
    local deltaTimeInSeconds = deltaTimeInMillis / 1000;
    local avoidAgentForce = agent:ForceToAvoidAgents(1.5);
    local avoidObjectForce = agent:ForceToAvoidObjects(1.5);
    local seekForce = agent:ForceToPosition(destination);
    local targetRadius = agent:GetTargetRadius();
    local radius = agent:GetRadius();
    local position = agent:GetPosition();
    local avoidanceMultiplier = 3;

    -- Sum all forces and apply higher priority to avoidance
    -- forces.
    local steeringForces =
        seekForce +
        avoidAgentForce * avoidanceMultiplier +
        avoidObjectForce * avoidanceMultiplier;

    AgentUtilities_ApplyForce(
        agent, steeringForces, deltaTimeInSeconds);

    ...

end
```

Sandbox.lua:

```
require "DebugUtilities";

function Sandbox_Update(sandbox, deltaTimeInMillis)
```

```
    -- Grab all Sandbox objects, not including agents.
    local objects = Sandbox.GetObjects(sandbox);

    -- Draw debug bounding sphere representations for objects with
    -- mass.
    DebugUtilities_DrawDynamicBoundingSpheres(objects);
end
```

Now when we run the sandbox, we can shoot boxes at our seeking agent and watch it steer around each object.

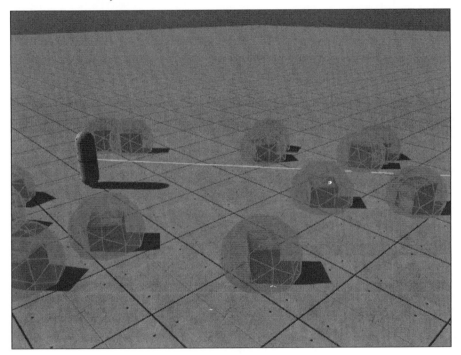

Avoiding obstacles using avoidance

Group steering

Group steering can be broken down into three main steering behaviors: alignment, cohesion, and separation. An alignment steering force has the agent's face in the same forward direction as the rest of the agents in the group. Cohesion is a force that keeps the agents within the group together. Separation is the opposite of cohesion and forces the agents within the group to keep minimum distance from one another.

Using a combination of these three steering behaviors, which are also known as flocking, you can create groups of agents that are driven to move together yet not run into each other.

Alignment

To calculate a steering vector that will align our agent to a group of other agents, we can use the `ForceToSeparate` function.

```
local forceToAlign =
    agent:ForceToSeparate(maxDistance, maxAngle, agents);
```

Cohesion

To keep our agent together with a group of other agents, we can calculate a steering force for combining using the `ForceToCombine` function.

```
local forceToCombine =
    agent:ForceToCombine(maxDistance, maxAngle, agents);
```

Separation

To keep our agent apart from a group of other agents, we can use the `ForceToSeparate` function.

```
local forceToSeparate =
    agent:forceToSeparate(minDistance, maxAngle, agents);
```

Creating a group of followers

In this example, we're going to build another AI type called a follower agent. This time, a group of followers will stay together and move toward their leader. The leader, on the other hand, is still the same seeking agent that will randomly move around the sandbox, completely oblivious to the group of followers behind it.

Group-based movement using separation, cohesion, and alignment

To create followers, we'll use multiple steering forces to combine, separate, and align our agents to the leader agent they are following.

Create the Lua file as follows:

```
src/my_sandbox/script/FollowerAgent.lua
```

FollowerAgent.lua:

```lua
require "AgentUtilities";

local leader;

function Agent_Initialize(agent)
    AgentUtilities_CreateAgentRepresentation(
        agent, agent:GetHeight(), agent:GetRadius());

    -- Randomly assign a position to the agent.
    agent:SetPosition(Vector.new(
        math.random(-50, 50), 0, math.random(-50, 50)));

    -- Assign the first valid agent as the leader to follow.
    local agents = Sandbox.GetAgents(agent:GetSandbox());
    for index = 1, #agents do
```

```
            if (agents[index] ~= agent) then
                leader = agents[index];
                break;
            end
        end
    end
end

function Agent_Update(agent, deltaTimeInMillis)
    local deltaTimeInSeconds = deltaTimeInMillis / 1000;
    local sandboxAgents = Sandbox.GetAgents(agent:GetSandbox());

    -- Calculate a combining force so long as the leader stays
    -- within a 100 meter range from the agent, and has less than
    -- 180 degree difference in forward direction.
    local forceToCombine =
        Agent.ForceToCombine(agent, 100, 180, { leader } );

    -- Force to stay away from other agents that are closer than
    -- 2 meters and have a maximum forward degree difference of
    -- less than 180 degrees.
    local forceToSeparate =
        Agent.ForceToSeparate(agent, 2, 180, sandboxAgents );

    -- Force to stay away from getting too close to the leader if
    -- within 5 meters of the leader and having a maximum forward
    -- degree difference of less than 45 degrees.
    local forceToAlign =
        Agent.ForceToSeparate(agent, 5, 45, { leader } );

    -- Summation of all separation and cohesion forces.
    local totalForces =
        forceToCombine + forceToSeparate * 1.15 + forceToAlign;

    -- Apply all steering forces.
    AgentUtilities_ApplyPhysicsSteeringForce(
        agent, totalForces, deltaTimeInSeconds);
    AgentUtilities_ClampHorizontalSpeed(agent);

    local targetRadius = agent:GetTargetRadius();
    local position = agent:GetPosition();
    local destination = leader:GetPosition();

    -- Draw debug information for target and target radius.
    Core.DrawCircle(
        position, 1, Vector.new(1, 1, 0));
    Core.DrawCircle(
        destination, targetRadius, Vector.new(1, 0, 0));
    Core.DrawLine(position, destination, Vector.new(0, 1, 0));
end
```

Our following agent is very similar to the pathing agent; it first finds a leader during the initialization and then uses cohesion and alignment steering forces to try and stay as close to the leader as possible while using a separation force at the same time to stay at least two meters away from all other agents, including the leader:

Sandbox.lua:

```
function Sandbox_Initialize(sandbox)

    ...

    -- Create a pursuing agent to follow the seeking agent.
    Sandbox.CreateAgent(sandbox, "PursuingAgent.lua");

    -- Create a group of followers that follow the seeking agent.
    for i=1, 5 do
        Sandbox.CreateAgent(sandbox, "FollowerAgent.lua");
    end

    ...

end
```

Creating five followers and drawing debug circles around them for their separation areas makes it very easy to see how each force applies to the agent's movements.

Creating a group leader and followers.

Summing steering forces

So far, we've been adding weighted steering forces together and applying forces when certain thresholds have been met, but what does all this really do to an agent's locomotion? The two most common techniques that are used to add different steering forces together are through a weighted sums approach or a priority-based approach.

Weighted sums

A weighted sums approach takes all the steering forces into account all the time using fixed coefficients that weigh each force against every other. While this is very intuitive with a small number of forces, it can get very hard to balance competing forces together when a large number of different steering forces are being used.

Typically, this should be your first approach to get the agents to move, but when complex situations need to be handled, it's better to go with a priority-based approach.

Priority-based forces

When dealing with priorities, only certain forces are taken into account based on some sort of priority or condition. For example, you can have a system that disregards all forces that are smaller than some amount or allow a round-robin style of applying forces, letting each force have a small fraction of time to apply the steering. Allowing a round robin approach can fix issues that appear in a weighted sums approach where steering forces cancel each other out and essentially leave the agent with no ability to move.

Neither the weighted sums nor the priority-based approach is perfect; both methods take a good amount of work to finely tune the agents to their expected locomotion behaviors.

Summary

So far we've created agents using steering forces such as seeking, pursuing, path following, and flocking. By now, you should be familiar with how Lua and the sandbox work together and where data and logic responsibilities lie.

In the next chapter, we'll start going over animation handling and how to create animation state machines in order to manage the stateful playback of animations and transitions. With a basic moving agent and an animating mesh, we'll move one step closer to a fully functioning AI agent.

3
Character Animations

In this chapter, we will cover the following topics:

- Loading animated meshes in the sandbox
- Attaching meshes to animating bones
- The sandbox soldier and weapon animations
- Blending multiple animations
- Creating a Lua animation state machine
- Building a soldier and weapon animation state machine

With a basic sandbox under our feet and a primitive agent representation, we can now move on to handling animations so that our agents can finally begin to look human. While we could assign a basic human mesh to our agents so far, they could never really look human without animations.

Animations play a key role in not only the visual aspect of the AI, but also the functionality of the AI. This might seem counter-intuitive, but the sandbox AI can only perform behaviors that the AI has animations for. If an animation takes 5 seconds to play out and can't be interrupted, our AI needs to take this into account before it decides to execute an animation; otherwise, our AI loses all reactiveness for these 5 seconds.

Skeletons and meshes

First, we need to cover some basics on how animations are represented and used by the sandbox.

Mesh skeletons

So far, we've learned how to create mesh representations within the sandbox. We're now going to deal with an additional asset called a skeleton. Ogre, which is the underlying renderer for the sandbox, stores the skeleton and animations within a single `.skeleton` file. Any animated Ogre mesh within the sandbox references its animations from the `media/animations` folder, and in the case of our soldier, animations are located at `media/animations/futuristic_soldier/futuristic_soldier.skeleton`.

Loading an animated mesh

Loading an animated mesh is exactly the same as loading a normal mesh within the sandbox. Simply create an animated mesh with the `Core.CreateMesh` function:

`Sandbox.lua`:

```
function Sandbox_Initialize(sandbox)
    local soldier = Core.CreateMesh(
        sandbox,
        "models/futuristic_soldier/" ..
        "futuristic_soldier_dark_anim.mesh");
```

Showing a skeleton

By default, there is nothing visually different when loading a standard mesh or an animated mesh unless we render the skeleton. The sandbox provides an easy debug representation of the skeleton with a `SetDisplaySkeleton` call:

`Sandbox.lua`:

```
function Sandbox_Initialize(sandbox)
    ...
    Animation.SetDisplaySkeleton(soldier, true);
```

The following screenshot shows you the soldier mesh with the debug skeleton information drawn. By default, animated meshes will show up typically in a T-pose when no animations are being applied to the skeleton.

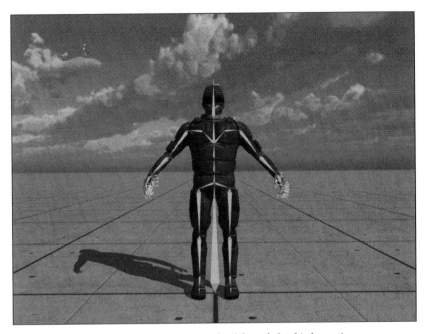

Animated mesh showing you the debug skeletal information

Attaching meshes to bones

Attaching a mesh to a bone is exactly what it sounds like. Each time the animation updates the skeleton, the attached mesh is repositioned to stay in sync with the bone it is attached to. The sandbox provides an `Animation.AttachToBone` function that attaches a mesh to a bone and allows for a position and rotation offset from the bone.

Once a mesh has been attached to the bone, you should discard the variable to the mesh, as it is no longer valid. It is best to assign the variable to nil in order to avoid errors.

Attaching a weapon to our soldier

Attaching a weapon to our soldier is very easy with the `Animation.AttachToBone` function. Given the correct offset values, we can position a sniper rifle grip into the soldier's hand:

`Sandbox.lua:`

```
function Sandbox_Initialize(sandbox)

    ...

    local weapon = Core.CreateMesh(
        sandbox,
        "models/futuristic_soldier/" ..
        "soldier_weapon.mesh");

    Animation.AttachToBone(
        soldier,
        "b_RightHand",
        weapon,
        Vector.new(0.04, 0.05, -0.01),   -- position offset
        Vector.new(98.0, 97.0, 0));   -- rotation offset in angles

    weapon = nil;
```

Running the sandbox now we'll see our soldier has a weapon attached to his right hand:

A weapon mesh attached to the soldier mesh with a given offset

Animation clips

Now that we have a mesh with a skeleton, we can start talking about how skeletons become animated. Ogre's animation system is based on animation clips and forward kinematics. What this all boils down to is the use of a hierarchical setup where each child bone is a position and orientation offset to its parent bone.

Each animation clip stores a number of key frames that pose the entire skeleton at a specific point in time. In between these key frames, Ogre will interpolate each bone position in order to create an animated skeleton.

Playing an animation on our soldier

Playing an animation on our soldier requires three important parts. First, we need to acquire the animation based on its name; then, we need to enable the animation; and then, we need to update the animation during our normal sandbox update loop.

 It is the sandbox's responsibility to step the animation based on the delta time the sandbox updates with.

Obtaining an animation is performed by the `Animation.GetAnimation` function, while enabling an animation is done through the `Animation.SetEnabled` function, and lastly stepping our animation is done with the `Animation.StepAnimation` function.

Sandbox.lua:

```
local idleAnimation;

function Sandbox_Initialize(sandbox)

    ...

    idleAnimation = Animation.GetAnimation(
        soldier, "stand_run_forward_weapon");

    -- Allow the animation to affect the soldier's skeleton.
    Animation.SetEnabled(idleAnimation, true);
end

function Sandbox_Update(sandbox, deltaTimeInMillis)
    Animation.StepAnimation(idleAnimation, deltaTimeInMillis);
end
```

Soldier animations

The soldier comes bundled with a number of animations for it to play with. The following is a list of all the animation names that can be used when referencing an animation with the `Animation.GetAnimation` function. Try out different animations in your own project to see everything that's available.

 Please note the `LICENSE.txt` file associated with the soldier in the `media\animations\futuristic_soldier` folder. The soldier, the soldier's weapon, images, and animations are licensed with the sandbox and must not be reused or distributed.

Crouching animations

The following animations animate the soldier in a crouching pose; typically, these animations can blend smoothly with each other without introducing blend artifacts:

- `crouch_backward_aim`
- `crouch_backward_weapon`
- `crouch_fire_one_shot`
- `crouch_forward_aim`
- `crouch_forward_weapon`
- `crouch_idle_aim`
- `crouch_left_aim`
- `crouch_left_weapon`
- `crouch_right_aim`
- `crouch_right_weapon`

Standing animations

The rest of the animations animate the soldier in a standing pose and allow for a wider variety of actions. As the crouching set and standing sets of animations are asymmetrical, this will require our soldiers to change to an intermediate pose before it is able to complete certain actions:

- `stand_dead_2`
- `stand_dead_headshot`
- `stand_fire_one_shot`
- `stand_grenade_toss`

- `stand_idle_aim`
- `stand_jump_land`
- `stand_jump_up`
- `stand_melee_1_with_weapon`
- `stand_melee_2_with_weapon`
- `stand_melee_3_fists`
- `stand_reload`
- `stand_roll_to_crouch_forward`
- `stand_run_backward_aim`
- `stand_run_backward_weapon`
- `stand_run_forward_aim`
- `stand_run_forward_weapon`
- `stand_smg_transform`
- `stand_sniper_transform`

Weapon animations

Our soldier's weapon also has a number of animations that will allow the sniper rifle to become a submachine gun and vice versa:

- `smg_idle`
- `smg_transform`
- `sniper_idle`
- `sniper_reload`
- `sniper_transform`

Soldier poses

Typically, animation clips are authored based on a set number of poses that an agent can be in. For example, our melee animations are only authored to be blended together with our soldier's standing idle aim pose.

Poses are very important when we lay out which animations our agent has at its disposal at any given time. Otherwise, we'll need to transition our agent into another pose first before playing our desired animation.

Our soldier model has five basic poses we need to be aware of: his standing idle aim pose, his running aim pose, his running pose, his crouch aim pose, and lastly, his crouch walk pose.

Almost all of the soldiers animations can be played quickly from the standing idle pose as the pose has no deviations in the movement during the playback.

The standing idle aim pose

In contrast, playing animations from the run pose will require some compensation for the animations' movement and possible foot positions.

The standing forward run aim pose

The standing forward run pose is even more difficult when it comes to handling consecutive animation playback, as most of our animations require the soldier to raise his weapon.

The standing forward run pose

The crouching idle pose is the ideal candidate to allow our soldiers to change their stance. As there are no leg or arm movements, for example, blending from crouching idle to the standing idle aim pose will look natural.

The crouching idle aim pose

The last pose, which is the crouching forward walk pose, allows for movement when crouching. Typically, this pose will blend well when our agents are moving and decide to change stance simultaneously without needing to first switch to an idle pose.

The crouching forward walk pose

Weapon poses

Our soldier's weapon has two main poses as well: a sniper gun pose and a **submachine gun (SMG)** pose.

The submachine gun pose (the SMG pose)

Just like the soldier, animations that were authored to play on the sniper pose, such as the reload animation, will not work correctly when the gun is in the submachine gun pose:

The sniper gun pose

Manipulating animations

A number of API calls allow you to manipulate the underlying animations backed by Ogre. While Ogre maintains the actual animation state, the sandbox is responsible for manipulating and updating these animation states.

Enabling and disabling animations

The enabling and disabling animations determine whether the animation will contribute to the skeleton's current pose. If multiple animations are enabled, they will combine in an additive manner to determine the skeleton's final pose.

> As none of our soldier's animations were authored to be played simultaneously with one another, additional steps are required to blend multiple animations together.

To determine if an animation is already enabled, we can use the `Animation.IsEnabled` function:

```
local enabled = Animation.IsEnabled(animation);
Animation.SetEnabled(animation, true);
```

Looping animations

Animation clips have an additional attribute, which is known as looping. Non-looping animations will freeze at their last keyframe pose, while looping animations will restart at the beginning of their animation when the animation is stepped past the animation length:

```
local looping = Animation.IsLooping(animation);
Animation.SetLooping(animation, true);
```

The animation length

The animation length is the number of seconds the animation plays for when stepped at the sandbox's update intervals:

```
local timeInSeconds = Animation.GetLength(animation);
```

The animation time

The animation time is how far the animation has progressed in seconds. A key aspect that must be noted is that looping animations will reset the animation's time whenever they loop. Any decisions based on an animation's time must remember to handle loop animations and deal with the amount of time the animation is stepped for.

To determine whether an animation will complete a loop within an update loop, take the animation's current time plus the amount the animation will be stepped for and see whether the result is greater than the animation's length:

```
local timeInSeconds = Animation.GetTime(animation);
Animation.SetTime(animation, timeInSeconds);
```

Normalized time

Normalized time is very similar to our animation's regular time, except that we receive a value between 0 and 1, which signifies how much of the animation has played. When using normalized time to determine whether an animation is complete, you must keep in mind the same restriction as the one while using animation time to determine whether the animation is complete:

```
local normalizedTime = Animation.GetNormalizedTime(animation);
Animation.SetNormalizedTime(animation, normalizedTime);
```

Restarting an animation

A convenient function that restarts an animation is the `Animation.Reset(animation)` function. This is essentially the same as calling `Animation.SetTime(animation, 0)`.

Playing a non-looping animation

Playing a non-looping melee animation while our soldier is already playing an idle animation takes a bit more effort than simply enabling a second animation. First, we need to disable looping on the melee animation, and then disable the animation completely during initialization.

Next, during the update loop, we determine whether the melee animation has completed; if it did complete, we disable the melee animation, reset its timing, and enable the idle animation.

To get our soldier to the melee on a command, we bind the `e_key` string to enable the melee animation and the idle animation:

Sandbox.lua:

```
local meleeAnimation;

function Sandbox_HandleEvent(sandbox, event)
    if (event.source == "keyboard" and
        event.pressed and
        event.key == "e_key") then
        if (not Animation.IsEnabled(meleeAnimation)) then
            Animation.Reset(meleeAnimation);
            Animation.SetEnabled(meleeAnimation, true);
            Animation.SetEnabled(idleAnimation, false);
        end
    end
end

function Sandbox_Initialize(sandbox)

    idleAnimation = Animation.GetAnimation(
        soldier, "stand_run_forward_weapon");

    -- Allow the animation to affect the soldier's skeleton.
    Animation.SetEnabled(idleAnimation, true);

    meleeAnimation = Animation.GetAnimation(
        soldier, "stand_melee_1_with_weapon");
    Animation.SetLooping(meleeAnimation, false);
```

```
        Animation.SetEnabled(meleeAnimation, false);
    end

    function Sandbox_Update(sandbox, deltaTimeInMillis)
        if (Animation.GetNormalizedTime(meleeAnimation) >= 1) then
            Animation.SetEnabled(idleAnimation, true);
            Animation.Reset(idleAnimation);
            Animation.SetEnabled(meleeAnimation, false);
        end

        if (Animation.IsEnabled(meleeAnimation)) then
            Animation.StepAnimation(
                meleeAnimation, deltaTimeInMillis);
        else
            Animation.StepAnimation(idleAnimation, deltaTimeInMillis);
        end
    end
```

The animation rate

As the sandbox is responsible for updating animations within the `Sandbox_Update` loop, it is also responsible for how fast the animation is playing; this is also known as the animation rate. Simply multiplying the `deltaTimeInMillis` time with a rate value will increase or decrease the animation's playback speed. We can also use negative values for the rate to have the animation play backward:

`Sandbox.lua`:

```
    function Sandbox_Update(sandbox, deltaTimeInMillis)
        if (idleAnimation) then
            local rate = 2;
            Animation.StepAnimation(
                idleAnimation, deltaTimeInMillis * rate);
        end
        ...
    end
```

Animation blending

Animation blending is the process of playing multiple animations on a single mesh at the same time. Some key things to note about animation blending are that the associated playing animations must be carefully balanced against one another; otherwise, this will result in artifacts such as clipping or impossible skeletal orientations.

We use animation blending to prevent what is commonly known as animation pops. These animation pops happen when the position of a bone becomes discontinuous as the bone moves. Typically, this shows up as an abrupt change in pose in a time span that is unbelievable to an observer.

Blending helps alleviate pops by smoothing out abrupt skeletal changes as well as allowing our soldier to blend together two animations that were not authored to be played back to back.

Animation weights

Animation blending is done through the manipulation of how much each animation contributes to the skeleton. As animation weights must be between 0 and 1, the animation system knows how much to contribute to the skeleton based on the weight's percentage to 1. Any values below 0 or above 1 are clamped by the sandbox:

```
local weight = Animation.GetWeight(animation);
Animation.SetWeight(animation, weight);
```

Blend window

The moment one animation blends into another animation is known as the blend window. For the sandbox, we consider the offset from the animation's total length as the blend window. To calculate the blend window, take the animation's length and subtract the blend window's offset:

```
Animation.Length(animation) - blendWindowOffset.
```

Blend curves

A blend curve determines how two animations will be blended together. Typically, we'll deal with a linear curve where one animation goes to 0 while the other animation goes to 1 at a steady rate. Other types of curves exist, such as exponential, quadratic, and sine curves, which blend both animations at different rates.

Linear blending

To implement linear blending, we create two types of linear blend functions. One function takes an animation and eases the animation's weight to zero over a duration of time, and another function takes an animation and eases the animation's weight to one over a duration of time. Both of these functions are meant to be called during the update loop till the animation is completely blended in or blended out.

Once these two functions are implemented, we can combine both of them into a `LinearBlendTo` function that will blend one animation out when another animation is blended in:

Sandbox.lua:

```lua
local function clamp(min, max, value)
    if (value < min) then
        return min;
    elseif (value > max) then
        return max;
    end

    return value;
end

function LinearBlendIn(
    animation, blendTime, startTime, currentTime)

    blendTime = clamp(0.01, blendTime, blendTime);
    local percent =
        clamp(0, 1, (currentTime - startTime) / blendTime);

    Animation.SetWeight(animation, percent);
end

function LinearBlendOut(
    animation, blendTime, startTime, currentTime)

    blendTime = clamp(0.01, blendTime, blendTime);
    local percent =
        clamp(0, 1, (currentTime - startTime) / blendTime);

    Animation.SetWeight(animation, 1 - percent);
end

function LinearBlendTo(
    startAnimation, endAnimation, blendTime, startTime,
        currentTime)
    LinearBlendIn(
        endAnimation, blendTime, startTime, currentTime);
    LinearBlendOut(
        startAnimation, blendTime, startTime, currentTime);
end
```

Playing with blend weights

Now that we have a function that can smoothly blend from one animation to another, we can modify out playback of the idle animation to the melee animation with our `LinearBlendTo` function. The key difference that using our `LinearBlendTo` function has is that we need to record the time when the blend begins so that it can process the blending based on our blend duration.

Instead of immediately controlling the melee animation within the `Sandbox_HandleEvent` function, we use a Boolean flag to specify whether the soldier should play the melee animation and handle the blending of the animations within the update function:

`Sandbox.lua`:

```
local melee, idle, shouldMelee, meleeStartTime, meleeStopTime;

function Sandbox_HandleEvent(sandbox, event)
    if (event.source == "keyboard" and
        event.pressed and event.key == "e_key") then

        if (not shouldMelee) then
            Animation.Reset(melee);
            shouldMelee = true;
            meleeStartTime = Sandbox.GetTimeInSeconds(sandbox);
        end
    end
end

function Sandbox_Initialize(sandbox)
    ...
    idle = Animation.GetAnimation(soldier, "stand_idle_aim");
    Animation.SetEnabled(idle, true);

    shouldMelee = false;
    melee = Animation.GetAnimation(
        soldier, "stand_melee_1_with_weapon");
    Animation.SetLooping(melee, false);
    Animation.SetEnabled(melee, true);
    Animation.SetWeight(melee, 0);
    Animation.SetTime(melee, Animation.GetLength(melee));
end

function Sandbox_Update(sandbox, deltaTimeInMillis)
    Animation.StepAnimation(idle, deltaTimeInMillis);
```

```
Animation.StepAnimation(melee, deltaTimeInMillis);

local currentTime = Sandbox.GetTimeInSeconds(sandbox);

if (shouldMelee) then
    if ((Animation.GetLength(melee) -
        Animation.GetTime(melee)) > 0.5) then
        LinearBlendTo(
            idle, melee, 0.2, meleeStartTime, currentTime);
    else
        meleeStopTime = currentTime;
        shouldMelee = false;
    end
else
    if ((Animation.GetLength(melee) -
        Animation.GetTime(melee)) > 0.05) then
        LinearBlendTo(
            melee, idle, 0.3, meleeStopTime, currentTime);
    end
end
end
```

Now, every time we press the *E* key, our soldier will blend into the melee animation and smoothly blend out into the idle animation.

Blending between idle and melee animations

Animation state machine (ASM)

Currently, our animation blending is a bit verbose and requires a lot of manual handling from Lua. Now, we're going to create a system that will manage animations and blends for us based on the concept of a **finite state machine** (**FSM**). We'll call this system an animation state machine but in essence, it's an FSM where states are animations and transitions between states represent the blend window, blend duration, and animation offsets.

States

Animation states in Lua will be represented by a table with a few key pieces of information. First, we need to store the animation, state name, whether the state is looping, and at what rate the animation will be played. The ASM will contain one animation state for each animation we support for our soldier.

 You can find the book's implementation of an animation state in the `src/demo_framework/script/AnimationState.lua` file.

Laying out the `AnimationState` class will create an initialization function which assigns default values for each instance of `AnimationState`.

Sandbox.lua:

```
AnimationState = {};

function AnimationState.new()
    local state = {};

    state.animation_ = nil;
    state.name_     = "";
    state.looping_  = false;
    state.rate_     = 1;

    return state;
end
```

 Setting a Lua table value to nil will remove the value from the table, but it is helpful to document exactly which variables we will be executing on.

Transitions

Transitions are represented in the same way with a Lua table and some basic information on how two animation states will blend together. The information we need to keep is the blend curve, blend-in window offset, blend-out window offset, and the duration of the animation blend.

 You can find the book's implementation of an animation state in the `src/demo_framework/script/AnimationTransition.lua` file.

Laying out the `AnimationTransition` class will create an initialization function which assigns default values for each instance of `AnimationTransition`.

`Sandbox.lua`:

```lua
AnimationTransition = {};

function AnimationTransition.new()
    local transition = {};

    transition.blendCurve_    = "linear";
    transition.blendInWindow_  = 0;
    transition.blendOutWindow_ = 0;
    transition.duration_       = 0.2;

    return transition;
end
```

Creating animation state machines

The animation state machine is created in a way that is very similar to transitions and states. We create a new Lua table and assign some basic attributes to the table. In this case, we'll need to know about the current state that is being played, whether there is a current transition happening, the next state the ASM is trying to transition to, the start time of the transition, as well as tables that represent the states and transitions of the ASM.

 You can find the book's implementation of an animation state in the `src/demo_framework/script/AnimationStateMachine.lua` file.

When we create an `AnimationStateMachine` instance we'll also assign default values, as well as create internal tables for store states and transitions.

`Sandbox.lua`:

```lua
require "AnimationUtilities";

AnimationStateMachine = {};

function AnimationStateMachine.new()
    local asm = {};

    -- data members
    asm.currentState_ = nil;
    asm.currentTransition_ = nil;
    asm.nextState_ = nil;
    asm.states_ = {};
    asm.transitions_ = {};
    asm.transitionStartTime_ = nil;

    return asm;
end
```

Creating helper functions

With our basic data structures out of the way, we need some helper functions to deal with animations. The `ClearAnimation` `InitializeAnimation` and `StepAnimation` functions will help when we need to transition to new states so that animations are in an expected enabled/disabled state. The StepAnimation function is slightly different and provides a means of handling the rate of animation playback.

`Sandbox.lua`:

```lua
local function ClearAnimation(animation)
    Animation.SetEnabled(animation, false);
end

local function InitializeAnimation(animation, startTime)
    Animation.Reset(animation);
    Animation.SetEnabled(animation, true);
    Animation.SetWeight(animation, 1);

    if (startTime ~= nil) then
        Animation.SetTime(animation, startTime);
    end
end

local function StepAnimation(animation, deltaTimeInMillis, rate)
```

```
        rate = rate or 1;

        Animation.StepAnimation(
            animation, deltaTimeInMillis * rate);
    end
```

Adding states

Adding states to our ASM will take in the required information in order to create a new animation state and assign the relevant information directly. We call ClearAnimation on the passed-in animation to make sure that it is in a known state.

Assigning the state to the ASM is done based on the state's name. This ensures the unique naming of states. As we will be interacting with an ASM through state names, this uniqueness is important:

Sandbox.lua:

```
    function AnimationStateMachine.AddState(
        self, name, animation, looping, rate)

        local state = AnimationState.new();
        state.name_    = name;
        state.animation_ = animation;
        state.rate_    = rate or state.rate_;
        state.looping_ = looping or state.looping_;

        self.states_[name] = state;

        ClearAnimation(animation);
        Animation.SetLooping(animation, state.looping_);
    end
```

Adding transitions

Adding transitions to the ASM is very similar to adding states, except that we need to check and make sure that the ASM contains the states we are transitioning to. Transitions are stored in a manner that is very similar to states, except that they are stored in a two-dimensional table based on their *from state* and their *to state*:

Sandbox.lua:

```
    function AnimationStateMachine.AddTransition(
        self, fromStateName, toStateName, blendOutWindow, duration,
```

```
    blendInWindow)

if (self:ContainsState(fromStateName) and
    self:ContainsState(toStateName)) then

    local transition = AnimationTransition.new();
    transition.blendOutWindow_ =
        blendOutWindow or transition.blendOutWindow_;
    transition.duration_ = duration or transition.duration_;
    transition.blendInWindow_ =
        blendInWindow or transition.blendInWindow_;

    if (self.transitions_[fromStateName] == nil) then
        self.transitions_[fromStateName] = {};
    end

    self.transitions_[fromStateName][toStateName] =
        transition;
    end
end
```

Adding external helper functions

Some additional helper functions come in handy when determining whether the ASM already has a state or transition and what is the current state the ASM is in:

Sandbox.lua:

```
function AnimationStateMachine.ContainsState(self, stateName)
    return self.states_[stateName] ~= nil;
end

function AnimationStateMachine.ContainsTransition(
    self, fromStateName, toStateName)

    return self.transitions_[fromStateName] ~= nil and
        self.transitions_[fromStateName][toStateName] ~= nil;
end

function AnimationStateMachine.GetCurrentStateName(self)
    if (self.currentState_) then
        return self.currentState_.name_;
    end
end
```

Forcefully setting states

Now that we have states and transitions, we need to be able to set the state of the ASM at any time. For this, we need to clear out any currently playing animations and set the current state while initializing the state's animation.

 Forcefully setting an ASM's state will immediately begin playing the animation for the set state. This will typically create an undesired *pop* for the requested animation.

Our SetState function will mainly be responsible for clearing a playing animation, and then immediately applying the animation for the corresponding forced state.

Sandbox.lua:

```
function AnimationStateMachine.SetState(self, stateName)
    if (self:ContainsState(stateName)) then
        if (self.currentState_) then
            ClearAnimation(self.currentState_.animation_);
        end
        if (self.nextState_) then
            ClearAnimation(self.nextState_.animation_);
        end

        self.nextState_ = nil;
        self.currentTransition_ = nil;
        self.transitionStartTime_ = nil;
        self.currentState_ = self.states_[stateName];
        InitializeAnimation(self.currentState_.animation_);
    end
end
```

Requesting states

Requesting a state in the ASM sets the next state the ASM will transition to without forcefully setting the state immediately. Requesting a state allows the ASM to transition between the current state's animation and the next state's animation based on the blend duration and the blend window:

Sandbox.lua:

```
function AnimationStateMachine.RequestState(self, stateName)
    if (self.nextState_ == nil and
        self:ContainsState(stateName)) then
        local currentState = self.currentState_;

        if (currentState == nil) then
```

```
        self:SetState(stateName);
      else
        self.nextState_ = self.states_[stateName];
      end

      return true;
    end
    return false;
  end
```

Updating the animation state machine

Updating the ASM is a bit of work. First, we need to check whether the ASM will be
transitioning to a new state, and secondly, we need to handle updating any animation
that is playing either the current state's animation or a blend of two animations.

Handling state transitions and state requests

During an update, we need to check whether a transition is already being processed
or whether we even have another state to transition to. If there is a next state, and no
transition is processing, we check to see whether the blend window has passed so
that we can start transitioning into the next state.

A special case is added to hand transitions moving to another state even though there
is no explicit transition to that state. While handling this case isn't entirely necessary,
it allows the ASM to finish playing the current animation before processing a request
to a new state that has no explicit transition:

Sandbox.lua:

```
function AnimationStateMachine.Update(
    self, deltaTimeInMillis, currentTimeInMillis)

    local deltaTimeInSeconds = deltaTimeInMillis/1000;
    local currentTimeInSeconds = currentTimeInMillis/1000;

    if (self.currentTransition_ == nil and self.nextState_) then
        local currentAnimTime =
            Animation.GetTime(self.currentState_.animation_);
        local currentAnimLength =
            Animation.GetLength(self.currentState_.animation_);

        if (self:ContainsTransition(
            self.currentState_.name_,
            self.nextState_.name_)) then

            local transition =
```

```
                        self.transitions_[self.currentState_.name_]
                            [self.nextState_.name_];

                if ((currentAnimTime + deltaTimeInSeconds) >=
                    (currentAnimLength -
                     transition.blendOutWindow_)) then

                    self.currentTransition_ = transition;
                    self.transitionStartTime_ =
                        currentTimeInSeconds;
                    InitializeAnimation(
                        self.nextState_.animation_,
                        transition.blendInWindow_);
                end
            else
                if ((currentAnimTime + deltaTimeInSeconds) >=
                    currentAnimLength) then

                    ClearAnimation(self.currentState_.animation_);
                    InitializeAnimation(self.nextState_.animation_);

                    self.currentState_ = self.nextState_;
                    self.nextState_ = nil;
                end
            end
        end
    end
```

Updating running animations

After checking whether the ASM is transitioning, we now need to handle
stepping animations. Two cases can exist in the ASM: either we are stepping
multiple animations when handling a transition, or we are stepping the current
state's animation only. When stepping multiple animations during a transition,
it's necessary to clear out a finished animation based on the animation's weight,
and then set the ASM to the next state:

Sandbox.lua:

```
    function AnimationStateMachine.Update(
        self, deltaTimeInMillis, currentTimeInMillis)

        ...

        if (self.currentTransition_) then
            AnimationUtilities_LinearBlendTo(
                self.currentState_.animation_,
```

```
            self.nextState_.animation_,
            self.currentTransition_.duration_,
            self.transitionStartTime_,
            currentTimeInSeconds);

        StepAnimation(
            self.currentState_.animation_,
            deltaTimeInMillis,
            self.currentState_.rate_);
        StepAnimation(
            self.nextState_.animation_,
            deltaTimeInMillis,
            self.currentState_.rate_);

        if (Animation.GetWeight(
            self.currentState_.animation_) == 0) then

            ClearAnimation(self.currentState_.animation_);
            self.currentState_     = self.nextState_;
            self.nextState_        = nil;
            self.currentTransition_ = nil;
            self.transitionStartTime_ = nil;
        end
    elseif (self.currentState_) then
        StepAnimation(
            self.currentState_.animation_,
            deltaTimeInMillis,
            self.currentState_.rate_);
    end
end
```

Adding functions to animation state machine instances

Now that we've flushed out our animation state machine functionality, we need to add each `AnimationStateMachine` function to every ASM instance. This is just an object-oriented way of adding class functions to our animation state machines:

Sandbox.lua:

```
function AnimationStateMachine.new()
    local asm = {};

    ...

    asm.AddState = AnimationStateMachine.AddState;
    asm.AddTransition = AnimationStateMachine.AddTransition;
```

```
    asm.ContainsState = AnimationStateMachine.ContainsState;
    asm.ContainsTransition =
        AnimationStateMachine.ContainsTransition;
    asm.GetCurrentStateName =
        AnimationStateMachine.GetCurrentStateName;
    asm.RequestState = AnimationStateMachine.RequestState;
    asm.SetState = AnimationStateMachine.SetState;
    asm.Update = AnimationStateMachine.Update;

    return asm;
end
```

Building a weapon animation state machine

Now that we've built an entire animation state machine system, it's time to build the ASMs our soldier will use. As the soldier's weapon is the simplest ASM, we'll start there first. With only five different animations, this is a relatively easy ASM to build.

First, we add each of the states with their corresponding animations and specify whether the animation is looping or non-looping. Next, we connect each state via transitions. Lastly, we request a state within the ASM to start playing a looping animation; in this case, this is the `sniper_idle` state.

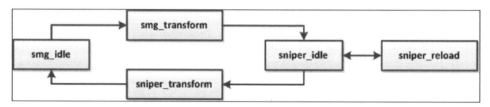

The sniper/submachine gun animation state machine

 The reload animation for the weapon only works when the weapon is in its sniper pose. The ASM must reflect this; otherwise, you will see a noticeable *pop* on the sniper pose before the reload animation plays.

Creating the weapon ASM primarily consists of adding each state, the states corresponding to the animation to play, and creating transitions between existing states.

Sandbox.lua:

```
require "AnimationStateMachine";

local weaponAsm;

function Sandbox_Initialize(sandbox)

    ...

    weaponAsm = AnimationStateMachine.new();

    weaponAsm:AddState(
        "smg_idle",
        Animation.GetAnimation(weapon, "smg_idle"),
        true);
    weaponAsm:AddState(
        "smg_transform",
        Animation.GetAnimation(weapon, "smg_transform"));
    weaponAsm:AddState(
        "sniper_idle",
        Animation.GetAnimation(weapon, "sniper_idle"),
        true);
    weaponAsm:AddState(
        "sniper_reload",
        Animation.GetAnimation(weapon, "sniper_reload"));
    weaponAsm:AddState(
        "sniper_transform",
        Animation.GetAnimation(weapon, "sniper_transform"));

    -- Add weapon transitions.
    local sniperLength = Animation.GetLength(
        Animation.GetAnimation(weapon, "sniper_idle"));
    local smgLength = Animation.GetLength(
        Animation.GetAnimation(weapon, "smg_idle"));

    weaponAsm:AddTransition(
        "sniper_idle", "sniper_reload", sniperLength, 0.2);
    weaponAsm:AddTransition(
        "sniper_idle", "sniper_transform", sniperLength, 0.2);
    weaponAsm:AddTransition(
        "sniper_reload", "sniper_idle", 0.2, 0.2);
    weaponAsm:AddTransition(
        "sniper_transform", "sniper_idle", 0.2, 0.2);
```

```
weaponAsm:AddTransition(
    "smg_idle", "smg_transform", smgLength , 0.2);
weaponAsm:AddTransition(
    "smg_transform", "smg_idle", 0.2, 0.2);

weaponAsm:RequestState("sniper_idle");

Animation.AttachToBone(
    soldier,
    "b_RightHand",
    weapon,
    Vector.new(0.04, 0.05, -0.01),
    Vector.new(98.0, 97.0, 0));

weapon = nil;
end
```

Building a soldier animation state machine

Building the soldier's ASM is very similar to the weapon ASM, except that we have a lot more animations to think about. In this case, we're only going to flush out the standing idle and standing run poses of the soldier. A spoke-wheel-designed ASM can easily accomplish each of the animation states with their corresponding transitions.

One large restriction to this simple design is that whenever an animation plays, we must return to the idle stand animation before being able to play another animation. In a fully connected ASM, you can add additional transition animations to go from **reload** to **fire** immediately, for example:

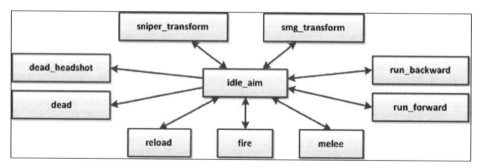

The soldier animation state machine

You should pay attention to where transitions exist as well as their blend durations, as this will ultimately affect how reactive your agent will appear. As this design requires going back to the `idle_aim` state for a minimum of the blend duration, there will always be a slight delay before an agent can select another animation.

Another key idea to take away is that when we add a transition from the `idle_aim` state to any other state, we want the `idle_aim` state to blend immediately with the next state. Setting the blend window of these transitions to the full length of the `idle_aim` state's animation will allow them to blend immediately, regardless of how far into the `idle_aim` animation's length we are:

Sandbox.lua:

```
local weaponAsm;
local soliderAsm;

function Sandbox_Initialize(sandbox)
    ...

    soliderAsm = AnimationStateMachine.new();

    soliderAsm:AddState(
        "idle_aim",
        Animation.GetAnimation(soldier, "stand_idle_aim"),
        true);
    soliderAsm:AddState(
        "dead",
        Animation.GetAnimation(soldier, "stand_dead_2"));
    soliderAsm:AddState(
        "dead_headshot",
        Animation.GetAnimation(soldier, "stand_dead_headshot"));
    soliderAsm:AddState(
        "fire",
        Animation.GetAnimation(soldier, "stand_fire_one_shot"),
        true);
    soliderAsm:AddState(
        "melee",
        Animation.GetAnimation(
            soldier, "stand_melee_1_with_weapon"));
    soliderAsm:AddState(
        "reload",
        Animation.GetAnimation(soldier, "stand_reload"));
    soliderAsm:AddState(
        "run_backward",
        Animation.GetAnimation(
            soldier, "stand_run_backward_aim"),
        true);
    soliderAsm:AddState(
        "run_forward",
```

```
        Animation.GetAnimation(
        soldier, "stand_run_forward_aim"), true);
    soliderAsm:AddState("
        smg_transform",
        Animation.GetAnimation(soldier, "stand_smg_transform"));
    soliderAsm:AddState(
        "sniper_transform",
        Animation.GetAnimation(
            soldier, "stand_sniper_transform"));

    -- Add soldier transitions.
    local idleAim =
        Animation.GetAnimation(soldier, "stand_idle_aim");
    local idleAimLength = Animation.GetLength(idleAim);

    soliderAsm:AddTransition(
        "idle_aim", "dead", idleAimLength, 0.2);
    soliderAsm:AddTransition(
        "idle_aim", "dead_headshot", idleAimLength, 0.2);
    soliderAsm:AddTransition(
        "idle_aim", "fire", idleAimLength, 0.1);
    soliderAsm:AddTransition(
        "idle_aim", "melee", idleAimLength, 0.2);
    soliderAsm:AddTransition(
        "idle_aim", "reload", idleAimLength, 0.2);
    soliderAsm:AddTransition(
        "idle_aim", "run_backward", idleAimLength, 0.2);
    soliderAsm:AddTransition(
        "idle_aim", "run_forward", idleAimLength, 0.2);
    soliderAsm:AddTransition(
        "idle_aim", "smg_transform", idleAimLength, 0.2);
    soliderAsm:AddTransition(
        "idle_aim", "sniper_transform", idleAimLength, 0.2);
    soliderAsm:AddTransition("fire", "idle_aim", 0.1, 0.1);
    soliderAsm:AddTransition("melee", "idle_aim", 0.2, 0.2);
    soliderAsm:AddTransition("reload", "idle_aim", 0.2, 0.2);
    soliderAsm:AddTransition(
        "run_backward", "idle_aim", 0.2, 0.2);
    soliderAsm:AddTransition(
        "run_forward", "idle_aim", 0.2, 0.2);
    soliderAsm:AddTransition(
        "smg_transform", "idle_aim", 0.2, 0.2);
    soliderAsm:AddTransition(
        "sniper_transform", "idle_aim", 0.2, 0.2);

    soliderAsm:RequestState("idle_aim");
end
```

Updating animation state machines

Now that we've created both the soldier and weapon ASMs, we need to add an update call within the sandbox update loop. This allows for both ASMs to update whatever animations they are playing:

Sandbox.lua:

```
function Sandbox_Update(sandbox, deltaTimeInMillis)
    soliderAsm:Update(
        deltaTimeInMillis, Sandbox.GetTimeInMillis(sandbox));
    weaponAsm:Update(
        deltaTimeInMillis, Sandbox.GetTimeInMillis(sandbox));
end
```

Playing with states

We can now start playing with animation states within our ASMs. In this case, we have two ASMs that need to be kept in sync, so we create a global `weaponState` variable that will check whether our weapon is in the sniper rifle pose or the SMG pose.

Next, we can bind each of the number pad keys to request specific states within our soldier and weapon ASMs. Special case handling is required for the transform states as well as the reload state:

Sandbox.lua:

```
local weaponState = "sniper";

local function IsNumKey(key, numKey)
    -- Match both numpad keys and numeric keys.
    return string.find(
        key, string.format("^[numpad_]*%d_key$", numKey));
end

function Sandbox_HandleEvent(sandbox, event)
    if (event.source == "keyboard" and event.pressed) then
        if (event.key == "f1_key") then
            Sandbox.SetCameraPosition(
                sandbox, Vector.new(0, 1, -3));
            Sandbox.SetCameraForward(
                sandbox, Vector.new(0, 0, -1));
        elseif (event.key == "f2_key") then
            UI.SetVisible(ui, not UI.IsVisible(ui));
```

```
        elseif (event.key == "f3_key") then
            displaySkeleton = not displaySkeleton;
            Animation.SetDisplaySkeleton(
                soldier, displaySkeleton);
        elseif (IsNumKey(event.key, 1)) then
            soldierAsm:RequestState("melee");
        elseif (IsNumKey(event.key, 2)) then
            if (weaponState == "sniper" and
                soldierAsm:RequestState("reload")) then

                weaponAsm:RequestState("sniper_reload");
            end
        elseif (IsNumKey(event.key, 3)) then
            if (weaponState == "sniper") then
                if (soldierAsm:RequestState("smg_transform")) then
                    weaponAsm:RequestState("smg_transform");
                    weaponState = "smg";
                end
            end
        elseif (IsNumKey(event.key, 4)) then
            if (weaponState == "smg") then
                if (soldierAsm:RequestState(
                    "sniper_transform")) then

                    weaponAsm:RequestState("sniper_transform");
                    weaponState = "sniper";
                end
            end
        elseif (IsNumKey(event.key, 5)) then
            soldierAsm:RequestState("fire");
        elseif (IsNumKey(event.key, 6)) then
            soldierAsm:RequestState("run_forward");
        elseif (IsNumKey(event.key, 7)) then
            soldierAsm:RequestState("run_backward");
        elseif (IsNumKey(event.key, 8)) then
            soldierAsm:RequestState("dead");
        elseif (IsNumKey(event.key, 9)) then
            soldierAsm:RequestState("dead_headshot");
        end
    end
end
```

As we want both the soldier's ASM and the weapon's ASM to return their idle states whenever a new state hasn't been requested, we can add a check during the update loop to request their idle states, if required:

Sandbox.lua:

```
function Sandbox_Update(sandbox, deltaTimeInMillis)
    -- Update the animation state machines to handle blending
    -- and animation playback.
    soldierAsm:Update(
        deltaTimeInMillis, Sandbox.GetTimeInMillis(sandbox));
    weaponAsm:Update(
        deltaTimeInMillis, Sandbox.GetTimeInMillis(sandbox));

    -- Always send both state machines back to the idle animation.
    if (soldierAsm:GetCurrentStateName() ~= "idle_aim") then
        soldierAsm:RequestState("idle_aim");
    end

    if (weaponState == "sniper") then
        if (weaponAsm:GetCurrentStateName() ~= "sniper_idle") then
            weaponAsm:RequestState("sniper_idle");
        end
    elseif (weaponState == "smg") then
        if (weaponAsm:GetCurrentStateName() ~= "smg_idle") then
            weaponAsm:RequestState("smg_idle");
        end
    end
end
```

Summary

From playing a simple animation clip to creating a full-fledged animation state machine, we've begun to bring life to characters. At the end of the day, animations play a very important role, not just in how our AIs will look, but what our AIs can do at any given moment.

Now that we have a stateful representation of when and what our agents will look like while executing specific behaviors, we can move forward to the next chapter and start binding the visual look of the agent with the agent's decision making.

4
Mind Body Control

In this chapter, we will cover the following topics:

- Attaching an animated mesh to an agent
- Adding callbacks to the Lua animation state machine
- Getting our soldier to shoot projectiles
- Creating an agent that directly controls the animation playback
- Creating an animation controller that handles the animation playback
- Running agents through an obstacle course

Now that we've learned how to move agents based on steering forces and created a system to handle animated meshes, it's time to join both of these systems to build a visual representation of an animated, moving agent.

Going forward, we'll implement two different approaches on how decision logic, the mind, the visual appearance, and the body can be implemented within the sandbox.

Creating a body

So far, we've hardcoded a lot of functionality directly inside our sandbox or agent Lua scripts. Now, we'll be using the same logic, but instead of duplicating it in multiple places, we'll be using helper functions provided by `src/demo_framework/script/Soldier.lua`. The functions within the soldier Lua script are specialized and tuned to provide the correct steering weights and animation representation in order to create a soldier going forward. The animation state machines found within the soldier script are a more flushed-out representation of the same state machines that we created previously.

Creating a soldier

Now, we'll take a brief look at what functionalities the soldier script provides and how we'll go about using them.

The `Soldier.SoldierStates` and `Soldier.WeaponStates` tables provide a list of all the available animation states for both the soldier and the soldier's weapon animation state machines.

The `Soldier_AttachWeapon` function will attach the soldier's weapon mesh to the proper bone with the correct position and rotation offsets:

```
function Soldier_AttachWeapon(soldier, weapon)
```

`Soldier_CalculateSlowSteering` will return a steering vector tuned toward the agents slowly moving throughout the environment. This will be the steering function we'll use when the agent is crouching:

```
function Soldier_CalculateSlowSteering(agent, deltaTimeInSeconds)
```

`Soldier_CalculateSteering` returns the original steering vector we calculated previously when our agent was running upright:

```
function Soldier_CalculateSteering(agent, deltaTimeInSeconds)
```

`Soldier_CreateLightSoldier` creates a soldier mesh attached to an agent with black and white armor:

```
function Soldier_CreateLightSoldier(agent)
```

`Soldier_CreateSoldier` creates a soldier mesh attached to an agent with black and red armor:

```
function Soldier_CreateSoldier(agent)
```

`Soldier_CreateSoldierStateMachine` creates and initializes an animation state machine already configured with states and transition setups for an animated soldier mesh. Additional crouch states and transitions are handled within this version of the state machine:

```
function Soldier_CreateSoldierStateMachine(soldier)
```

`Soldier_CreateWeapon` creates an animated weapon mesh attached to the agent:

```
function Soldier_CreateWeapon(agent)
```

`Soldier_CreateWeaponStateMachine` creates and initializes a fully connected animation state machine configured for our weapon mesh:

```
function Soldier_CreateWeaponStateMachine(weapon)
```

`Soldier_IsFalling` returns a true or false Boolean value depending on whether the soldier is considered free-falling in air. Small falls such as brief steps off the ground running down a ramp, will not return true from this function:

```
function Soldier_IsFalling(agent)
```

`Soldier_IsMoving` returns true or false if the agent is considered to be moving in any direction; again, small amounts of movements will return false:

```
function Soldier_IsMoving(agent)
```

`Soldier_OnGround` returns true or false if the agent is considered to be touching the ground. Small fluctuations of the agent off the ground will still return true:

```
function Soldier_OnGround(agent)
```

`Soldier_SetHeight` properly adjusts the agent's collision capsule with the physics environment and properly offsets the soldier's mesh to the new height:

```
function Soldier_SetHeight(agent, soldierMesh, newHeight)
```

`Soldier_SetPath` assigns a path to an agent and adjusts the agent's facing direction toward the starting position of the path, if required:

```
function Soldier_SetPath(agent, path, cyclic)
```

`Soldier_SlowMovement` artificially dampens the agent's velocity based on the rate of deceleration. This function is useful in order to adjust the speed of the agent, when it goes from running to idle, to matching the animation playback:

```
function Soldier_SlowMovement(agent, deltaTimeInMillis, rate)
```

`Soldier_Shoot` is a helper function that shoots a laser projectile out of the agent's weapon muzzle. This function is only meant to be used as a callback for the animation state machine:

```
function Soldier_Shoot(stateName, callbackData)
```

`Soldier_Update` wraps additional soldier logic that is required during the soldier's update loop:

```
function Soldier_Update(agent, deltaTimeInMillis)
```

Attaching an animated mesh to an agent

First, we'll attach a soldier mesh to an actual agent. The only difference while creating a mesh in this fashion is passing the agent into the `Core.CreateMesh` function instead of the sandbox. This allows the sandbox to automatically update the mesh based on the agent's position and orientation.

As the sandbox automatically updates the mesh's position and orientation based on the agent's forward direction, we will always consider the agent's forward vector as the vector of movement and not necessarily the direction the agent is facing. Intuitively, this division will allow our agent to move backwards, for example, while still having the mesh facing forward:

SoldierAgent.lua:

```
require "Soldier"

local _soldier;
local _soldierAsm;
local _weaponAsm;

function Agent_Cleanup(agent)
end

function Agent_HandleEvent(agent, event)
end

function Agent_Initialize(agent)
    -- Initialize the soldier and weapon models.
    _soldier = Soldier_CreateSoldier(agent);
    local weapon = Soldier_CreateWeapon(agent);

    -- Create the soldier and weapon animation state machines.
    _soldierAsm = Soldier_CreateSoldierStateMachine(_soldier);
    _weaponAsm = Soldier_CreateWeaponStateMachine(weapon);

    -- Request a default looping state in both animation state
    -- machines.
    _soldierAsm:RequestState(
        Soldier.SoldierStates.STAND_RUN_FORWARD);
    _weaponAsm:RequestState(Soldier.WeaponStates.SMG_IDLE);

    -- Attach the weapon model after the animation state machines
    -- have been created.
    Soldier_AttachWeapon(_soldier, weapon);
    weapon = nil;
end

function Agent_Update(agent, deltaTimeInMillis)
end
```

Creating an obstacle course

Now, we're going to replace the plane we've been using for the sandbox with something that is a bit more interesting. The `SandboxUtilities_CreateLevel` function internally creates a number of boxes that represent a level with more variation in height and terrain.

 Take a look at the `SandboxUtilities_CreateBox` function to know how you can change the layout of the level or create additional sandbox geometry.

`Sandbox.lua`:

```
require "SandboxUtilities"

function Sandbox_Initialize(sandbox)
    SandboxUtilities_CreateLevel(sandbox);

    Sandbox.CreateAgent(sandbox, "SoldierAgent.lua");
end
```

In the following screenshot, you can see that we have introduced some obstacles for the agent:

Displaying the physics world

So far, we've been using physics but never actually displayed any physics representation within the sandbox. To know whether our agent has been set up properly, though, we need to make sure that the soldier's mesh and agent's height line up. We can enable drawing a debug representation of the physics world within the sandbox in order to understand representations of our physics objects.

 Drawing the physics world can be expensive, as it requires continuous updates and should not be enabled by default.

Sandbox.lua:

```lua
function Sandbox_HandleEvent(sandbox, event)
    if (event.source == "keyboard" and event.pressed) then
        if ( event.key == "f1_key" ) then
            local drawDebug =
                Sandbox.GetDrawPhysicsWorld(sandbox);
            Sandbox.SetDrawPhysicsWorld(sandbox, not drawDebug);
        end
    end
end
```

The following screenshot shows you the physics world that we have created:

Adding callbacks to the animation state machine

So far, our animation state machine could control animations and transitions; now, we'll extend the ASM to notify functions whenever a new state begins playing. This functionality is extremely useful for actions that require synchronization with animations, such as reloading and shooting.

Previously, we've implemented our animation state machine within the Sandbox. lua script. Now, you can either copy that implementation into a new AnimationStateMachine.lua file or take a look at the implementation provided by the sandbox.

 The sandbox will always load a demo's specific implementation of a Lua file instead of the file provided by default within the demo_framework project. This allows you to replace the default implementation of the AnimationStateMachine.lua script, for instance, without needing to change any other script references.

Handling callbacks

A callback is essentially another Lua function that is stored as a variable. A helper function iterates over all callbacks associated with a state and invokes them accordingly, passing an additional data value along with the state name and whether the state is looping:

AnimationStateMachine.lua:

```
local function CallCallbacks(callbacks, stateName, looping)
    for index = 1, #callbacks do
        callbacks[index].callback(
            stateName, looping, callbacks[index].data);
    end
end
```

Adding callbacks to the ASM

To add a callback to the ASM, we store the callback function as well as an arbitrary data member to be passed back to the callback when invoked. This data member allows for any specific information the callback might require, such as a reference to the agent or the soldier mesh:

AnimationStateMachine.lua:

```
function AnimationStateMachine.AddStateCallback(
    self, name, callback, data)

    if (self:ContainsState(name)) then
        if (not self.stateCallbacks_[name]) then
            self.stateCallbacks_[name] = {};
        end
        table.insert(
            self.stateCallbacks_[name],
            { callback = callback, data = data });
    end
end

function AnimationStateMachine.new()
    ...

    asm.stateCallbacks_ = {};
    asm.AddStateCallback =
        AnimationStateMachine.AddStateCallback;

    ...
end
```

Updating the ASM to call callbacks

Handling callbacks within the ASM must occur in three different places. A helper HandleCallbacks function is useful in order to reduce duplicating code.

The first case we need to handle is when the ASM transitions to a state that contains callbacks. This particular case has two different variations: one where a transition exists within the ASM and another when no transition exists.

The last case we handle is when animations loop. When updating the current state of the ASM, an additional check is required in order to see whether stepping the ASM will cause the animation to loop. A while loop is used to handle callbacks in this case, as it's possible for an animation to loop multiple times within a single step of the ASM.

While an animation can loop multiple times within a single ASM time step, this typically doesn't happen, and any example callbacks we write won't consider this case.

AnimationStateMachine.lua:

```lua
local function HandleCallbacks(self, stateName)
    if (self.stateCallbacks_[stateName]) then
        CallCallbacks(
            self.stateCallbacks_[stateName], stateName);
    end
end

function AnimationStateMachine.Update(
    self, deltaTimeInMillis, currentTimeInMillis)

    ...

            if ((currentAnimTime + deltaTimeInSeconds) >=
                currentAnimLength) then

                ClearAnimation(self.currentState_.animation_);
                InitializeAnimation(self.nextState_.animation_);

                self.currentState_ = self.nextState_;
                self.nextState_ = nil;

                HandleCallbacks(self, self.nextState_.name_);
            end
        else
            if ((currentAnimTime + deltaTimeInSeconds) >=
                currentAnimLength) then

                ClearAnimation(self.currentState_.animation_);
                InitializeAnimation(self.nextState_.animation_);

                self.currentState_ = self.nextState_;
                self.nextState_ = nil;

                HandleCallbacks(self, self.currentState_.name_);
            end
        end
    end

    -- Step animations that are currently playing.
```

```
        if (self.currentTransition_) then

        ...

        elseif (self.currentState_) then
            local currentAnimTime =
                Animation.GetTime(self.currentState_.animation_);
            local currentAnimLength =
                Animation.GetLength(self.currentState_.animation_);
            local deltaTime =
                deltaTimeInSeconds * self.currentState_.rate_;

            local timeStepped = (currentAnimTime + deltaTime);

            while timeStepped >= currentAnimLength do
                HandleCallbacks(self, self.currentState_.name_);

                timeStepped = timeStepped - currentAnimLength;
            end

            StepAnimation(
                self.currentState_.animation_,
                deltaTimeInMillis,
                self.currentState_.rate_);
        end
    end
```

Getting our soldier to shoot

Before we use the `Soldier_Shoot` helper function provided by the sandbox, we
should implement our soldier shooting by hand. Overall, the process of shooting a
bullet requires a look up of the bone position and rotation for the soldier, creating
a physics representation for the bullet, attaching a particle system to the bullet,
launching the profile, and then handling the impact of a bullet with any other
physics simulated object.

The bone position

Getting a bone position requires passing a sandbox object or mesh to the `Animation.`
`GetBonePosition` function. `GetBonePosition` also works for any attached object
that contains bones as well. This allows you to retrieve the bone position of a bone
within the weapon while it is attached to the soldier, for example:

```
local position =
    Animation.GetBonePosition(sandboxObject, boneName);
```

The bone rotation

Bone rotation is exactly the same as getting the bone's position, except that it returns a vector that represents the rotation around the *x*, *y*, and *z* axes in degrees:

```
local rotation =
    Animation.GetBoneRotation(sandboxObject, boneName);
```

Creating particle effects

Creating a particle system is similar to creating a mesh within the sandbox. The particle's name is the Ogre3D `particle_system` name that is specific in a `.particle` file:

 The sandbox has a few predefined particle systems located within the `media/particle` folder.

The `CreateParticle` function requires attaching the particle to some type of sandbox object to provide position and rotation information on where to play the particle.

```
local particle = Core.CreateParticle(sandboxObject, particleName);
```

The particle direction

Setting a particle's direction changes how the particle is oriented based on its `.particle` script. Bullet impacts, for example, set the particle's direction to change how particles are emitted based on the surface the bullet impacts:

```
Core.SetParticleDirection(particle, vectorNormal);
```

Object removal

As bullets have a very short lifespan within the sandbox, it's necessary to remove them once they've collided. Calling `Sandbox.RemoveObject` will destroy the passed-in sandbox object from the sandbox.

 Destroying objects happens at the end of the sandbox's update loop. Objects can still be referenced until the sandbox's update call has finished.

The `RemoveObject` function requires passing both the sandbox instance as well as the sandbox objects to delete.

```
Sandbox.RemoveObject(sandbox, sandboxObject);
```

The collision impact callback

Acting on collisions within the sandbox happens through the use of callbacks. To register for a collision callback, you pass in the Lua function you want to be called whenever the `SandboxObject` instance you're interested in collides with something. Callbacks happen on a per-frame basis and only one invocation of a callback occurs even if there are multiple collision points between two objects. For example, if `ObjectA` and `ObjectB` are colliding at three different points, the callback function will be invoked once per sandbox update.

 Removing sandbox objects during a collision callback will disable any additional callback functions that the sandbox might invoke within the sandbox's current update loop.

Assigning a collision callback function to a sandbox object is done through the `AddCollisionCallback` function.

```
Sandbox.AddCollisionCallback(sandbox, sandboxObject, function);
```

Shooting a projectile

Shooting a bullet projectile ends up with creating a physics capsule, setting the position and orientation through the `Core.SetAxis` function, attaching a particle to the bullet, and then applying an impulse to that bullet:

`SoldierAgent.lua`:

```
local function _ShootBullet(sandbox, position, rotation)
    local forward = Vector.Rotate(Vector.new(1, 0, 0), rotation);
    local up = Vector.Rotate(Vector.new(0, 1, 0), rotation);
    local left = Vector.Rotate(Vector.new(0, 0, -1), rotation);

    -- Create a capsule shaped bullet to launch forward given the
    -- weapons muzzle orientation.
    local bullet = Sandbox.CreatePhysicsCapsule(
        sandbox, 0.3, 0.01);
    Core.SetMass(bullet, 0.1);
    Core.SetPosition(bullet, position + forward * 0.2);
    Core.SetAxis(bullet, left, -forward, up);

    -- Create a particle to visibly show the bullet.
    local bulletParticle = Core.CreateParticle(bullet, "Bullet");
```

```
        Core.SetRotation(bulletParticle, Vector.new(-90, 0, 0));

        -- Instantaneously apply a force in the forward direction.
        Core.ApplyImpulse(bullet, forward * 750);

        return bullet;
    end
```

Handling projectile collision impacts

Bullets aren't very interesting unless we show where they impacted the environment.
First, let's take a look at the collision object that's passed into a collision callback.
The collision object has the two sandbox objects that collided and will always set the
object that registered with the callback as objectA and the other object as objectB.
PointA and PointB are the positions on each object that the collision took place on.
The normalOnB value represents the normal vector to the collision point relative
to objectB:

```
Collision Object
collision.objectA
collision.objectB
collision.pointA
collision.pointB
collision.normalOnB
```

Creating a particle impact for a bullet creates a new particle system, which is
BulletImpact, and then sets the particle's direction based on the normal vector
of the collision. The callback also removes the bullet from the sandbox:

SoldierAgent.lua:

```
    local function _ParticleImpact(sandbox, collision)
        -- Remove the bullet particle.
        Sandbox.RemoveObject(sandbox, collision.objectA);

        -- Create an impact particle where the bullet collided with
        -- another object.
        local particleImpact = Core.CreateParticle(
            sandbox, "BulletImpact");

        Core.SetPosition(particleImpact, collision.pointA);
        Core.SetParticleDirection(
```

```
                    particleImpact, collision.normalOnB);
    end

    local function _ShootBullet(sandbox, position, rotation)

        ...

        -- Add a particle impact callback to remove the bullet and
        -- create an impact particle effect.
        Sandbox.AddCollisionCallback(
            sandbox, particle, _ParticleImpact);

        return bullet;
    end
```

Shooting

Getting our agent to shoot ends up with an ASM callback function that shoots a bullet each time the *fire* animation plays. The position and rotation of the muzzle bone is looked up and a single bullet is fired by the `Agent_ShootBullet` function:

SoldierAgent.lua:

```
    local function _Shoot(stateName, callbackData)
        local agent = callbackData.agent;
        local sandbox = agent:GetSandbox();
        local soldier = callbackData.soldier;
        local position =
            Animation.GetBonePosition(soldier, "b_muzzle");
        local rotation =
            Animation.GetBoneRotation(soldier, "b_muzzle");

        _ShootBullet(sandbox, position, rotation);
    end

    function Agent_Initialize(agent)

        ...

        -- Data that is passed into _Shoot, expects an agent, and
        -- soldier attribute.
        local callbackData = {
            agent = agent,
            soldier = _soldier
        };

        -- Add the shoot callback to handle bullet creation.
        _soldierAsm:AddStateCallback(
            Soldier.SoldierStates.STAND_FIRE, _Shoot, callbackData);
```

```
    end

function Agent_HandleEvent(agent, event)
    if (event.source == "keyboard" and event.pressed) then
        if ( event.key == "f2_key" ) then
            _soldierAsm:RequestState(
                Soldier.SoldierStates.STAND_FIRE);
            -- Disable moving while shooting.
            agent:SetMaxSpeed(0);
        end
    end
end
```

The program, when executed, makes our agent shoot, as shown in the following screenshot:

Getting our soldier to run

Now that we have an animated agent, we can get the agent to run around the obstacle course while animating with the same steering techniques we used previously. First, we set the agent's path, which is provided by the `SandboxUtilities_GetLevelPath` function, and then we request the ASM to let the agent play the `run_forward` animation.

Setting a path through the obstacle course

You can set a path through the obstacle course as follows:

SoldierAgent.lua:

```
require "SandboxUtilities"

function Agent_Initialize(agent)

    . . .

    _soldierAsm:RequestState(
        Soldier.SoldierStates.STAND_RUN_FORWARD);

    -- Assign the default level path and adjust the agent's speed
    -- to match the soldier's steering scalars.
    agent:SetPath(SandboxUtilities_GetLevelPath());
    agent:SetMaxSpeed(agent:GetMaxSpeed() * 0.5);
end
```

Running the obstacle course

Actually getting our agent to move requires us to calculate the steering forces based on the set path and then apply these forces to the agent. Instead of having to set up the same summation of steering forces we used previously, we can use the `Soldier_CalculateSteering` function to calculate the appropriate forces and use the `Soldier_ApplySteering` function to apply the forces to the agent:

SoldierAgent.lua:

```
require "DebugUtilities"

function Agent_Update(agent, deltaTimeInMillis)
    -- Returns the amount of time that has passed in the sandbox,
    -- this is not the same as Lua's os.time();
    local sandboxTimeInMillis =
        Sandbox.GetTimeInMillis(agent:GetSandbox());
```

```
        local deltaTimeInSeconds = deltaTimeInMillis / 1000;

        -- Allow the soldier to update any soldier's specific data.
        Soldier_Update(agent, deltaTimeInMillis);

        -- Update the animation state machines to process animation
        -- requests.
        _soldierAsm:Update(deltaTimeInMillis, sandboxTimeInMillis);
        _weaponAsm:Update(deltaTimeInMillis, sandboxTimeInMillis);

        -- Draw the agent's cyclic path, offset slightly above the
        -- level geometry.
        DebugUtilities_DrawPath(
            agent:GetPath(), true, Vector.new(0, 0.02, 0));

        -- Apply a steering force to move the agent along the path.
        if (agent:HasPath()) then
            local steeringForces = Soldier_CalculateSteering(
                agent, deltaTimeInSeconds);
            Soldier_ApplySteering(
                agent, steeringForces, deltaTimeInSeconds);
        end
    end
end
```

The following screenshot shows you the agent running near to the obstacle:

Creating a brain

So far, we have a very basic binding between an agent and an animating mesh. Now, we are going to implement two different approaches that will help us have the decision logic control the agent's animated state machines.

Approaches for mind body control

The two main approaches we will be implementing are direct control over the ASM by the agent, where the decision logic can directly control which state the ASM transitions to, and a second approach where the agent issues commands to another system that is responsible for figuring out which animations are appropriate to be played for the agent.

Direct animation control

The first approach we'll implement is direct control over the ASM, as it is the simplest approach to understand and implement. While the agent has a lot of advantages as it knows exactly what animation is playing on its body, this technique tends to scale very poorly as more and more animation states are introduced. Although scaling becomes a problem, this approach allows for the lowest grain of control in terms of animation selection and response times from the agent.

As the agent must be responsible for animation selection, we'll create some basic actions that the agent can perform and represent as states:

DirectSoldierAgent.lua:

```
-- Supported soldier states.
local _soldierStates = {
    DEATH = "DEATH",
    FALLING = "FALLING",
    IDLE = "IDLE",
    MOVING = "MOVING",
    SHOOTING = "SHOOTING"
}
```

The death state

The first action we'll implement is the death state of the agent. As the ASM provides both a crouch and standing death variation, the action simply slows the agent's movement and requests the ASM to play the death animation. Once the agent begins to animate, the agent's physics representation is removed from the sandbox and the agent's health is set to zero, so no additional actions will be processed once death has occurred:

DirectSoldierAgent.lua:

```
function Agent_DeathState(agent, deltaTimeInMillis)
    local currentState = _soldierAsm:GetCurrentStateName();

    if (Soldier_IsMoving(agent)) then
        -- Slow movement at twice the rate to blend to a death
        -- pose.
        Soldier_SlowMovement(agent, deltaTimeInMillis, 2);
    end

    -- Only request a death state if not currently playing.
    if (_soldierStance == _soldierStances.STAND) then
        if (currentState ~= Soldier.SoldierStates.STAND_DEAD) then
            _soldierAsm:RequestState(
                Soldier.SoldierStates.STAND_DEAD);
        end
    else
        if (currentState ~=
            Soldier.SoldierStates.CROUCH_DEAD) then

            _soldierAsm:RequestState(
                Soldier.SoldierStates.CROUCH_DEAD);
        end
    end

    -- Remove the soldier from physics once the death animation
    -- starts playing to prevent other agents from colliding with
    -- the agent's physics capsule.
    if (currentState == Soldier.SoldierStates.STAND_DEAD or
        currentState == Soldier.SoldierStates.CROUCH_DEAD) then
        agent:RemovePhysics();
        agent:SetHealth(0);
    end
end
```

The following screenshot shows you our agent in the death state:

The idle state

The idle state also supports standing and crouching while slowing down the movement of the agent at different rates depending on whether the agent is standing or crouching. As the ASM is fully connected, we don't need to know which state the ASM is currently in and merely have to request the idle state. This allows the agent to go from a standing run to a crouch idle animation without the agent knowing specifically what animation transitions the ASM supports:

DirectSoldierAgent.lua:

```
    function Agent_IdleState(agent, deltaTimeInMillis)
        local currentState = _soldierAsm:GetCurrentStateName();

        if (_soldierStance == _soldierStances.STAND) then
            if (Soldier_IsMoving(agent)) then
                -- Slow movement to blend to an idle pose.
                Soldier_SlowMovement(agent, deltaTimeInMillis);
```

```
            end

        -- Only request the STAND_IDLE_AIM state if not currently
        -- playing.
        if (currentState ~=
            Soldier.SoldierStates.STAND_IDLE_AIM) then

            _soldierAsm:RequestState(
                Soldier.SoldierStates.STAND_IDLE_AIM);
        end
    else
        if (Soldier_IsMoving(agent)) then
            -- Slow movement at twice the rate to blend to an idle
            -- pose.
            Soldier_SlowMovement(agent, deltaTimeInMillis, 2);
        end

        -- Only request the CROUCH_IDLE_AIM state if not currently
        -- playing.
        if (currentState ~=
            Soldier.SoldierStates.CROUCH_IDLE_AIM) then

            _soldierAsm:RequestState(
                Soldier.SoldierStates.CROUCH_IDLE_AIM);
        end
    end
end
```

The falling state

As the soldier's ASM doesn't have a falling animation directly, two different animation states are used to simulate a falling death. When an agent begins to fall, we play the standing idle animation and immediately play the fall_dead animation once the agent is no longer falling. The same physics removal takes place when the agent gets killed or dies from a fall:

DirectSoldierAgent.lua:

```
function Agent_FallingState(agent, deltaTimeInMillis)
    local currentState = _soldierAsm:GetCurrentStateName();

    -- Since there's no falling animation, move the soldier into
    -- an idle animation.
    if (currentState ~= Soldier.SoldierStates.STAND_IDLE_AIM and
        currentState ~= Soldier.SoldierStates.STAND_FALL_DEAD)
        then

        _soldierAsm:RequestState(
            Soldier.SoldierStates.STAND_IDLE_AIM);
```

```
        end

        -- Once the soldier is no longer falling, kill the soldier.
        if (not Soldier_IsFalling(agent)) then
            if (currentState ~=
                Soldier.SoldierStates.STAND_FALL_DEAD) then

                -- Play a death animation once the soldier stops
                -- falling.
                _soldierAsm:RequestState(
                    Soldier.SoldierStates.STAND_FALL_DEAD);
            elseif (currentState ==
                Soldier.SoldierStates.STAND_FALL_DEAD) then

                -- Remove the soldier from physics once the death
                -- animation starts playing.
                agent:RemovePhysics();
                agent:SetHealth(0);
            end
        end
    end
```

The moving state

Handling movements takes care of both standing and crouched movements.
Standing movements apply the maximum amount of speed to our agent, while
crouched movements apply one third of our agent's maximum speed. Calculating
and applying steering forces happens exactly the same way as the previous agent
movement techniques we've used:

DirectSoldierAgent.lua:

```
    function Agent_MovingState(agent, deltaTimeInMillis)
        local currentState = _soldierAsm:GetCurrentStateName();
        local deltaTimeInSeconds = deltaTimeInMillis / 1000;
        local steeringForces;

        if (_soldierStance == _soldierStances.STAND) then
            -- Only request the STAND_RUN_FORWARD state if not
            -- currently playing.
            if (currentState ~=
                Soldier.SoldierStates.STAND_RUN_FORWARD) then
                -- Change the agent's desired speed for quick
                -- movement.
                agent:SetMaxSpeed(Soldier.Speed.Stand);
                _soldierAsm:RequestState(
                    Soldier.SoldierStates.STAND_RUN_FORWARD);
            end

            -- Calculate steering forces tuned for quick movement.
```

```
        steeringForces = Soldier_CalculateSteering(
            agent, deltaTimeInSeconds);
    else
        -- Only request the CROUCH_FORWARD state if not currently
        -- playing.
        if (currentState ~=
            Soldier.SoldierStates.CROUCH_FORWARD) then

            -- Change the agent's desired speed for slow movement.
            agent:SetMaxSpeed(Soldier.Speed.Crouch);
            _soldierAsm:RequestState(
                Soldier.SoldierStates.CROUCH_FORWARD);
        end

        -- Calculate steering forces tuned for slow movement.
        steeringForces = Soldier_CalculateSlowSteering(
            agent, deltaTimeInSeconds);
    end

    Soldier_ApplySteering(
        agent, steeringForces, deltaTimeInSeconds);
end
```

The following screenshot shows you the agent in the moving state:

The shooting state

The shooting state will be the first state to take advantage of ASM callbacks that actually perform shooting. The only action required by the state is to request the fire or crouch_fire animation from the ASM.

 You can play with the rate of the fire and crouch_fire animations in the Soldier.lua file to change how quickly the agent fires its weapon.

DirectSoldierAgent.lua:

```
function Agent_ShootState(agent, deltaTimeInMillis)
    local currentState = _soldierAsm:GetCurrentStateName();

    if (_soldierStance == _soldierStances.STAND) then
        -- Slow movement to blend to a shooting pose.
        if (Soldier_IsMoving(agent)) then
            Soldier_SlowMovement(agent, deltaTimeInMillis);
        end

        -- Only request the STAND_FIRE state if not currently
        -- playing.
        if (currentState ~= Soldier.SoldierStates.STAND_FIRE) then
            _soldierAsm:RequestState(
                Soldier.SoldierStates.STAND_FIRE);
        end
    else
        -- Slow movement at twice the rate to blend to a shooting
        -- pose.
        if (Soldier_IsMoving(agent)) then
            Soldier_SlowMovement(agent, deltaTimeInMillis, 2);
        end

        -- Only request the CROUCH_FIRE state if not currently
        -- playing.
        if (currentState ~=
            Soldier.SoldierStates.CROUCH_FIRE) then

            _soldierAsm:RequestState(
                Soldier.SoldierStates.CROUCH_FIRE);
        end
    end
end
```

A simple, finite state machine

Now that we've implemented the internals of each state, we can flush out the basic FSM that controls when each state function is to be called. We'll begin by getting some local variables out of the way and different flags for stance variation:

DirectSoldierAgent.lua:

```
local _soldier;
local _soldierAsm;
local _soldierStance;
local _soldierState;
local _weaponAsm;

-- Supported soldier stances.
local _soldierStances = {
    CROUCH = "CROUCH",
    STAND = "STAND"
};
```

Initializing the agent

Initializing our direct control agent is very similar to the other agents we created previously. This time, we add the ASM callbacks during the initialization so that our soldier will shoot during the fire and crouch_fire animation states. The Soldier_Shoot function expects to receive a table that contains both the agent and soldier mesh in order to shoot projectiles and handle projectile collisions:

DirectSoldierAgent.lua:

```
function Agent_Initialize(agent)
    -- Initialize the soldier and weapon models.
    _soldier = Soldier_CreateLightSoldier(agent);
    local weapon = Soldier_CreateWeapon(agent);

    -- Create the soldier and weapon animation state machines.
    _soldierAsm = Soldier_CreateSoldierStateMachine(_soldier);
    _weaponAsm = Soldier_CreateWeaponStateMachine(weapon);

    -- Data that is passed into Soldier_Shoot, expects an agent,
    -- and soldier attribute.
    local callbackData = {
        agent = agent;
        soldier = _soldier
    };

    -- Add callbacks to shoot a bullet each time the shooting
```

```
-- animation is played.
_soldierAsm:AddStateCallback(
    Soldier.SoldierStates.STAND_FIRE,
    Soldier_Shoot,
    callbackData);
_soldierAsm:AddStateCallback(
    Soldier.SoldierStates.CROUCH_FIRE,
    Soldier_Shoot,
    callbackData);

-- Attach the weapon model after the animation state machines
-- have been created.
Soldier_AttachWeapon(_soldier, weapon);
weapon = nil;

-- Set the default state and stance.
_soldierState = _soldierStates.IDLE;
_soldierStance = _soldierStances.STAND;
end
```

Agent FSM state handling

All the actual FSM states get handled during the update loop. The direct control soldier is very similar to other agents except that it handles which of the state functions we call. As this is a very simple FSM without a real system providing state updates, all that you need to do is match which state the soldier is in and call the appropriate function. Some checks for death and falling occur before this happens, as they take precedence regardless of what the agent actually wants to do:

DirectSoldierAgent.lua:

```
function Agent_Update(agent, deltaTimeInMillis)
    -- Returns the amount of time that has passed in the sandbox,
    -- this is not the same as lua's os.time();
    local sandboxTimeInMillis = Sandbox.GetTimeInMillis(
        agent:GetSandbox());

    -- Allow the soldier to update any soldier's specific data.
    Soldier_Update(agent, deltaTimeInMillis);

    -- Update the animation state machines to process animation
    -- requests.
    _soldierAsm:Update(deltaTimeInMillis, sandboxTimeInMillis);
    _weaponAsm:Update(deltaTimeInMillis, sandboxTimeInMillis);

    -- Draw the agent's cyclic path, offset slightly above the
    -- level geometry.
```

```
DebugUtilities_DrawPath(
    agent:GetPath(), true, Vector.new(0, 0.02, 0));

-- Ignore all state requests once the agent is dead.
if (agent:GetHealth() <= 0) then
    return;
end

-- Force the soldier into falling, this overrides all other
-- requests.
if (Soldier_IsFalling(agent)) then
    _soldierState = _soldierStates.FALLING;
end

-- Handle the current soldier's requested state.
if (_soldierState == _soldierStates.IDLE) then
    Agent_IdleState(agent, deltaTimeInMillis);
elseif (_soldierState == _soldierStates.SHOOTING) then
    Agent_ShootState(agent, deltaTimeInMillis);
elseif (_soldierState == _soldierStates.MOVING) then
    Agent_MovingState(agent, deltaTimeInMillis);
elseif (_soldierState == _soldierStates.FALLING) then
    Agent_FallingState(agent, deltaTimeInMillis);
elseif (_soldierState == _soldierStates.DEATH) then
    Agent_DeathState(agent, deltaTimeInMillis);
end
end
```

Indirect animation control

Now that we've implemented direct ASM control from the agent's point of view, we're going to create a system that manages the ASM while taking commands from the agent. One layer of abstraction above the ASM helps separate decision-making logic that resides in the agent and low-level animation handling.

Take falling, for example—does it make sense for the agent to constantly care about knowing that the agent is falling, or would it make things simpler if another system forces the agent to play a falling animation until the agent can interact with the environment again?

The system we'll be creating is called an animation controller. As animation controllers are very specific to the type of agent we create, you'll tend to create a new animation controller for each and every agent type.

The animation controller

Creating an animation controller will follow an object-oriented style that is similar to the ASM. First, we create a new function that creates variables for holding commands and command callbacks for the controller:

SoldierController.lua:

```
require "AnimationStateMachine"
require "Soldier"

function SoldierController.new(agent, soldier, weapon)
    local controller = {};

    -- The SoldierController's data members.
    controller.commands = {};
    controller.commandCallbacks = {};
    controller.asms = {};
    controller.executingCommand = nil;
    controller.previousCommand = nil;

    return controller;
end
```

Commands

Commands for an animation controller dictate exactly how the agent communicates with the body. Instead of directly acting on each command the agent issues to the body, the animation controller is free to decide how each command is executed. This might seem counter-intuitive to what would be desirable from an agent's point of view, but this freedom allows the body to easily handle things such as falling, pain animations, and death animations:

SoldierController.lua:

```
SoldierController = {};

-- Supported commands that can be requested.
SoldierController.Commands = {
    CHANGE_STANCE = "CHANGE_STANCE",
    DIE = "DIE",
    IDLE = "IDLE",
```

```
        MOVE = "MOVE",
        SHOOT = "SHOOT"
};

-- Supported soldier stances.
SoldierController.Stances = {
        CROUCH =      "CROUCH",
        STAND =       "STAND"
};

-- Additional supported commands that cannot be requested.
SoldierController.PrivateCommands = {
        FALLING = "FALLING"
};
```

The command queue

The structure that holds all the commands issued from the agent is called the command queue. Typically, this structure acts as a **First In First Out (FIFO)** data structure, which is also known as a queue. The agent is able to communicate with the controller by queuing commands or by issuing an immediate command that the controller prioritizes:

SoldierController.lua:

```
function SoldierController.QueueCommand(self, agent, command)
    -- Add the new command to the back of the queue.
    table.insert(self.commands, command);
end

function SoldierController.ClearCommands(self, agent)
    self.commands = {};
end

function SoldierController.CurrentCommand(self)
    return self.executingCommand;
end

function SoldierController.ImmediateCommand(
    self, agent, command)

    -- Adds the command to the beginning of the queue.
    table.insert(self.commands, 1, command);
end
```

Manipulating commands

Internally, the animation controller uses three main functions to manipulate the command queue. `AddCommandCallback` adds a function callback to handle a specific command, `AdvanceExecutingCommand` will remove the top command from the command queue if there is no currently executing command, and `ExecuteCommand` will call the associate callback for an executing command once per frame:

`SoldierController.lua`:

```lua
local function _AddCommandCallback(self, commandName, callback)
    self.commandCallbacks[commandName] = callback;
end

local function _AdvanceExecutingCommand(self)
    -- Moves the first queued command into execution if the
    -- previous command has finished.
    if (#self.commands > 0 and not self.executingCommand) then
        local command = self.commands[1];
        self.executingCommand = command;
        table.remove(self.commands, 1);
    end
end

local function _ExecuteCommand(self, agent, deltaTimeInMillis)
    local callback = self.commandCallbacks[self.executingCommand];

    -- Handle any callback that is associated with an executing
    -- command.
    if (callback) then
        callback(self, agent, deltaTimeInMillis);
    end
end
```

The change stance command

Creating a command handler typically follows a similar style to previous command handlers regardless of the command being handled. First, you handle any manipulation of the command queue that needs to happen, perform the specific action associated with the command, and then remove the command once it finishes. As commands can run over multiple update loops, each command must take this into account.

The change stance command slightly differs from other commands, as it can push an additional command back onto the queue. The change stance command looks whether any additional commands are already queued; if not, then the previous executing command is pushed back onto the queue. This allows the controller to change the agent's stance and then return to what the agent was previously doing, as the change stance command does not loop:

SoldierController.lua:

```lua
local function _ExecuteChangeStanceCommand(
    self, agent, deltaTimeInMillis)

    -- Requeues the previous command since change stance isn't a
    -- state the soldier can stay in.
    if (#self.commands == 0) then
        self:ImmediateCommand(agent, self.previousCommand);
    end

    -- Immediately changes the stance of the agent.  The requeued
    -- command is responsible for actually transitioning the agent
    -- to the correct stance visually.
    if (_stance == SoldierController.Stances.CROUCH) then
        _stance = SoldierController.Stances.STAND;
        Soldier_SetHeight(
            agent, _soldierMesh, Soldier.Height.Stand);
    else
        _stance = SoldierController.Stances.CROUCH;
        Soldier_SetHeight(
            agent, _soldierMesh, Soldier.Height.Crouch);
    end

    -- Remove the change stance command since it finishes
    -- immediately.
    _ClearExecutingCommand(self);
end
```

The die command

The die command is the first command that interacts with the ASM directly. In this case, the animation controller requests a particular ASM state based on the stance and then sets the controller to dead, preventing any additional commands from getting executed:

SoldierController.lua:

```
local function _ExecuteDieCommand(self, agent, deltaTimeInMillis)
    local currentState =
        self.asms["soldier"]:GetCurrentStateName();

    if (Soldier_IsMoving(agent)) then
        -- Slow movement at twice the rate to blend to a death
        -- pose.
        Soldier_SlowMovement(agent, deltaTimeInMillis, 2);
    end

    -- Request the appropriate stance death and immediately remove
    -- physics to prevent other agents from colliding with the
    -- agent's physics capsule.
    if (_stance == SoldierController.Stances.STAND) then
        if (currentState ~= Soldier.SoldierStates.STAND_DEAD) then
            self.asms["soldier"]:RequestState(
                Soldier.SoldierStates.STAND_DEAD);
            agent:RemovePhysics();
        end
    else
        if (currentState ~=
            Soldier.SoldierStates.CROUCH_DEAD) then

            self.asms["soldier"]:RequestState(
                Soldier.SoldierStates.CROUCH_DEAD);
            agent:RemovePhysics();
        end
    end

    -- Never clears the executing command since this is a terminal
    -- state.
end
```

The fall command

The fall command acts similar to the fall state we've implemented previously, except that it's implemented as an animation controller command callback:

SoldierController.lua:

```lua
local function _ExecuteFallingCommand(
    self, agent, deltaTimeInMillis)

    local currentState =
        self.asms["soldier"]:GetCurrentStateName();

    -- Since there's no falling animation, move the soldier into
    -- an idle animation.
    if (currentState ~= Soldier.SoldierStates.STAND_FALL_IDLE and
        currentState ~=
        Soldier.SoldierStates.STAND_FALL_DEAD) then

        self.asms["soldier"]:RequestState(
            Soldier.SoldierStates.STAND_FALL_IDLE);
    end

    -- Once the soldier is no longer falling, play a death
    -- animation.
    if (not Soldier_IsFalling(agent)) then
        if (currentState ~=
            Soldier.SoldierStates.STAND_FALL_DEAD) then

            self.asms["soldier"]:RequestState(
                Soldier.SoldierStates.STAND_FALL_DEAD);
            -- Remove the soldier from physics once the death
            -- animation starts playing.
            agent:RemovePhysics();
        end
    end

    -- Never clears the executing command since this is a terminal
    -- state.
end
```

The idle command

The idle command is implemented in almost the same way as the idle state function, except that the command clears itself once a new command is actively waiting in the command queue. The reason behind this is that the idle command will continue to loop and must terminate itself when a new command is waiting. As the responsibility to clear an executing command resides with the command itself, it is critical that the command handles this; otherwise, the agent will stop being responsive to new commands:

SoldierController.lua:

```lua
local function _ExecuteIdleCommand(self, agent, deltaTimeInMillis)
    local currentState =
        self.asms["soldier"]:GetCurrentStateName();

    if (_stance == SoldierController.Stances.STAND) then
        if (Soldier_IsMoving(agent)) then
            -- Slow movement to blend to an idle pose.
            Soldier_SlowMovement(agent, deltaTimeInMillis);
        end

        if (currentState ~=
            Soldier.SoldierStates.STAND_IDLE_AIM) then

            -- Only request the STAND_IDLE_AIM state if not
            -- currently playing.
            self.asms["soldier"]:RequestState(
                Soldier.SoldierStates.STAND_IDLE_AIM);
        elseif (#self.commands > 0) then
            -- Continue executing till a new command is queued.
            _ClearExecutingCommand(self);
        end
    else
        if (Soldier_IsMoving(agent)) then
            -- Slow movement at twice the rate to blend to an idle
            -- pose.
            Soldier_SlowMovement(agent, deltaTimeInMillis, 2);
        end

        if (currentState ~=
            Soldier.SoldierStates.CROUCH_IDLE_AIM) then

            -- Only request the CROUCH_IDLE_AIM state if not
            -- currently playing.
            self.asms["soldier"]:RequestState(
            Soldier.SoldierStates.CROUCH_IDLE_AIM);
```

```
        elseif (#self.commands > 0) then
            -- Continue executing till a new command is queued.
            _ClearExecutingCommand(self);
        end
    end
end
```

The move command

The move command handles both crouched- and standing-based movements and
changes the speed of the agent. Once another command is queued, the movement
is halted:

SoldierController.lua:

```
local function _ExecuteMoveCommand(self, agent, deltaTimeInMillis)
    local currentState =
        self.asms["soldier"]:GetCurrentStateName();
    local deltaTimeInSeconds = deltaTimeInMillis / 1000;
    local steeringForces = nil

    if (_stance == SoldierController.Stances.STAND) then
        -- Only request the STAND_RUN_FORWARD state if not
        -- currently playing.
        if (currentState ~=
            Soldier.SoldierStates.STAND_RUN_FORWARD) then
            -- Change the agent's desired speed for quick
            -- movement.
            agent:SetMaxSpeed(Soldier.Speed.Stand);
            self.asms["soldier"]:RequestState(
                Soldier.SoldierStates.STAND_RUN_FORWARD);
        elseif (#self.commands > 0) then
            -- Continue executing till a new command is queued.
            _ClearExecutingCommand(self);
        end

        -- Calculate steering forces tuned for quick movement.
        steeringForces =
            Soldier_CalculateSteering(agent, deltaTimeInSeconds);
    else
        -- Only request the CROUCH_FORWARD state if not currently
        -- playing.
        if (currentState ~=
            Soldier.SoldierStates.CROUCH_FORWARD) then

            -- Change the agent's desired speed for slow movement.
            agent:SetMaxSpeed(Soldier.Speed.Crouch);
            self.asms["soldier"]:RequestState(
                Soldier.SoldierStates.CROUCH_FORWARD);
```

```
        elseif (#self.commands > 0) then
            -- Continue executing till a new command is queued.
            _ClearExecutingCommand(self);
        end

        -- Calculate steering forces tuned for slow movement.
        steeringForces = Soldier_CalculateSlowSteering(
            agent, deltaTimeInSeconds);
    end

    Soldier_ApplySteering(
        agent, steeringForces, deltaTimeInSeconds);
end
```

The shoot command

As shooting is completely based on the weapon's muzzle position and orientation for now, we let the ASM callback shoot a projectile into the environment. The shoot command is merely responsible for requesting the appropriate animation state. Here, you can see the agent ready to shoot in the shoot state:

SoldierController.lua:

```lua
local function _ExecuteShootCommand(
    self, agent, deltaTimeInMillis)

    local currentState =
        self.asms["soldier"]:GetCurrentStateName();

    if (_stance == SoldierController.Stances.STAND) then
        -- Slow movement to blend to a shooting pose.
        if (Soldier_IsMoving(agent)) then
            Soldier_SlowMovement(agent, deltaTimeInMillis);
        end

        -- Only request the STAND_FIRE state if not currently
        -- playing.
        if (currentState ~= Soldier.SoldierStates.STAND_FIRE) then
            self.asms["soldier"]:RequestState(
                Soldier.SoldierStates.STAND_FIRE);
        elseif (#self.commands > 0) then
            -- Continue executing till a new command is queued.
            _ClearExecutingCommand(self);
        end
    else
        -- Slow movement at twice the rate to blend to a shooting
        -- pose.
        if (Soldier_IsMoving(agent)) then
            Soldier_SlowMovement(agent, deltaTimeInMillis, 2);
        end

        -- Only request the CROUCH_FIRE state if not currently
        -- playing.
        if (currentState ~=
            Soldier.SoldierStates.CROUCH_FIRE) then

            self.asms["soldier"]:RequestState(
                Soldier.SoldierStates.CROUCH_FIRE);
        elseif (#self.commands > 0) then
            -- Continue executing till a new command is queued.
            _ClearExecutingCommand(self);
        end
    end
end
```

Assigning member functions

Now that we have local implementations of functions, we need to assign them to each instance of a soldier controller. Exposing these functions allows for an object-oriented way of manipulating the solder controller from our agent Lua scripts:

SoldierController.lua:

```
    function SoldierController.new(agent, soldier, weapon)

        ...

        -- The SoldierController's accessor functions.
        controller.ClearCommands = SoldierController.ClearCommands;
        controller.CurrentCommand =
            SoldierController.CurrentCommand;
        controller.ImmediateCommand =
            SoldierController.ImmediateCommand;
        controller.QueueCommand = SoldierController.QueueCommand;
        controller.Update = SoldierController.Update;

        SoldierController.Initialize(
            controller, agent, soldier, weapon);

        return controller;
    end
```

Initializing the controller

The initialization of the controller creates the ASMs responsible for animation handling of the soldier mesh and weapon mesh. The important thing to note is that the soldier controller places a command immediately into the queue so that the agent can be placed into an idle state upon creation:

SoldierController.lua:

```
    function SoldierController.Initialize(
        self, agent, soldier, weapon)

        self.asms["soldier"] =
            Soldier_CreateSoldierStateMachine(soldier);
        self.asms["weapon"] =
            Soldier_CreateWeaponStateMachine(weapon);

        -- Data that is passed into Soldier_Shoot, expects an agent,
        -- and soldier attribute.
        local callbackData = {
            agent = agent,
```

```
            soldier = soldier
        };

        -- Add callbacks to shoot a bullet each time the shooting
        -- animation is played.
        self.asms["soldier"]:AddStateCallback(
            Soldier.SoldierStates.STAND_FIRE,
            Soldier_Shoot,
            callbackData );
        self.asms["soldier"]:AddStateCallback(
            Soldier.SoldierStates.CROUCH_FIRE,
            Soldier_Shoot,
            callbackData );

        _soldierMesh = soldier;

        -- Sets the default state and stance of the controller.
        self:QueueCommand(agent, SoldierController.Commands.IDLE);
        _stance = SoldierController.Stances.STAND;
    end
```

Adding handlers for commands

Now that we've implemented each command handler, we add each command callback function during the initialization:

SoldierController.lua:

```
    function SoldierController.Initialize(
        self, agent, soldier, weapon)

        ...

        -- Associate a callback function to handle each command.
        _AddCommandCallback(
            self,
            SoldierController.Commands.CHANGE_STANCE,
            _ExecuteChangeStanceCommand);
        _AddCommandCallback(
            self,
            SoldierController.Commands.DIE,
            _ExecuteDieCommand);
        _AddCommandCallback(
            self,
            SoldierController.Commands.IDLE,
            _ExecuteIdleCommand);
        _AddCommandCallback(
            self,
            SoldierController.Commands.MOVE,
```

```
        _ExecuteMoveCommand);
    _AddCommandCallback(
        self,
        SoldierController.Commands.SHOOT,
        _ExecuteShootCommand);
    _AddCommandCallback(
        self,
        SoldierController.PrivateCommands.FALLING,
        _ExecuteFallingCommand);
end
```

Updating the controller

Updating the controller itself is responsible for updating the associated ASMs as well as handling internal checks for agent changes such as dying and falling. Advancing the executing command also happens during updates when a command is queued and no command is currently executing. If a command is currently executing, the associated callbacks are invoked:

SoldierController.lua:

```
    function SoldierController.Update(
        self, agent, deltaTimeInMillis)

        -- Returns the amount of time that has passed in the sandbox,
        -- this is not the same as lua's os.time();
        local sandboxTimeInMillis =
            Sandbox.GetTimeInMillis(agent:GetSandbox());

        -- Allow the soldier to update any soldier's specific data.
        Soldier_Update(agent, deltaTimeInMillis);

        -- Update the animation state machines to process animation
        -- requests.
        _UpdateAsms(self, deltaTimeInMillis, sandboxTimeInMillis);

        -- Ignore all state requests once the agent is dead.
        if (agent:GetHealth() <= 0) then
            return;
        end

        -- Force the soldier into falling, this overrides all other
        -- requests.
        if (Soldier_IsFalling(agent)) then
            self:ImmediateCommand(
                agent, SoldierController.PrivateCommands.FALLING);
            _ClearExecutingCommand(self);
```

```
    end

    -- Select a new command to execute if the current command has
    -- finished and a new command is queued.
    _AdvanceExecutingCommand(self);

    -- Process the current command.
    _ExecuteCommand(self, agent, deltaTimeInMillis);
end
```

Running the obstacle course

Now that we've implemented both approaches to animation control, it's time to create both of these agent types within the obstacle course. As there's no actual agent decision-making logic, we'll be binding each different state to a keyboard hotkey so that we can influence what actions the agents perform. Here, we can see a few agents running the obstacle course:

Creating a direct control agent

As all the animation control for our direct control agents exists within the agent Lua script, all that remains is setting the soldier's state based on hotkeys. Note that as we have no direct change state, we handle this completely within the hotkey itself:

`DirectSoldierAgent.lua`:

```lua
local function _IsNumKey(key, numKey)
    -- Match both numpad keys and numeric keys.
    return string.find(
        key, string.format("^[numpad_]*%d_key$", numKey));
end

function Agent_HandleEvent(agent, event)
    if (event.source == "keyboard" and event.pressed) then
        -- Ignore new state requests if the agent is dead or about
        -- to die.
        if (_soldierState == _soldierStates.DEATH or
            _soldierState == _soldierStates.FALLING) then
            return;
        end

        -- Immediately switch the current state of the soldier.
        if (_IsNumKey(event.key, 1)) then
            _soldierState = _soldierStates.IDLE;
        elseif (_IsNumKey(event.key, 2)) then
            _soldierState = _soldierStates.SHOOTING;
        elseif (_IsNumKey(event.key, 3)) then
            _soldierState = _soldierStates.MOVING;
        elseif (_IsNumKey(event.key, 4)) then
            _soldierState = _soldierStates.DEATH;
        elseif (_IsNumKey(event.key, 5)) then
            -- Immediately switch the stance of the soldier, does
            -- not switch the current state of the soldier. Doing
            -- this assumes all possible states can transitions to
            -- both stances.
            if (_soldierStance == _soldierStances.CROUCH) then
                _soldierStance = _soldierStances.STAND;
                Soldier_SetHeight(
                    agent, _soldier, Soldier.Height.Stand);
            else
                _soldierStance = _soldierStances.CROUCH;
                Soldier_SetHeight(
                    agent, _soldier, Soldier.Height.Crouch);
            end
        end
    end
end
```

With the ability to change the soldier's state, it's time to spawn a new
`DirectSoldierAgent` agent within the sandbox. We can add a key press
handler in the sandbox script to spawn a `DirectSoldierAgent` variation
at a semi-randomized location:

`Sandbox.lua`:

```
function Sandbox_HandleEvent(sandbox, event)
    if (event.source == "keyboard" and event.pressed) then
        if ( event.key == "f1_key" ) then
            local agent = Sandbox.CreateAgent(
                sandbox, "DirectSoldierAgent.lua");

            agent:SetPosition(
                agent:GetPosition() +
                Vector.new(
                    math.random(-5, 5), 0, math.random(-5, 5)));
        end
    end
end
```

Creating an indirect control agent

Creating an indirect control agent is relatively simple, as all the animation logic is
contained within the `SoldierController.lua` script:

`IndirectSoldierAgent.lua`:

```
require "DebugUtilities"
require "SandboxUtilities"
require "Soldier"
require "SoldierController"

local _soldierController;
```

Indirect control agent initialization

The initialization of the agent requires creating both the soldier and weapon mesh
and then handing them over to a soldier controller:

`IndirectSoldierAgent.lua`:

```
function Agent_Initialize(agent)
    -- Initialize the soldier and weapon models.
    local soldier = Soldier_CreateSoldier(agent);
    local weapon = Soldier_CreateWeapon(agent);

    -- Create the soldier controller, responsible for handling
```

```
    -- animation state machines.
    _soldierController =
        SoldierController.new(agent, soldier, weapon);

    -- Attach the weapon model after the animation state machines
    -- have been created.
    Soldier_AttachWeapon(soldier, weapon);
    weapon = nil;
end
```

Indirect control agent update

Updating an animation controller agent simply requires you to step up the controller to handle commands:

IndirectSoldierAgent.lua:

```
function Agent_Update(agent, deltaTimeInMillis)
    -- Draw the agent's cyclic path, offset slightly above the
    -- level geometry.
    DebugUtilities_DrawPath(
        agent:GetPath(), true, Vector.new(0, 0.02, 0));

    -- Allow the soldier controller to update animations and
    -- handle new commands.
    _soldierController:Update(agent, deltaTimeInMillis);
end
```

Indirect control agent control

Interfacing with the animation controller only requires queuing up additional commands. We can bind different key events in order to queue each available command:

IndirectSoldierAgent.lua:

```
local function _IsNumKey(key, numKey)
    -- Match both numpad keys and numeric keys.
    return string.find(
        key, string.format("^[numpad_]*%d_key$", numKey));
end

function Agent_HandleEvent(agent, event)
    -- Queue a new command with the soldier controller.
```

```
    if (event.source == "keyboard" and event.pressed) then
        if (_IsNumKey(event.key, 1)) then
            _soldierController:QueueCommand(
                agent, SoldierController.Commands.IDLE);
        elseif (_IsNumKey(event.key, 2)) then
            _soldierController:QueueCommand(
                agent, SoldierController.Commands.SHOOT);
        elseif (_IsNumKey(event.key, 3)) then
            _soldierController:QueueCommand(
                agent, SoldierController.Commands.MOVE);
        elseif (_IsNumKey(event.key, 4)) then
            _soldierController:ImmediateCommand(
                agent, SoldierController.Commands.DIE);
        elseif (_IsNumKey(event.key, 5)) then
            _soldierController:QueueCommand(
                agent, SoldierController.Commands.CHANGE_STANCE);
        end
    end
end
```

Spawning an indirect control agent

Spawning the agent is identical to how we spawn a direct control soldier:

Sandbox.lua:

```
function Sandbox_HandleEvent(sandbox, event)
    if (event.source == "keyboard" and event.pressed) then

        ...

        elseif ( event.key == "f2_key" ) then
            local agent = Sandbox.CreateAgent(
                sandbox, "IndirectSoldierAgent.lua");

            agent:SetPosition(
                agent:GetPosition() +
                Vector.new(
                    math.random(-5, 5), 0, math.random(-5, 5)));
        end
    end
end
```

Action latency

Now that we've created both approaches for animation handling, we'll take a look at the pros and cons of each implementation. Direct control gives our agents absolute control over animations and allows the decision logic to account for the cost of animation playback. While it might seem counter-intuitive to mix animation logic with decision logic, this allows a direct control agent to be in absolute control over the minimum amount of latency required to go from a decision to a visible action within the sandbox.

With the indirect animation controller taking control over the body, the agent now faces a new issue, which is action latency. Action latency is the time between when a command is queued till it is acted upon. With our current setup of a fully connected ASM, this latency is minimized as any command can go directly to any queued command. A fully connected ASM is not a typical representation of an ASM, though. For many game types, this responsiveness won't affect the gameplay to a visible degree, but for other game genres, this latency might become a constant source of problem between decision-making and animation playback.

Since there are a number of tradeoffs to both methods, which aspects are more important is left to the implementer, responsiveness trading off animation quality or animation quality and maintainability trading off with decision response.

Summary

With movement and animation working together, we've finally created an agent that resembles more of what we would consider in the game AI. Going forward, we'll expand when and how our agents perform actions that create a robust game AI capable of movement, shooting, interacting, and finally, death.

Now that we've implemented a basic soldier agent, we can take a step back and begin to analyze the environment that agents reside in. In the next chapter, we'll integrate the navigation mesh generation and pathfinding in environments and finally move away from the fixed paths we've been using so far.

5
Navigation

In this chapter, we will cover the following topics:

- Generating navigation meshes
- Pathfinding with navigation meshes
- Accessing the path information
- Moving soldiers with navigation meshes
- Multiple navigation meshes

So far, we've focused on agents; now, we'll take a look at the environments that our agents occupy. To get agents to move around, we're going to use navigation meshes, which are also known as navmeshes. A navmesh is simply a polygon representation of all possible areas our agents can move to.

Pathfinding

Unlike other systems we've implemented in Lua, the navigation mesh and pathfinding will be provided by the open source Recast and Detour libraries. Recast is the library and toolset that is responsible for building a navigation mesh from our sandbox-level geometry, while Detour is responsible for pathfinding on the mesh.

The agents within the sandbox will use Detour as a service where paths are requested, and the agents then become responsible for following these paths. This separation of data allows you to reuse the navmesh as well as multiple navmeshes within the sandbox without having Detour or Recast interface with our agents.

Creating a navigation mesh

Creating a navmesh utilizes all the fixed geometry within the sandbox. The C++ side of the navmesh generation takes care of representing the sandbox to the Recast library. Any SandboxObject instance with a mass of zero, which is a fixed object, will be used for the navmesh generation.

 Planes are excluded from navmesh generation, so make sure that the ground is represented by a mesh or box.

We see a navigation mesh in the following screenshot:

Configuring navigation meshes

Generating a navmesh requires some basic information about the type of agents that will use pathfinding with the mesh. By default, the sandbox will autopopulate navmesh configuration, unless overriding values are provided during the generation.

Passing overrides to Recast happens through a Lua table. The properties shown in the following code snippet are the default values that are used when generating a navmesh without passing any override values to `Sandbox.CreateNavigationMesh`:

```lua
local configuration = {
    MinimumRegionArea = 50,
    WalkableClimbHeight = agent:GetHeight() / 10,
    WalkableHeight = agent:GetHeight(),
    WalkableRadius = agent:GetRadius() * 1.25,
    WalkableSlopeAngle = 15
};
```

The walkable height

The walkable height of the navmesh represents the height at which agents can walk under objects. If multiple agents of different heights exist within the sandbox, the tallest height should be used, as this will preclude any agents from bumping into overhangs. An adverse effect of using the tallest agent's height might limit shorter agents from pathfinding under objects they should otherwise be able to walk under.

A navigation mesh with a walkable height of 1.6 meters

The default height of our agents is 1.6 meters, as shown in the preceding screenshot. Note how the overhang prevents navigation mesh generation within the area. If we generate a new navigation for agents that are 0.5 meters tall, the area that was previously precluded from pathfinding is now accessible.

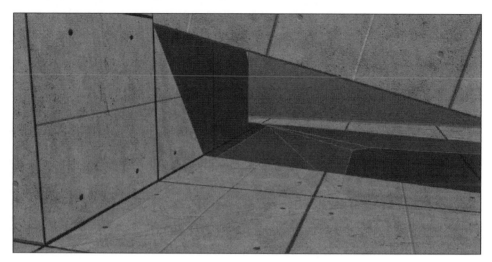

A navigation mesh with a walkable height of 0.5 meters

The walkable radius

The agents' radius is used during mesh generation to determine areas where the agent can walk. As agents can be on any part of the navigation mesh, the border is trimmed to prevent the agent from bumping into walls. Usually, it's advisable to give a bit extra to the walkable radius in order to distance how close the agent will move alongside walls. In particular, steering behaviors might push the agent slightly off their path, causing agents to collide with our sandbox geometry.

A navigation mesh with a 0.075 radius padding on top of the agent's default radius of 0.3

Padding our agent's walkable radius to 0.375 meters makes the navmesh shown in the preceding screenshot proceed. If our agents had a smaller radius of 0.1875, the generated navmesh would look similar to the following screenshot:

A navigation mesh with a walkable radius of 0.1875 meters

The walkable climb height

As our agents are represented by capsules, they will inherently walk over small, uneven areas in the environment. The walkable climb height represents the maximum vertical height of an obstacle our agents can step over. If the value is too large, our agents will get stuck on geometry that Detour thinks the agent should be able to pass over. A reasonable default value is half of the radius of the agent, which accounts for the curvature in the capsule.

A navigation mesh with a climb height of 0.15 meters

As our agents have a radius of 0.3 meters, using half of the radius as the climb height will produce the navigation mesh seen in the previous screenshot. If our agents can step over objects as tall as a meter, we can generate a navmesh with a climb height of 1 meter, as shown in the following screenshot:

A navigation mesh with a climb height of 1.0 meter

The walkable slope angle

The walkable slope angle is the maximum slope on which an agent can walk. If the slope angle is set too high, our agents will attempt to walk on inclines where gravity and friction will cause them to stop or fall backwards. Our default soldier agent can travel over inclines as steep as 45 degrees, based on their maximum speed and acceleration.

A navigation mesh with a walkable slope angle of 45.0 degrees

By default, our navigation mesh is generated to allow angles up to but not exceeding 45 degrees, as shown in the previous screenshot. Setting the walkable slope angle to a much smaller value—for instance, 15 degrees—will prevent navmesh from being generated on the exact same ramp.

A navigation mesh with a walkable slope angle of 15.0 degrees

The minimum region area

As all possible walkable areas will be added to the navigation mesh, we have criteria that specifies the minimum area size, which will prune out any small isolated islands of navigation. Lowering this value based on your sandbox layout will decrease the amount of time it takes to pathfind on the navmesh. By default, a minimum region of 50 meters squared (50 meters times 50 meters) works well for the obstacle course geometry.

A navigation mesh with a minimum region size of 50.0 square meters

With a default minimum region area of 50 meters squared, the navigation mesh will not be generated on the small concrete outcroppings on the top of the map, as shown in the preceding screenshot. If we lower the minimum region area to 15 meters squared, these outcroppings will no longer be discarded.

A navigation mesh with a minimum region of 15.0 square meters

A big downside to having disconnected regions in the sandbox's navigation mesh stems from the use of randomly picked points. If all areas within the sandbox are traversable for agents, then Lua scripts won't have to consider the edge case where two valid points on the navigation mesh have no possible path between them.

Building the navigation mesh

Constructing a navigation mesh is an expensive operation that will halt the execution of the sandbox till the mesh has been generated. Usually, the generation should happen during the sandbox's initialization, but nothing prevents the navigation mesh from being regenerated at any time.

While the sandbox doesn't support serializing the navigation mesh and loading a previously serialized navmesh by default, the underlying Recast library supports the storing and loading of the binary navmesh data.

When creating a navmesh, we assign a name to the mesh; this allows any further manipulation or querying of the mesh to be referenced by name.

As navmeshes are meant to be shared between similar AI agents, it's best to generate the navmesh in the sandbox's initialization and reference the navmesh by name in each agent script. Creating a navmesh with the same name as an existing navmesh will destroy the previous mesh.

Creating a navmesh is done through the `CreateNavigationMesh` function provided by the sandbox.

```
function Sandbox_Initialize(sandbox)
    Sandbox.CreateNavigationMesh(
        sandbox, "default", configuration);
end
```

Drawing the navigation mesh

Displaying the navmesh is accessible through the `Sandbox.SetDebugNavigationMesh` function. Drawing the navmesh is typically a cheap operation, as a renderable form of the navmesh is generated during the original navmesh's construction.

As the navmesh is static, the debug graphics used to render the mesh utilizes a different underlying system compared to the debug graphics used by the physics system.

Passing either true or false will toggle drawing the debug navmesh.

```
function Sandbox_Initialize(sandbox)
    Sandbox.CreateNavigationMesh(sandbox, "default");
    Sandbox.SetDebugNavigationMesh(sandbox, "default", true);
end
```

Pathfinding on a navigation mesh

Pathfinding on the navmesh requires the start and end locations as well as the navmesh that needs to be queried. The position of the start point and end point isn't required to be directly on the navmesh, but can, instead, be up to 5 meters vertically or 2 meters horizontally away from the mesh. The path returned will have the nearest start point and end point on the navmesh if the original point resides outside the mesh. Snapping search points on the navmesh allows agents to navigate back to the navmesh in case they navigate off the mesh due to steering.

Path query

Path queries are performed based on the shortest distance from the start point to the end point. The sandbox doesn't distinguish any area of the navmesh from being more costly to traverse over   , so pathfinding only considers the Euclidean distance when performing a search:

```
path = Sandbox.FindPath(sandbox, "default", startPoint, endPoint);
```

Query results

Pathfinding results are returned as a table of points to the caller. If no path is found, an empty table is returned in order to signify no possible path exists:

```
local path = Sandbox.FindPath(
    sandbox, "default", agent:GetPosition(), endPoint);
```

The following is the result of running the preceding code:

Random navigation points

To randomly select a point on the navmesh, the Sandbox.RandomPoint function will perform a small query and return a point. If there are multiple navmesh regions, there is no guarantee that this random point will be pathable to every other point:

```
local randomPoint = Sandbox.RandomPoint(sandbox, "default");
```

The path information

Now that we have generated paths from the navmesh, there are additional accessor functions that can retrieve useful information about the paths themselves. Once we've assigned a path to an agent, we can retrieve the nearest point on the path the agent is close to.

Typically, the nearest point on the path will be very close to the agent's current position, but our agents can navigate away from their paths due to steering. Finding the closest point on our agent's path can be useful in order to know the direction our agent has to move in order to return to its path:

```
local nearestPoint = Agent.GetNearestPointOnPath(
    agent, agent:GetPosition());
```

Once we know a point on the path, we can perform an additional query to find out how far that point is from the start position. The distance returned from the `Agent.GetDistanceAlongPath` function is not the Euclidean distance between the two points but is the actual traveled distance along the path to the point:

```
local distance = Agent.GetDistanceAlongPath(agent, nearest);
```

Finding out a point along the agent's path given a specific distance along the agent's path is available from the `Agent.GetPointOnPath` function. Typically, once we've calculated the current distance our agent has traveled along their path, we can add an offset to the distance in order to find a future position along the path our agents will navigate toward:

```
local pointOnPath = Agent.GetPointOnPath(
    agent, distance + offset);
```

Adding random pathfinding to our soldier

Now that we have navmesh generation and pathfinding out of the way, we can add pathfinding to our agents. As our agents currently have no decision making—and therefore, no ability to select a goal to reach—we'll randomly pick a point on the navmesh and send our agent to that point. Once it reaches its target, a new location will be selected.

Our sandbox Lua script will be very similar to previous scripts we've written, and it will take advantage of the previous controller-based agents we've created so far:

Sandbox.lua:

```
require "DebugUtilities"
require "SandboxUtilities"
local agents = {};
```

Updating agent paths

We can use a helper function to generate new paths for agents that have reached their target. As we're randomly selecting a point on the navmesh, we need to check whether the agent can actually use a path to that point, as the obstacle course geometry isn't fully connected. We'll continue trying to generate new paths until a path is successfully found, and then we update the agent's path and target accordingly:

Sandbox.lua:

```
local function _UpdatePaths(sandbox)
    for index, agent in pairs(_agents) do
        local navPosition = Sandbox.FindClosestPoint(
            sandbox, "default", agent:GetPosition());
        local targetRadiusSquared =
            agent:GetTargetRadius() * agent:GetTargetRadius();
        local distanceSquared = Vector.DistanceSquared(
            navPosition, agent:GetTarget());

        -- Determine if the agent is within the target radius to
        -- their target position.
        if (distanceSquared < targetRadiusSquared) then
            local endPoint;
            local path = {};

            -- Randomly try and pathfind to a new navmesh point,
            -- keep trying until a valid path is found.
            while #path == 0 do
                endPoint = Sandbox.RandomPoint(
                    sandbox, "default");
                path = Sandbox.FindPath(
                    sandbox,
                    "default",
                    agent:GetPosition(),
                    endPoint);
            end

            -- Assign a new path and target position.
            Soldier_SetPath(agent, path);
            agent:SetTarget(endPoint);
        end
    end
end
```

Drawing paths

Drawing each path uses the same `DebugUtilities_DrawPath` helper function we've used previously:

`Sandbox.lua:`

```
local function _DrawPaths()
    for index, agent in pairs(_agents) do
        -- Draw the agent's cyclic path, offset slightly above the
        -- level geometry.
        DebugUtilities_DrawPath(
            agent:GetPath(), false, Vector.new(0, 0.02, 0));
        Core.DrawSphere(
            agent:GetTarget(), 0.1, DebugUtilities.Red, true);
    end
end
```

Initializing the navmesh

The creation of the navmesh occurs only once and uses default values, as our agents also use the sandbox's default values. When we spawn a new agent, we'll randomly place them somewhere in the navmesh:

`Sandbox.lua:`

```
local _agents = {};

function Sandbox_Initialize(sandbox)
    -- Create the sandbox level, handles creating geometry,
    -- skybox, and lighting.
    SandboxUtilities_CreateLevel(sandbox);

    -- Override the default navigation mesh config generation.
    local navMeshConfig = {
        MinimumRegionArea = 100,
        WalkableRadius = 0.4,
        WalkableClimbHeight = 0.2,
```

```
            WalkableSlopeAngle = 45 };

    Sandbox.CreateNavigationMesh(
        sandbox, "default", navMeshConfig);

    Sandbox.SetDebugNavigationMesh(sandbox, "default", true);

    -- Create agents and randomly place them on the navmesh.
    for i=1, 5 do
        local agent = Sandbox.CreateAgent(
            sandbox, "IndirectSoldierAgent.lua");
        table.insert(_agents, agent);

        agent:SetPosition(
            Sandbox.RandomPoint(sandbox, "default"));

        -- Use the Agent's closest point to the navmesh as their
        -- target position.
        local navPosition = Sandbox.FindClosestPoint(
            sandbox, "default", agent:GetPosition());

        agent:SetTarget(navPosition);

        -- Increase the target radius to prevent agents from
        -- slowing to reach their target position.
        agent:SetTargetRadius(1);
    end
end

function Sandbox_Update(sandbox, deltaTimeInMillis)
    -- Select new paths if agents have reached the end of their
    -- current path.
    _UpdatePaths(sandbox);

    -- Draw every agent's path.
    _DrawPaths();
end
```

Now that our agents have their own unique paths, we can start seeing how steering, path following, and avoidance play a part in the movement. As each generated path will be the shortest possible path, many path segments will overlap when agents move around the sandbox. Notice that as agents move close to each other, they will deviate off their path in order to prevent bumping into each other.

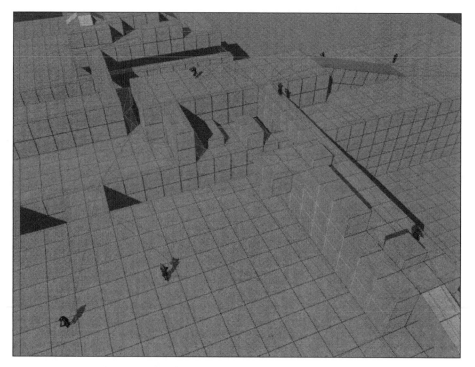

Agents randomly pathfinding through the obstacle course

Randomly running agents

Now that we have a number of agents running around in the sandbox, there are some critical things that we need to be aware of. As the sandbox geometry has a lot of bridges and ledges, our agents will most certainly fall to their death from time to time. This is because of the way the agent chooses to follow its path. As we're using a steering function that maximizes the agent's speed regardless of the turning angle, when agents generate a new path to follow, they will sometimes have a large turning radius that takes them far enough off the navmesh to fall off a ledge.

Fixing the problem requires you to tune the steering function or replace it all together so that agents have a quicker turning radius or slower speed. Try experimenting with crouching and standing agents in order to see how the maximum speed and acceleration can change the effects of path following.

Creating additional navigation meshes

So far, we've only been using one navigation mesh in the sandbox; nothing stops you from using multiple navmeshes for multiple types of agents. Different sets of configurations can generate radically different navmeshes that can suit the needs of nearly any agent that walks.

Summary

Now that our agents have a basic understanding of navigable areas within our sandbox, we can start creating decision logic that utilizes movement and animation. In the next chapter, we'll create multiple decision structures that will let our agents become autonomous within the sandbox.

6
Decision Making

In this chapter, we will cover the following topics:

- Creating reusable actions for agent behaviors
- Building conditional evaluators for decision making
- Creating a decisions tree structure that builds autonomous agents
- Creating a finite state machine that handles state-based agents
- Creating behavior trees for reactive agents

Now that we have agents that can animate and maneuver through their environments, we'll add high-level decision making to our agents. These data structures will finally give our agents autonomy in how they interact with the world as well as other agents.

Creating userdata

So far we've been using global data to store information about our agents. As we're going to create decision structures that require information about our agents, we'll create a local userdata table variable that contains our specific agent data as well as the agent controller in order to manage animation handling:

```
local userData =
{
    alive, -- terminal flag
    agent, -- Sandbox agent
    ammo, -- current ammo
    controller, -- Agent animation controller
    enemy, -- current enemy, can be nil
    health, -- current health
    maxHealth -- max Health
};
```

Moving forward, we will encapsulate more and more data as a means of isolating our systems from global variables. A `userData` table is perfect for storing any arbitrary piece of agent data that the agent doesn't already possess and provides a common storage area for data structures to manipulate agent data. So far, the listed data members are some common pieces of information we'll be storing; when we start creating individual behaviors, we'll access and modify this data.

Agent actions

Ultimately, any decision logic or structure we create for our agents comes down to deciding what action our agent should perform. Actions themselves are isolated structures that will be constructed from three distinct states:

- Uninitialized
- Running
- Terminated

The typical lifespan of an action begins in uninitialized state and will then become initialized through a onetime initialization, and then, it is considered to be running. After an action completes the running phase, it moves to a terminated state where cleanup is performed. Once the cleanup of an action has been completed, actions are once again set to uninitialized until they wait to be reactivated.

We'll start defining an action by declaring the three different states in which actions can be as well as a type specifier, so our data structures will know that a specific Lua table should be treated as an action.

 Remember, even though we use Lua in an object-oriented manner, Lua itself merely creates each instance of an object as a primitive table. It is up to the code we write to correctly interpret different tables as different objects. The use of a `Type` variable that is moving forward will be used to distinguish one class type from another.

`Action.lua:`

```
Action = {};

Action.Status = {
    RUNNING = "RUNNING",
    TERMINATED = "TERMINATED",
    UNINITIALIZED = "UNINITIALIZED"
};

Action.Type = "Action";
```

Adding data members

To create an action, we'll pass three functions that the action will use for the initialization, updating, and cleanup. Additional information such as the name of the action and a `userData` variable, used for passing information to each callback function, is passed in during the construction time.

 Moving our systems away from global data and into instanced object-oriented patterns requires each instance of an object to store its own data. As our `Action` class is generic, we use a custom data member, which is `userData`, to store action-specific information.

Whenever a callback function for the action is executed, the same `userData` table passed in during the construction time will be passed into each function. The update callback will receive an additional `deltaTimeInMillis` parameter in order to perform any time specific update logic.

To flush out the `Action` class' constructor function, we'll store each of the callback functions as well as initialize some common data members:

`Action.lua`:

```
function Action.new(name, initializeFunction, updateFunction,
        cleanUpFunction, userData)

    local action = {};

    -- The Action's data members.
    action.cleanUpFunction_   = cleanUpFunction;
    action.initializeFunction_ = initializeFunction;
    action.updateFunction_    = updateFunction;
    action.name_   = name or "";
    action.status_ = Action.Status.UNINITIALIZED;
    action.type_   = Action.Type;
    action.userData_ = userData;

    return action;
end
```

Initializing an action

Initializing an action begins by calling the action's initialize callback and then immediately sets the action into a running state. This transitions the action into a standard update loop that is moving forward:

Action.lua:

```lua
function Action.Initialize(self)
    -- Run the initialize function if one is specified.
    if (self.status_ == Action.Status.UNINITIALIZED) then
        if (self.initializeFunction_) then
            self.initializeFunction_(self.userData_);
        end
    end
    -- Set the action to running after initializing.
    self.status_ = Action.Status.RUNNING;
end
```

Updating an action

Once an action has transitioned to a running state, it will receive callbacks to the update function every time the agent itself is updated, until the action decides to terminate. To avoid an infinite loop case, the update function must return a terminated status when a condition is met; otherwise, our agents will never be able to finish the running action.

 An update function isn't a hard requirement for our actions, as actions terminate immediately by default if no callback function is present.

Action.lua:

```lua
function Action.Update(self, deltaTimeInMillis)
    if (self.status_ == Action.Status.TERMINATED) then
        -- Immediately return if the Action has already
        -- terminated.
        return Action.Status.TERMINATED;
    elseif (self.status_ == Action.Status.RUNNING) then
        if (self.updateFunction_) then
            -- Run the update function if one is specified.
            self.status_ = self.updateFunction_(
                deltaTimeInMillis, self.userData_);
            -- Ensure that a status was returned by the update
            -- function.
            assert(self.status_);
        else
```

```
            -- If no update function is present move the action
            -- into a terminated state.
            self.status_ = Action.Status.TERMINATED;
        end
    end
    return self.status_;
end
```

Action cleanup

Terminating an action is very similar to initializing an action, and it sets the status of the action to uninitialized once the cleanup callback has an opportunity to finish any processing of the action.

 If a cleanup callback function isn't defined, the action will immediately move to an uninitialized state upon cleanup.

During action cleanup, we'll check to make sure the action has fully terminated, and then run a cleanup function if one is specified.

Action.lua:

```
function Action.CleanUp(self)
    if (self.status_ == Action.Status.TERMINATED) then
        if (self.cleanUpFunction_) then
            self.cleanUpFunction_(self.userData_);
        end
    end

    self.status_ = Action.Status.UNINITIALIZED;
end
```

Action member functions

Now that we've created the basic, initialize, update, and terminate functionalities, we can update our action constructor with CleanUp, Initialize, and Update member functions:

Action.lua:

```
function Action.new(name, initializeFunction, updateFunction,
        cleanUpFunction, userData)

    ...
    -- The Action's accessor functions.
    action.CleanUp = Action.CleanUp;
```

```
        action.Initialize = Action.Initialize;
        action.Update = Action.Update;

        return action;
    end
```

Creating actions

With a basic action class out of the way, we can start implementing specific action logic that our agents can use. Each action will consist of three callback functions—initialization, update, and cleanup—that we'll use when we instantiate our action instances.

The idle action

The first action we'll create is the basic and default choice from our agents that are going forward. The idle action wraps the IDLE animation request to our soldier's animation controller. As the animation controller will continue looping our IDLE command until a new command is queued, we'll time our idle action to run for 2 seconds, and then terminate it to allow another action to run:

SoldierActions.lua:

```
    function SoldierActions_IdleCleanUp(userData)
        -- No cleanup is required for idling.
    end

    function SoldierActions_IdleInitialize(userData)
        userData.controller:QueueCommand(
            userData.agent,
            SoldierController.Commands.IDLE);

        -- Since idle is a looping animation, cut off the idle
        -- Action after 2 seconds.
        local sandboxTimeInMillis = Sandbox.GetTimeInMillis(
            userData.agent:GetSandbox());
        userData.idleEndTime = sandboxTimeInMillis + 2000;
    end
```

Updating our action requires that we check how much time has passed; if the 2 seconds have gone by, we terminate the action by returning the terminated state; otherwise, we return that the action is still running:

SoldierActions.lua:

```
    function SoldierActions_IdleUpdate(deltaTimeInMillis, userData)
        local sandboxTimeInMillis = Sandbox.GetTimeInMillis(
```

```
        userData.agent:GetSandbox());
    if (sandboxTimeInMillis >= userData.idleEndTime) then
        userData.idleEndTime = nil;
        return Action.Status.TERMINATED;
    end
    return Action.Status.RUNNING;
end
```

As we'll be using our idle action numerous times, we'll create a wrapper around initializing our action based on our three functions:

SoldierLogic.lua:

```
local function IdleAction(userData)
    return Action.new(
        "idle",
        SoldierActions_IdleInitialize,
        SoldierActions_IdleUpdate,
        SoldierActions_IdleCleanUp,
        userData);
end
```

The die action

Creating a basic death action is very similar to our idle action. In this case, as death in our animation controller is a terminating state, all we need to do is request that the DIE command be immediately executed. From this point, our die action is complete, and it's the responsibility of a higher-level system to stop any additional processing of logic behavior.

Typically, our agents will request this state when their health drops to zero. In the special case that our agent dies due to falling, the soldier's animation controller will manage the correct animation playback and set the soldier's health to zero:

SoldierActions.lua:

```
function SoldierActions_DieCleanUp(userData)
    -- No cleanup is required for death.
end

function SoldierActions_DieInitialize(userData)
    -- Issue a die command and immediately terminate.
    userData.controller:ImmediateCommand(
        userData.agent,
        SoldierController.Commands.DIE);

    return Action.Status.TERMINATED;
```

```
    end

    function SoldierActions_DieUpdate(deltaTimeInMillis, userData)
        return Action.Status.TERMINATED;
    end
```

Creating a wrapper function to instantiate a death action is identical to our idle action:

SoldierLogic.lua:

```
    local function DieAction(userData)
        return Action.new(
            "die",
            SoldierActions_DieInitialize,
            SoldierActions_DieUpdate,
            SoldierActions_DieCleanUp,
            userData);
    end
```

The reload action

Reloading is the first action that requires an animation to complete before we can consider the action complete, as the behavior will refill our agent's current ammunition count. As our animation controller is queue-based, the action itself never knows how many commands must be processed before the reload command has finished executing.

To account for this during the update loop of our action, we wait till the command queue is empty, as the reload action will be the last command that will be added to the queue. Once the queue is empty, we can terminate the action and allow the cleanup function to award the ammo:

SoldierActions.lua:

```
    function SoldierActions_ReloadCleanUp(userData)
        userData.ammo = userData.maxAmmo;
    end

    function SoldierActions_ReloadInitialize(userData)
        userData.controller:QueueCommand(
            userData.agent,
            SoldierController.Commands.RELOAD);
        return Action.Status.RUNNING;
    end

    function SoldierActions_ReloadUpdate(deltaTimeInMillis, userData)
        if (userData.controller:QueueLength() > 0) then
            return Action.Status.RUNNING;
```

```
        end

        return Action.Status.TERMINATED;
    end
```

SoldierLogic.lua:

```
    local function ReloadAction(userData)
        return Action.new(
            "reload",
            SoldierActions_ReloadInitialize,
            SoldierActions_ReloadUpdate,
            SoldierActions_ReloadCleanUp,
            userData);
    end
```

The shoot action

Shooting is the first action that directly interacts with another agent. In order to apply damage to another agent, we need to modify how the soldier's shots deal with impacts. Previously, when the soldier shot bullets out of his rifle, we added a callback function to handle the cleanup of particles; now, we'll add an additional functionality in order to decrement an agent's health if the particle impacts an agent:

Soldier.lua:

```
    local function ParticleImpact(sandbox, collision)
        Sandbox.RemoveObject(sandbox, collision.objectA);

        local particleImpact = Core.CreateParticle(
            sandbox, "BulletImpact");
        Core.SetPosition(particleImpact, collision.pointA);
        Core.SetParticleDirection(
            particleImpact, collision.normalOnB);

        table.insert(
            impactParticles,
            { particle = particleImpact, ttl = 2.0 } );

        if (Agent.IsAgent(collision.objectB)) then
            -- Deal 5 damage per shot.
            Agent.SetHealth(
                collision.objectB,
                Agent.GetHealth(collision.objectB) - 5);
        end
    end
```

Creating the shooting action requires more than just queuing up a shoot command to the animation controller. As the SHOOT command loops, we'll queue an IDLE command immediately afterward so that the shoot action will terminate after a single bullet is fired. To have a chance at actually shooting an enemy agent, though, we first need to orient our agent to face toward its enemy. During the normal update loop of the action, we will forcefully set the agent to point in the enemy's direction.

> Forcefully setting the agent's forward direction during an action will allow our soldier to shoot but creates a visual artifact where the agent will pop to the correct forward direction. See whether you can modify the shoot action's update to interpolate to the correct forward direction for better visual results.

SoldierActions.lua:

```lua
function SoldierActions_ShootCleanUp(userData)
    -- No cleanup is required for shooting.
end

function SoldierActions_ShootInitialize(userData)
    userData.controller:QueueCommand(
        userData.agent,
        SoldierController.Commands.SHOOT);
    userData.controller:QueueCommand(
        userData.agent,
        SoldierController.Commands.IDLE);

    return Action.Status.RUNNING;
end

function SoldierActions_ShootUpdate(deltaTimeInMillis, userData)
    -- Point toward the enemy so the Agent's rifle will shoot
    -- correctly.
    local forwardToEnemy = userData.enemy:GetPosition() -
        userData.agent:GetPosition();
    Agent.SetForward(userData.agent, forwardToEnemy);

    if (userData.controller:QueueLength() > 0) then
        return Action.Status.RUNNING;
    end

    -- Subtract a single bullet per shot.
    userData.ammo = userData.ammo - 1;
    return Action.Status.TERMINATED;
end
```

SoldierLogic.lua:

```lua
local function ShootAction(userData)
    return Action.new(
        "shoot",
        SoldierActions_ShootInitialize,
        SoldierActions_ShootUpdate,
        SoldierActions_ShootCleanUp,
        userData);
end
```

The random move action

Randomly moving is an action that chooses a random point on the navmesh to be moved to. This action is very similar to other actions that move, except that this action doesn't perform the moving itself. Instead, the random move action only chooses a valid point to move to and requires the move action to perform the movement:

SoldierActions.lua:

```lua
function SoldierActions_RandomMoveCleanUp(userData)

end

function SoldierActions_RandomMoveInitialize(userData)
    local sandbox = userData.agent:GetSandbox();

    local endPoint = Sandbox.RandomPoint(sandbox, "default");
    local path = Sandbox.FindPath(
        sandbox,
        "default",
        userData.agent:GetPosition(),
        endPoint);

    while #path == 0 do
        endPoint = Sandbox.RandomPoint(sandbox, "default");
        path = Sandbox.FindPath(
            sandbox,
            "default",
            userData.agent:GetPosition(),
            endPoint);
    end

    userData.agent:SetPath(path);
    userData.agent:SetTarget(endPoint);
    userData.movePosition = endPoint;

    return Action.Status.TERMINATED;
```

```
        end

    function SoldierActions_RandomMoveUpdate(userData)
        return Action.Status.TERMINATED;
    end
```

```
SoldierLogic.lua:
```

```
    local function RandomMoveAction(userData)
        return Action.new(
            "randomMove",
            SoldierActions_RandomMoveInitialize,
            SoldierActions_RandomMoveUpdate,
            SoldierActions_RandomMoveCleanUp,
            userData);
    end
```

The move action

Our movement action is similar to an idle action, as the agent's walk animation will loop infinitely. In order for the agent to complete a move action, though, the agent must reach within a certain distance of its target position or timeout. In this case, we can use 1.5 meters, as that's close enough to the target position to terminate the move action and half a second to indicate how long the move action can run for:

```
SoldierActions.lua:
```

```
    function SoldierActions_MoveToCleanUp(userData)
        userData.moveEndTime = nil;
    end

    function SoldierActions_MoveToInitialize(userData)
        userData.controller:QueueCommand(
            userData.agent,
            SoldierController.Commands.MOVE);

        -- Since movement is a looping animation, cut off the move
        -- Action after 0.5 seconds.
        local sandboxTimeInMillis =
            Sandbox.GetTimeInMillis(userData.agent:GetSandbox());
        userData.moveEndTime = sandboxTimeInMillis + 500;

        return Action.Status.RUNNING;
    end
```

When applying the move action onto our agents, the indirect soldier controller will manage all animation playback and steer our agent along their path.

The agent moving to a random position

Setting a time limit for the move action will still allow our agents to move to their final target position, but gives other actions a chance to execute in case the situation has changed. Movement paths can be long, and it is undesirable to not handle situations such as death until the move action has terminated:

SoldierActions.lua:

```
function SoldierActions_MoveToUpdate(deltaTimeInMillis, userData)
    -- Terminate the action after the allotted 0.5 seconds.  The
    -- decision structure will simply repath if the Agent needs
    -- to move again.
    local sandboxTimeInMillis =
        Sandbox.GetTimeInMillis(userData.agent:GetSandbox());
    if (sandboxTimeInMillis >= userData.moveEndTime) then
        userData.moveEndTime = nil;
        return Action.Status.TERMINATED;
    end

    path = userData.agent:GetPath();
    if (#path ~= 0) then
        offset = Vector.new(0, 0.05, 0);
```

```
            DebugUtilities_DrawPath(
                path, false, offset, DebugUtilities.Orange);
            Core.DrawCircle(
                path[#path] + offset, 1.5, DebugUtilities.Orange);
        end

        -- Terminate movement is the Agent is close enough to the
        -- target.
        if (Vector.Distance(userData.agent:GetPosition(),
            userData.agent:GetTarget()) < 1.5) then

            Agent.RemovePath(userData.agent);
            return Action.Status.TERMINATED;
        end

        return Action.Status.RUNNING;
    end
```

SoldierLogic.lua:

```
    local function MoveAction(userData)
        return Action.new(
            "move",
            SoldierActions_MoveToInitialize,
            SoldierActions_MoveToUpdate,
            SoldierActions_MoveToCleanUp,
            userData);
    end
```

The flee action

To create a flee action that causes our agent to run away from its enemy, we need to first find a valid path that is at least 4.0 meters away. Picking an arbitrary point on the navmesh will work, but we must ensure that there is a valid path to that point from the agent's current position:

SoldierActions.lua:

```
    function SoldierActions_FleeCleanUp(userData)
        -- No cleanup is required for fleeing.
    end

    function SoldierActions_FleeInitialize(userData)
        local sandbox = userData.agent:GetSandbox();

        if (userData.enemy) then
            local endPoint = Sandbox.RandomPoint(sandbox, "default");
```

```
        local path = Sandbox.FindPath(
            sandbox,
            "default",
            userData.agent:GetPosition(),
            endPoint);

        -- Find a valid position at least 16 units away from the
        -- current enemy.
        -- Note: Since pathfinding is not affected by the enemy,
        -- it is entirely possible to generate paths that move the
        -- Agent into the enemy, instead of away from the enemy.
        while #path == 0 do
            endPoint = Sandbox.RandomPoint(sandbox, "default");
            while Vector.DistanceSquared(endPoint,
                userData.enemy:GetPosition()) < 16.0 do

                endPoint = Sandbox.RandomPoint(
                    sandbox, "default");
            end
            path = Sandbox.FindPath(
                sandbox,
                "default",
                userData.agent:GetPosition(),
                endPoint);
        end

        Soldier_SetPath(userData.agent, path, false);
        userData.agent:SetTarget(endPoint);
        userData.movePosition = endPoint;
    else
        -- Randomly move anywhere if the Agent has no current
        -- enemy.
        SoldierActions_RandomMoveInitialize(userData);
    end

    userData.controller:QueueCommand(
        userData.agent,
        SoldierController.Commands.MOVE);

    return Action.Status.RUNNING;
end
```

Once a valid target position and path is found, the flee action acts very similar to a move action with one exception, which is health. As our flee action continues to move our agent until it reaches the target position, we must check whether the agent is still alive; otherwise, we have to terminate the action early:

SoldierActions.lua:

```lua
function SoldierActions_FleeUpdate(deltaTimeInMillis, userData)
    -- Terminate the Action if the agent is dead.
    if (Agent.GetHealth(userData.agent) <= 0) then
        return Action.Status.TERMINATED;
    end

    path = userData.agent:GetPath();
    DebugUtilities_DrawPath(
        path, false, Vector.new(), DebugUtilities.Blue);
    Core.DrawCircle(
        path[#path], 1.5, DebugUtilities.Blue);

    if (Vector.Distance(
        userData.agent:GetPosition(),
        userData.agent:GetTarget()) < 1.5) then

        Agent.RemovePath(userData.agent);
        return Action.Status.TERMINATED;
    end

    return Action.Status.RUNNING;
end
```

When our agents start fleeing from their pursuers, they will now draw a blue path indicating the position they are fleeing to.

Agents fleeing from one another

Instantiating the flee action requires creating a new action and specifying the initialize, update, and cleanup functions.

SoldierLogic.lua:

```
local function FleeAction(userData)
    return Action.new(
        "flee",
        SoldierActions_FleeInitialize,
        SoldierActions_FleeUpdate,
        SoldierActions_FleeCleanUp,
        userData);
end
```

The pursue action

Pursue is the exact opposite of flee, as our agent will track down its enemy instead of running from it. For this, we first find a path to the enemy and then begin moving toward it. Typically, our agents will default to this behavior if they have a known enemy and sufficient health to engage the enemy:

SoldierActions.lua:

```
function SoldierActions_PursueCleanUp(userData)
    -- No cleanup is required for pursuit.
end

function SoldierActions_PursueInitialize(userData)
    local sandbox = userData.agent:GetSandbox();
    local endPoint = userData.enemy:GetPosition();
    local path = Sandbox.FindPath(
        sandbox,
        "default",
        userData.agent:GetPosition(),
        endPoint);

    -- Path to the enemy if possible, otherwise idle and
    -- constantly try to repath to the enemy.
    if (#path ~= 0) then
        Soldier_SetPath(userData.agent, path, false);
        userData.agent:SetTarget(endPoint);
        userData.movePosition = endPoint;

        userData.controller:QueueCommand(
            userData.agent,
            SoldierController.Commands.MOVE);
    end

    return Action.Status.RUNNING;
end
```

As the enemy agent will typically be moving, we need to update our agent's path during the update loop so that the agent can track down the enemy's new position. If our agent gets within 3.0 meters of the enemy, the pursuit ends and another action can be run. As pursuit is a long running action, we also check for the health condition of our agent that can terminate pursuits early:

SoldierActions.lua:

```lua
function SoldierActions_PursueUpdate(deltaTimeInMillis, userData)
    -- Terminate the Action if the agent dies.
    if (Agent.GetHealth(userData.agent) <= 0) then
        return Action.Status.TERMINATED;
    end

    -- Constantly repath to the enemy's new position.
    local sandbox = userData.agent:GetSandbox();
    local endPoint = userData.enemy:GetPosition();
    local path = Sandbox.FindPath(
        sandbox,
        "default",
        userData.agent:GetPosition(),
        endPoint);

    if (#path ~= 0) then
        Soldier_SetPath(userData.agent, path, false);
        userData.agent:SetTarget(endPoint);
        userData.movePosition = endPoint;

        offset = Vector.new(0, 0.1, 0);
        path = userData.agent:GetPath();
        DebugUtilities_DrawPath(
            path, false, offset, DebugUtilities.Red);
        Core.DrawCircle(
            path[#path] + offset, 3, DebugUtilities.Red);
    end

    -- Terminate the pursuit Action when the Agent is within
    -- shooting distance to the enemy.
    if (Vector.Distance(userData.agent:GetPosition(),
        userData.agent:GetTarget()) < 3) then

        Agent.RemovePath(userData.agent);
```

```
        return Action.Status.TERMINATED;
    end

    return Action.Status.RUNNING;
end
```

When our soldiers are pursuing their enemy, we'll now see a red path that is constantly updated to move toward the enemy position.

Agents pursuing one another

Instantiating a pursue action is identical to the previous actions we've created and requires passing our pursue initialize, update, and cleanup functions to each new action instance.

SoldierLogic.lua:

```
local function PursueAction(userData)
    return Action.new(
        "pursue",
        SoldierActions_PursueInitialize,
        SoldierActions_PursueUpdate,
        SoldierActions_PursueCleanUp,
        userData);
end
```

Evaluators

Evaluators are the principal method of handling conditional checks in our decision structures. While actions perform the eventual behaviors that our agents exhibit, it's the responsibly of evaluators to determine which action is allowed to run at what time.

Creating an evaluator object simply wraps a function call that returns true or false when the userData table is passed into the function:

Evaluator.lua:

```
function Evaluator.Evaluate(self)
    return self.function_(self.userData_);
end

function Evaluator.new(name, evalFunction, userData)
    local evaluator = {};

    -- data members
    evaluator.function_ = evalFunction;
    evaluator.name_  = name or "";
    evaluator.type_  = Evaluator.Type;
    evaluator.userData_ = userData;

    -- object functions
    evaluator.evaluate_ = Evaluate;

    return evaluator;
end
```

Creating evaluators

Creating evaluators relies on simple functions that perform isolated operations on the agent's userData table. Typically, most evaluators will only perform calculations based on userData instead of modifying the data itself, although there is no limitation on doing this. As the same evaluator might appear within a decision structure, care must be taken to create consistent decision choices.

> Evaluators that modify userData can easily become a source of bugs; try to avoid this if at all possible. Actions should modify the agent's state, when evaluators begin to modify the agent's state as a decision structure is processed; it becomes very difficult to tell how and why any eventual action was chosen, as the order of operations will affect the outcome.

Constant evaluators

First, we'll need to create the two most basic evaluators; one that always returns true, and another that always returns false. These evaluators come in handy as a means of enabling or disabling actions during development:

SoldierEvaluators.lua:

```
function SoldierEvaluators_True(userData)
    return true;
end

function SoldierEvaluators_False(userData)
    return false;
end
```

Has ammo evaluator

Next, we can perform a simple ammo check to see whether the agent has any remaining ammo, as well as the inverse to check whether the agent has no ammo:

SoldierEvaluators.lua:

```
function SoldierEvaluators_HasAmmo(userData)
    return userData.ammo ~= nil and userData.ammo > 0;
end

function SoldierEvaluators_HasNoAmmo(userData)
    return not SoldierEvaluators_HasAmmo(userData);
end
```

Has critical health evaluator

A critical health check evaluator returns true if our agent has less than 20 percent of its health; otherwise, it evaluates to false:

SoldierEvaluators.lua:

```
function SoldierEvaluators_HasCriticalHealth(userData)
    return Agent.GetHealth(userData.agent) <
        (userData.maxHealth * 0.2);
end
```

Has enemy evaluator

Has enemy is the first evaluator that actually modifies the `userData` table passed in to the evaluator. The `HasEnemy` function calculates the best enemy the agent should consider to be its enemy. Iterating over all agents in the sandbox, the closest pathable enemy will be selected. If no enemy that meets these requirements is found, the `HasEnemy` evaluator returns false.

 As `HasEnemy` modifies and performs non-simple calculations, it should be used sparingly within any logic structure.

Since our agents will need to know when they have an enemy as well as when there are no valid enemies, we'll create a normal `HasEnemy` function evaluator and the inverse `HasNoEnemy` function.

`SoldierEvaluators.lua`:

```
function SoldierEvaluators_HasEnemy(userData)
    local sandbox = userData.agent:GetSandbox();
    local position = Agent.GetPosition(userData.agent);
    local agents = Sandbox.GetAgents(userData.agent:GetSandbox());

    local closestEnemy;
    local distanceToEnemy;

    for index=1, #agents do
        local agent = agents[index];
        if (Agent.GetId(agent) ~= Agent.GetId(userData.agent) and
            Agent.GetHealth(agent) > 0) then
            -- Find the closest enemy.
            local distanceToAgent = Vector.DistanceSquared(
                position, Agent.GetPosition(agent));
            if (closestEnemy == nil or
                distanceToAgent < distanceToEnemy) then

                local path = Sandbox.FindPath(
                    sandbox,
                    "default",
                    position,
                    agent:GetPosition());

                -- If the agent can path to the enemy, use this
                -- enemy as the best possible enemy.
                if (#path ~= 0) then
                    closestEnemy = agent;
                    distanceToEnemy = distanceToAgent;
```

```
                        end
                    end
                end
            end

        userData.enemy = closestEnemy;

        return userData.enemy ~= nil;
    end

    function SoldierEvaluators_HasNoEnemy(userData)
        return not SoldierEvaluators_HasEnemy(userData);
    end
```

Has move position evaluator

The HasMovePosition evaluator calculates whether the agent is within 1.5 meters of its target position. This allows for agents to terminate their move behaviors once they've reached their target position:

SoldierEvaluators.lua:

```
    function SoldierEvaluators_HasMovePosition(userData)
        return userData.movePosition ~= nil and
            (Vector.Distance(
                userData.agent:GetPosition(),
                userData.movePosition) > 1.5);
    end
```

Is alive evaluator

IsAlive simply informs you whether the agent has health left, and the IsNotAlive evaluator returns the negation:

SoldierEvaluators.lua:

```
    function SoldierEvaluators_IsAlive(userData)
        return Agent.GetHealth(userData.agent) > 0;
    end

    function SoldierEvaluators_IsNotAlive(userData)
        return not SoldierEvaluators_IsAlive(userData);
    end
```

Can shoot enemy evaluator

To determine if our agent can shoot an enemy agent, we can perform a distance check to see whether our agent is within 3.0 meters of the enemy. While this might produce some false positives, it's effective enough to allow our agents to shoot one another with a relatively high accuracy:

SoldierEvaluators.lua:

```
function SoldierEvaluators_CanShootAgent(userData)
    if (userData.enemy ~= nil and
        Agent.GetHealth(userData.enemy) > 0 and
        Vector.Distance(
            userData.agent:GetPosition(),
            userData.enemy:GetPosition()) < 3) then
        return true;
    end;
    return false;
end
```

50/50 chance evaluator

A 50/50 chance evaluator is a random roll and returns true half of the time:

SoldierEvaluators.lua:

```
function SoldierEvaluators_Random(userData)
    return math.random() >= 0.5;
end
```

Decision structures

With actions and evaluators at our disposal, we'll begin to create different types of logic structures that use both of these primitive operators to build our agent's behaviors. While each decision structure uses different approaches and techniques, we'll create similar behaving agents based on the actions and evaluators we have.

Decision trees

Decision trees will be the first structure we'll implement and are, by far, the easiest way to understand how a decision was made. A decision tree is composed of branches and leaves. Each branch in the tree will wrap an evaluator, while each leaf will be composed of an action. Through a sequence of branch conditions, our decision tree will always result in a final action that our agent will perform.

To create a decision tree structure, we'll implement an update loop for our tree, which evaluates the root branch within the tree and then proceeds to process the resulting action. Once the action has been initialized, updated, and eventually, terminated, the decision tree will re-evaluate the tree from the root branch to determine the next action to be executed:

DecisionTree.lua:

```
require "Action"

DecisionTree = {};

function DecisionTree.SetBranch(self, branch)
    self.branch_ = branch;
end

function DecisionTree.Update(self, deltaTimeInMillis)
    -- Skip execution if the tree hasn't been setup yet.
    if (self.branch_ == nil) then
        return;
    end

    -- Search the tree for an Action to run if not currently
    -- executing an Action.
    if (self.currentAction_ == nil) then
        self.currentAction_ = self.branch_:Evaluate();

        self.currentAction_:Initialize();
    end

    local status = self.currentAction_:Update(deltaTimeInMillis);

    -- Clean up the Action once it has terminated.
    if (status == Action.Status.TERMINATED) then
        self.currentAction_:CleanUp();
        self.currentAction_ = nil;
```

```
        end
    end

function DecisionTree.new()
    local decisionTree = {};

        -- The DecisionTree's data members.
        decisionTree.branch_   = nil;
        decisionTree.currentAction_   = nil;

        -- The DecisionTree's accessor functions.
        decisionTree.SetBranch = DecisionTree.SetBranch;
        decisionTree.Update = DecisionTree.Update;

        return decisionTree;
    end
```

Branches

Branches in a decision tree consist of a conditional evaluator that determines which child is executed. It is the responsibility of the evaluator to return a value that ranges from 1 to the maximum number of children in the branch. Even though we'll only be creating binary decision trees, the structure itself can branch out to any number of children, as shown in the following diagram:

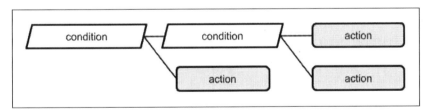

An example of a decision tree branch

Our decision branch class will have basic assessors such as adding additional children as well as setting the evaluator function used during branch calculation.

DecisionBranch.lua:

```
DecisionBranch = {}

DecisionBranch.Type = "DecisionBranch";

function DecisionBranch.new()
    local branch = {};

        -- The DecisionBranch's data members.
        branch.children_ = {};
```

```
        branch.evaluator_ = nil;
        branch.type_ = DecisionBranch.Type;

        -- The DecisionBranch's accessor functions.
        branch.AddChild = DecisionBranch.AddChild;
        branch.Evaluate = DecisionBranch.Evaluate;
        branch.SetEvaluator = DecisionBranch.SetEvaluator;

        return branch;
    end
    function DecisionBranch.AddChild(self, child, index)
        -- Add the child at the specified index, or as the last child.
        index = index or (#self.children_ + 1);

        table.insert(self.children_, index, child);
    end
    function DecisionBranch.SetEvaluator(self, evaluator)
        self.evaluator_ = evaluator;
    end
```

Decision leaves

As the leaves of the decision tree are merely actions, we can completely encase each leaf action into the branches themselves without the need for any additional structures. The use of the `type_` variable allows us to determine whether a child of the branch is another branch or an action to be executed.

Branch evaluation

To evaluate a branch, we execute the evaluator and use the return value to further process the tree. Once a choice is made, we either return an action node if the selected child is a leaf, otherwise we recursively evaluate another branch until an action is found.

 Every branch within a decision tree must eventually end with an action node; trees without actions as leafs are malformed and will not evaluate properly.

To implement evaluation, we'll use the `type_` field to determine if a child should be considered as a branch or as an action to return.

`DecisionBranch.lua`:

```
    function DecisionBranch.Evaluate(self)
        -- Execute the branch's evaluator function, this much return a
        -- numeric value which indicates what child should execute.
```

```
    local eval = self.evaluator_();

    local choice = self.children_[eval];

    if (choice.type_ == DecisionBranch.Type) then
        -- Recursively evaluate children that are decisions
        -- branches.
        return choice:Evaluate();
    else
        -- Return the leaf action.
        return choice;
    end
end
```

Building a decision tree

Building a decision tree starts with instantiating an instance of a decision tree, creating each branch within our tree, connecting the conditional branches, and adding actions:

SoldierLogic.lua:

```
function SoldierLogic_DecisionTree(userData)
    local tree = DecisionTree.new();
    return tree;
end
```

Creating branches

The tree we'll be creating combines each of the actions and evaluators we implemented previously and gives our agents the ability to pursue, flee, move, shoot, idle, reload, and die.

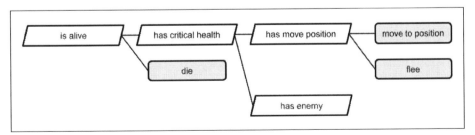

Critical health decision branch

First we'll create each branch instance that our decision tree will contain before adding any evaluators or actions.

SoldierLogic.lua:

```lua
function SoldierLogic_DecisionTree(userData)
    local tree = DecisionTree.new();

    local isAliveBranch = DecisionBranch.new();
    local criticalBranch = DecisionBranch.new();
    local moveFleeBranch = DecisionBranch.new();
    local enemyBranch = DecisionBranch.new();
    local ammoBranch = DecisionBranch.new();
    local shootBranch = DecisionBranch.new();
    local moveRandomBranch = DecisionBranch.new();
    local randomBranch = DecisionBranch.new();

    tree:SetBranch(isAliveBranch);
    return tree;
end
```

Once we've created each branch in our decision tree, we'll begin to hook up the parent-child relationships between branches as well as add leaf node actions.

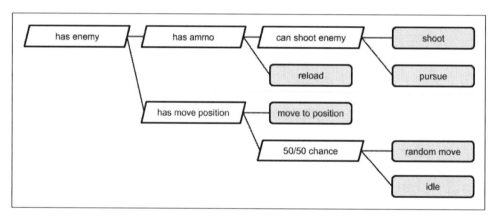

Enemy and no enemy decision branches

As our decision tree follows a binary tree design, each branch will typically have one action and another branch. Branches at the tips of the tree will end with two different actions:

SoldierLogic.lua:

```lua
function SoldierLogic_DecisionTree(userData)

    ...

    isAliveBranch:AddChild(criticalBranch);
```

```
isAliveBranch:AddChild(DieAction(userData));
isAliveBranch:SetEvaluator(
    function()
        if SoldierEvaluators_IsNotAlive(userData) then
            return 2;
        end
        return 1;
    end);

criticalBranch:AddChild(moveFleeBranch);
criticalBranch:AddChild(enemyBranch);
criticalBranch:SetEvaluator(
    function()
        if SoldierEvaluators_HasCriticalHealth(
                userData) then

            return 1;
        end
        return 2;
    end);

moveFleeBranch:AddChild(MoveAction(userData));
moveFleeBranch:AddChild(FleeAction(userData));
moveFleeBranch:SetEvaluator(
    function()
        if SoldierEvaluators_HasMovePosition(userData) then
            return 1;
        end
        return 2;
    end);

tree:SetBranch(isAliveBranch);
return tree;
end
```

So far, we've added death, move, and flee actions; now, we'll add the remaining reload, shoot, pursue, move, random move, and idle actions:

SoldierLogic.lua:

```
function SoldierLogic_DecisionTree(userData)

    ...

    enemyBranch:AddChild(ammoBranch);
    enemyBranch:AddChild(moveRandomBranch);
```

```
enemyBranch:SetEvaluator(
    function()
        if SoldierEvaluators_HasAmmo(userData) then
            return 2;
        end
        return 1;
    end);

ammoBranch:AddChild(shootBranch);
ammoBranch:AddChild(ReloadAction(userData));
ammoBranch:SetEvaluator(
    function()
        if SoldierEvaluators_HasAmmo(userData) then
            return 1;
        end
        return 2;
    end);

shootBranch:AddChild(ShootAction(userData));
shootBranch:AddChild(PursueAction(userData));
shootBranch:SetEvaluator(
    function()
        if SoldierEvaluators_CanShootAgent(userData) then
            return 1;
        end
        return 2;
    end);

moveRandomBranch:AddChild(MoveAction(userData));
moveRandomBranch:AddChild(randomBranch);
moveRandomBranch:SetEvaluator(
    function()
        if SoldierEvaluators_HasMovePosition(userData) then
            return 1;
        end
        return 2;
    end);

randomBranch:AddChild(RandomMoveAction(userData));
randomBranch:AddChild(IdleAction(userData));
randomBranch:SetEvaluator(
    function()
        if SoldierEvaluators_Random(userData) then
            return 1;
        end
        return 2;
```

```
                end);

        tree:SetBranch(isAliveBranch);
        return tree;
    end
```

Creating a decision tree agent

To create an agent whose logic is controlled by our decision tree, we'll modify our indirect soldier agent, as the initial setup of an animation state machine and soldier controller is already done for us.

We'll first create the userData table and associate the initial values so that our decision tree can interact with the agent. Once we've populated the userData table, we can instantiate our decision tree. We'll change the agent's update loop to process the decision tree as well as the soldier controller. As our decision tree expects that the execution will end when an agent dies, we'll add a conditional check that halts updates when this occurs:

IndirectSoldierAgent.lua:

```
    local soldier;
    local soldierController;
    local soldierDecisionTree;
    local soldierUserData;

    function Agent_Initialize(agent)
        Soldier_InitializeAgent(agent);
        soldier = Soldier_CreateSoldier(agent);
        weapon = Soldier_CreateWeapon(agent);

        soldierController = SoldierController.new(
            agent, soldier, weapon);

        Soldier_AttachWeapon(soldier, weapon);
        weapon = nil;

        soldierUserData = {};
        soldierUserData.agent = agent;
        soldierUserData.controller = soldierController;
        soldierUserData.maxHealth = soldierUserData.health;
        soldierUserData.alive = true;
        soldierUserData.ammo = 10;
```

```
            soldierUserData.maxAmmo = 10;

        soldierDecisionTree = SoldierLogic_DecisionTree(
            soldierUserData);
    end

    function Agent_Update(agent, deltaTimeInMillis)
        if (soldierUserData.alive) then
            soldierDecisionTree:Update(deltaTimeInMillis);
        end

        soldierController:Update(agent, deltaTimeInMillis);
    end
```

Strengths of decision trees

After implementing a decision tree, it's relatively easy to tell how decisions are made, as evaluators essentially serve as nested if...else structures. Any possible case can be modeled by the decision tree, as every action our agent supports will be a leaf node within the tree.

Pitfalls of decision trees

Although decision trees are easy to understand, their weaknesses stem from trying to implement complicated logical conditions where every possible outcome must also be accounted for. With a large number of branch possibilities, a decision tree will also need to be balanced; otherwise, parts of the tree will end up needing to being replicated, further increasing the complexity of the tree.

Finite state machines

Creating a **finite state machine (FSM)** for modeling logic will resemble the animation state machines we've created previously, except that transitioning to a new state within the state machine is handled automatically through the evaluation of transitions. Once one evaluator returns true, the state machine will transition to the new state and invoke the associated state's action.

States

States within an FSM are responsible for associating an action with the state. We create a state by passing an action and naming the state for debug convenience:

FiniteState.lua:

```
require "Action";
require "FiniteState";
require "FiniteStateTransition";

FiniteState = {};

function FiniteState.new(name, action)
    local state = {};

    -- The FiniteState's data members.
    state.name_   = name;
    state.action_ = action;

    return state;
end
```

Transitions

Transitions encapsulate the state to be transitioned to as well as the evaluator that determines whether the transition should be taken. The responsibility for evaluating transitions is left to the finite state machine itself:

FiniteStateTransition.lua:

```
FiniteStateTransition = {};

function FiniteStateTransition.new(toStateName, evaluator)
    local transition = {};

    -- The FiniteStateTransition's data members.
    transition.evaluator_  = evaluator;
    transition.toStateName_ = toStateName;

    return transition;
end
```

Finite state machine structure

The FSM consists of ever logical state the agent can execute on, as well as a two-dimensional table of every possible state transition. The `transition_` variable is keyed by the state name and consists of transition objects:

FiniteStateMachine.lua:

```lua
require "Action";
require "FiniteState";
require "FiniteStateTransition";

function FiniteStateMachine.new(userData)
    local fsm = {};

    -- The FiniteStateMachine's data members.
    fsm.currentState_ = nil;
    fsm.states_       = {};
    fsm.transitions_  = {};
    fsm.userData_     = userData;
end
```

Helper functions

We can implement additional helper functions in order to allow interactions with the FSM in a safe manner:

FiniteStateMachine.lua:

```lua
function FiniteStateMachine.ContainsState(self, stateName)
    return self.states_[stateName] ~= nil;
end

function FiniteStateMachine.ContainsTransition(
    self, fromStateName, toStateName)

    return self.transitions_[fromStateName] ~= nil and
        self.transitions_[fromStateName][toStateName] ~= nil;
end

function FiniteStateMachine.GetCurrentStateName(self)
    if (self.currentState_) then
        return self.currentState_.name_;
    end
end

function FiniteStateMachine.GetCurrentStateStatus(self)
    if (self.currentState_) then
        return self.currentState_.action_.status_;
    end
```

```
end

function FiniteStateMachine.SetState(self, stateName)
    if (self:ContainsState(stateName)) then
        if (self.currentState_) then
            self.currentState_.action_:CleanUp();
        end

        self.currentState_ = self.states_[stateName];
        self.currentState_.action_:Initialize();
    end
end
```

Adding states and transitions

As states are contained in a table where the state's name is the look-up key, we simply create a new `FiniteState` instance and add it to the table. Adding transitions requires checking whether each of the transitions to and from states exist within the FSM, and then inserting the transition within the `transitions_` class variable.

Going forward, as we create states and transitions, we'll represent each state as well as every possible transition using the following diagram:

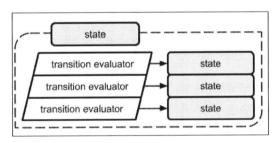

A finite state machine

Creating our `AddState` and `AddTransition` functions will modify the internal tables held by the FSM in order to add additional states and map one state to another using transitions

FiniteStateMachine.lua:

```
function FiniteStateMachine.AddState(self, name, action)
    self.states_[name] = FiniteState.new(name, action);
end

function FiniteStateMachine.AddTransition(
    self, fromStateName, toStateName, evaluator)
    -- Ensure both states exist within the FSM.
    if (self:ContainsState(fromStateName) and
```

```
        self:ContainsState(toStateName)) then
        if (self.transitions_[fromStateName] == nil) then
            self.transitions_[fromStateName] = {};
        end

        -- Add the new transition to the "from" state.
        table.insert(
            self.transitions_[fromStateName],
            FiniteStateTransition.new(toStateName, evaluator));
    end
end
```

Updating the finite state machine

Updating the state machine internally performs two different operations. The first is to execute or continue executing a running action, and the second is to select a new state once the action is complete. As transitions exist in a priority order, we iterate over all transitions executing their evaluators to determine the next state for the FSM to transition to. The first evaluator that returns true determines the state the FSM moves to.

Note that there is no validation that the finite state machine actually picks an action to transition to. If this occurs, the FSM will attempt to iterate over each transition in the next update call in order to find a valid transition. Using an evaluator that always returns true as the last possible transition is a best practice to prevent cases where our agent is unable to select any action to perform.

First we'll create an EvaluateTransitions function to determine the next state our FSM will move to once a state has finished. Afterwards we can create the FSM Update function that manages a running action and determines when state transitions occur.

FiniteStateMachine.lua:

```
    local function EvaluateTransitions(self, transitions)
        for index = 1, #transitions do
            -- Find the first transition that evaluates to true,
            -- return the state the transition points to.
            if (transitions[index].evaluator_(self.userData_)) then
                return transitions[index].toStateName_;
            end
        end
    end

    function FiniteStateMachine.Update(self, deltaTimeInMillis)
        if (self.currentState_) then
```

```
        local status = self:GetCurrentStateStatus();

        if (status == Action.Status.RUNNING) then
            self.currentState_.action_:Update(deltaTimeInMillis);
        elseif (status == Action.Status.TERMINATED) then
            -- Evaluate all transitions to find the next state
            -- to move the FSM to.
            local toStateName = EvaluateTransitions(
                self,
                self.transitions_[self.currentState_.name_]);
            if (self.states_[toStateName] ~= nil) then
                self.currentState_.action_:CleanUp();
                self.currentState_ = self.states_[toStateName];
                self.currentState_.action_:Initialize();
            end
        end
    end
end
```

Adding instance functions

With helper functions and the main update loop out of the way, we can modify our
FSM mapping to point to our new local functions:

FiniteStateMachine.lua:

```
function FiniteStateMachine.new()
    local fsm = {};

    ...

    -- The FiniteStateMachine's accessor functions.
    fsm.AddState = FiniteStateMachine.AddState;
    fsm.AddTransition = FiniteStateMachine.AddTransition;
    fsm.ContainsState = FiniteStateMachine.ContainsState;
    fsm.ContainsTransition =
        FiniteStateMachine.ContainsTransition;
    fsm.GetCurrentStateName =
        FiniteStateMachine.GetCurrentStateName;
    fsm.GetCurrentStateStatus =
        FiniteStateMachine.GetCurrentStateStatus;
    fsm.SetState = FiniteStateMachine.SetState;
    fsm.Update = FiniteStateMachine.Update;

    return fsm;
end
```

Building a finite state machine

To build a finite state machine for our agent, we'll create the initial states that wrap each possible action. As the state machine needs a starting point, we'll set the state explicitly to the idle state to begin with. Once the idle state has finished, our state machine will automatically pick the most relevant action to execute afterward:

SoldierLogic.lua:

```
function SoldierLogic_FiniteStateMachine(userData)
    local fsm = FiniteStateMachine.new(userData);
    fsm:AddState("die", DieAction(userData));
    fsm:AddState("flee", FleeAction(userData));
    fsm:AddState("idle", IdleAction(userData));
    fsm:AddState("move", MoveAction(userData));
    fsm:AddState("pursue", PursueAction(userData));
    fsm:AddState("randomMove", RandomMoveAction(userData));
    fsm:AddState("reload", ReloadAction(userData));

    fsm:SetState("idle");
    return fsm;
end
```

The idle state

Creating the idle state consists of adding every possible transition from the idle, which also allows for looping back to itself.

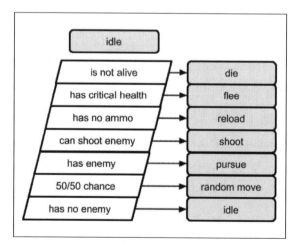

The soldier's FSM idle state

As transitions are evaluated in a priority order, it is imperative to add the most important actions first, followed by less important actions. In this case, death will always be the most important action, followed by our agent's sense of preservation to flee from their enemies. If both of these cases don't exist, our agent will move into combat behaviors such as reload, shoot, pursue, or randomly wander around:

SoldierLogic.lua:

```lua
function SoldierLogic_FiniteStateMachine(userData)

    ...

    -- idle action
    fsm:AddTransition(
        "idle", "die", SoldierEvaluators_IsNotAlive);
    fsm:AddTransition(
        "idle", "flee", SoldierEvaluators_HasCriticalHealth);
    fsm:AddTransition(
        "idle", "reload", SoldierEvaluators_HasNoAmmo);
    fsm:AddTransition(
        "idle", "shoot", SoldierEvaluators_CanShootAgent);
    fsm:AddTransition(
        "idle", "pursue", SoldierEvaluators_HasEnemy);
    fsm:AddTransition(
        "idle", "randomMove", SoldierEvaluators_Random);
    fsm:AddTransition("idle", "idle", SoldierEvaluators_True);

    fsm:SetState("idle");
    return fsm;
end
```

The movement state

The move state is nearly identical to the idle state, as every possibility is equally valid except for the addition of the looping movement.

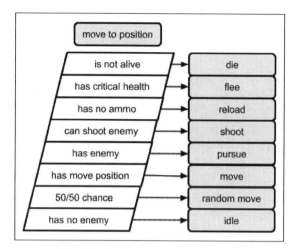

The soldier's FSM move to position state

As our move action is time-based, instead of terminating when our agent reaches its target position, we need to continue looping within the state until a better option becomes available:

SoldierLogic.lua:

```
function SoldierLogic_FiniteStateMachine(userData)

    ...

    -- move action
    fsm:AddTransition(
        "move", "die", SoldierEvaluators_IsNotAlive);
    fsm:AddTransition(
        "move", "flee", SoldierEvaluators_HasCriticalHealth);
    fsm:AddTransition(
        "move", "reload", SoldierEvaluators_HasNoAmmo);
    fsm:AddTransition(
        "move", "shoot", SoldierEvaluators_CanShootAgent);
    fsm:AddTransition(
        "move", "pursue", SoldierEvaluators_HasEnemy);
    fsm:AddTransition(
        "move", "move", SoldierEvaluators_HasMovePosition);
    fsm:AddTransition(
        "move", "randomMove", SoldierEvaluators_Random);
```

```
fsm:AddTransition("move", "idle", SoldierEvaluators_True);

fsm:SetState("idle");
return fsm;
end
```

The random movement state

A random movement state is only responsible for picking a location to move to; once a location is found, our agent will proceed to the move position state to complete the action.

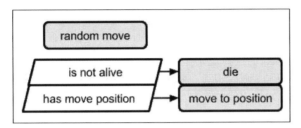

The soldier's FSM random move state

Separating position selection and processing of a position allows us to minimize all possible transitions that need to be taken care of from the random movement state:

SoldierLogic.lua:

```
function SoldierLogic_FiniteStateMachine(userData)

    ...

    -- random move action
    fsm:AddTransition(
        "randomMove", "die", SoldierEvaluators_IsNotAlive);
    fsm:AddTransition(
        "randomMove", "move", SoldierEvaluators_True);

    fsm:SetState("idle");
    return fsm;
end
```

The shoot state

Shooting is another state that is nearly identical to our idle state.

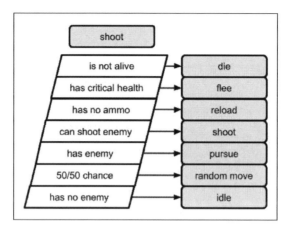

The soldier's FSM shoot state

As our state machine only has eight possible states, states such as idle and shoot are nearly fully connected to any possible action our agent can perform. Having fully connected states produces more reactive agents overall:

SoldierLogic.lua:

```lua
function SoldierLogic_FiniteStateMachine(userData)

    ...

    -- shoot action
    fsm:AddTransition(
        "shoot", "die", SoldierEvaluators_IsNotAlive);
    fsm:AddTransition(
        "shoot", "flee", SoldierEvaluators_HasCriticalHealth);
    fsm:AddTransition(
        "shoot", "reload", SoldierEvaluators_HasNoAmmo);
    fsm:AddTransition(
        "shoot", "shoot", SoldierEvaluators_CanShootAgent);
    fsm:AddTransition(
        "shoot", "pursue", SoldierEvaluators_HasEnemy);
    fsm:AddTransition(
        "shoot", "randomMove", SoldierEvaluators_Random);
    fsm:AddTransition("shoot", "idle", SoldierEvaluators_True);

    fsm:SetState("idle");
    return fsm;
end
```

The flee state

As fleeing is a state our agents cannot exit from, we can loop directly into another flee action until our agents die.

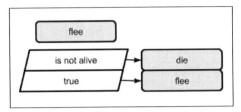

The soldier's FSM flee state

The only way for our agent to exit from fleeing its enemy is through death:

SoldierLogic.lua:

```
function SoldierLogic_FiniteStateMachine(userData)

    ...

    -- flee action
    fsm:AddTransition(
        "flee", "die", SoldierEvaluators_IsNotAlive);
    fsm:AddTransition("flee", "move", SoldierEvaluators_True);

    fsm:SetState("idle");
    return fsm;
end
```

The die state

The death state is the only terminal state within the state machine and has no transitions. The processing of the state machine is expected to seize once the death state finishes.

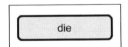

The soldier's FSM die state

The pursue state

As pursuing an enemy generates new paths during each update call, our agent doesn't need another state to handle movements.

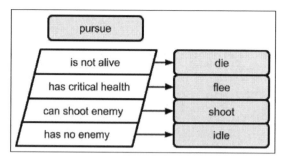

The soldier's FSM pursue state

In this case, the only thing our agent cares about while pursuing an enemy is to flee in order to prevent death, shoot the enemy when it comes within range, or idle if the enemy is no longer valid. As there are limited transitions from pursuit, our agent will sometimes need to jump through another state to find a valid action, such as reload. Even though cases like these exist, very little noticeable latency is introduced, and the finite state machine is less complex because of the reduced number of transitions:

SoldierLogic.lua:

```
function SoldierLogic_FiniteStateMachine(userData)

    ...

    -- pursue action
    fsm:AddTransition(
        "pursue", "die", SoldierEvaluators_IsNotAlive);
    fsm:AddTransition(
        "pursue", "shoot", SoldierEvaluators_CanShootAgent);
    fsm:AddTransition(
        "pursue", "move", SoldierEvaluators_HasMovePosition);
    fsm:AddTransition("pursue", "idle", SoldierEvaluators_True);

    fsm:SetState("idle");
    return fsm;
end
```

The reload state

As reloading is such a short-lived action, every transition out of reload is either a combat action or an idling action.

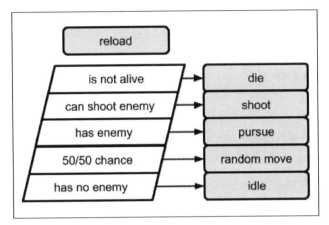

The soldier's FSM reload state

This reduced number of transitions will also incur latency in behavior selection, but it further reduces the complexity of our agent:

SoldierLogic.lua:

```
function SoldierLogic_FiniteStateMachine(userData)

    ...

    -- reload action
    fsm:AddTransition(
        "reload", "die", SoldierEvaluators_IsNotAlive);
    fsm:AddTransition(
        "reload", "shoot", SoldierEvaluators_CanShootAgent);
    fsm:AddTransition(
        "reload", "pursue", SoldierEvaluators_HasEnemy);
    fsm:AddTransition(
        "reload", "randomMove", SoldierEvaluators_Random);
    fsm:AddTransition("reload", "idle", SoldierEvaluators_True);

    fsm:SetState("idle");
    return fsm;
end
```

Creating a finite state machine agent

Now that we've created a finite state machine, we can simply replace the decision tree that powers our indirect soldier agent with a finite state machine. The initialization, updating, and termination of our FSM are identical to the decision tree.

With an abstract data structure, we can now create both decision-tree-based agents and finite state machine agents simultaneously:

IndirectSoldierAgent.lua:

```lua
local soldier;
local soldierController;
local soldierFSM;
local soldierUserData;

function Agent_Initialize(agent)

    ...

    soldierFSM = SoldierLogic_FiniteStateMachine(
        soldierUserData);
end

function Agent_Update(agent, deltaTimeInMillis)
    if (soldierUserData.alive) then
        soldierFSM:Update(deltaTimeInMillis);
    end

    soldierController:Update(agent, deltaTimeInMillis);
end
```

Strengths of finite state machines

The straightforwardness of a state machine relies heavily on large amounts of data. One of the key strengths with such a structure lies in the fact that the statefulness of an agent is inherent within the logical structure.

Compared to a decision tree, finite states isolate the amount of possible actions that can follow from another action. To create the same sort of flow in a decision tree would be inherently difficult and would require embedding some sort of userdata that maintains the statefulness we get for free with a finite state machine.

Pitfalls of finite state machines

The downside of state machines, though, are the exponential possible connections that come with the addition of each new state. To reduce latency or unexpected chains of actions, state machines need to be well connected so that agents can quickly select the best action.

Our implementation of state transitions is a simple, priority-based approach that might not fit all circumstances, in which case, a weighted or search-based approach might become necessary. This additional complexity can further complicate logic selection, where actions are chosen for reasons that aren't apparent.

Behavior trees

With decision trees focusing on the `if...else` style of action selection and state machines focusing on the statefulness of actions, behavior trees fill a nice middle ground with reaction-based decision making.

The behavior tree node

Behavior trees are composed solely of different types of nodes. Based on the node type, the behavior tree will interpret child nodes as actions and evaluators. As we'll need to distinguish each node instance type from one another, we can create an enumeration of all supported node types: actions, conditions, selectors, and sequences.

Creating an instance of a behavior tree node merely sets the node type and the name of the node:

BehaviorTreeNode.lua:

```
BehaviorTreeNode = {};

BehaviorTreeNode.Type = {
    ACTION = "ACTION",
    CONDITION = "CONDITION",
    SELECTOR = "SELECTOR",
    SEQUENCE = "SEQUENCE"
};

function BehaviorTreeNode.new(name, type)
    local node = {};

    -- The BehaviorTreeNode's data members.
```

```lua
        node.action_    = nil;
        node.children_  = {};
        node.evaluator_ = nil;
        node.name_      = name or "";
        node.parent_    = nil;
        node.type_      = type or BehaviorTreeNode.Type.ACTION;
end
```

Helper functions

Adding some object-oriented helper functions to handle child management as well as a backward link to the nodes parent will allow the behavior tree to evaluate the nodes more efficiently:

BehaviorTreeNode.lua:

```lua
    function BehaviorTreeNode.AddChild(self, child, index)
        index = index or (#self.children_ + 1);

        table.insert(self.children_, index, child);

        child.parent_ = self;
    end

    function BehaviorTreeNode.ChildIndex(self, child)
        for index=1, #self.children_ do
            if (self.children_[index] == child) then
                return index;
            end
        end

        return -1;
    end

    function BehaviorTreeNode.GetChild(self, childIndex)
        return self.children_[childIndex];
    end

    function BehaviorTreeNode.GetNumberOfChildren(self)
        return #self.children_;
    end

    function BehaviorTreeNode.GetParent(self)
        return self.parent_;
```

```
end

function BehaviorTreeNode.SetAction(self, action)
    self.action_ = action;
end

function BehaviorTreeNode.SetEvaluator(self, evaluator)
    self.evaulator_ = evaluator;
end

function BehaviorTreeNode.SetType(self, type)
    self.type_ = type;
end
```

Updating the behavior tree node

With local functions fleshed out, we can fully encapsulate our behavior tree
node functionality:

BehaviorTreeNode.lua:

```
function BehaviorTreeNode.new(name, type)
    local node = {};

    ...

    -- The BehaviorTreeNode's accessor functions.
    node.AddChild = BehaviorTreeNode.AddChild;
    node.ChildIndex = BehaviorTreeNode.ChildIndex;
    node.GetChild = BehaviorTreeNode.GetChild;
    node.GetNumberOfChildren =
        BehaviorTreeNode.GetNumberOfChildren;
    node.GetParent = BehaviorTreeNode.GetParent;
    node.SetAction = BehaviorTreeNode.SetAction;
    node.SetEvaluator = BehaviorTreeNode.SetEvaluator;
    node.SetType = BehaviorTreeNode.SetType;

    return node;
end
```

Actions

The first node type is a basic action. We can create a wrapper function that will instantiate an action node and set the internal action accordingly. Actions are only designed to execute behaviors on an agent and shouldn't be assigned any children. They should be considered leaves in a behavior tree:

SoldierLogic.lua:

```
local function CreateAction(name, action)
    local node = BehaviorTreeNode.new(
        name, BehaviorTreeNode.Type.ACTION);
    node:SetAction(action);
    return node;
end
```

Conditions

Conditions are similar to actions and are also leaves in a behavior tree. Condition nodes will execute the evaluator assigned to them and return the result to the caller to determine how they should be processed.

SoldierLogic.lua:

```
local function CreateCondition(name, evaluator)
    local condition = BehaviorTreeNode.new(
        name, BehaviorTreeNode.Type.CONDITION);
    condition:SetEvaluator(evaluator);
    return condition;
end
```

Selectors

Selectors are the first type of nodes that can have children within the behavior tree. A selector can have any number of children, but will only execute the first child that is available for execution. Essentially, selectors act as if, if...else, and else structures within behavior trees. A selector will return true if at least one child node is able to run; otherwise, the selector returns false:

SoldierLogic.lua:

```
local function CreateSelector()
    return BehaviorTreeNode.new(
        "selector", BehaviorTreeNode.Type.SELECTOR);
end
```

Sequences

Lastly, we have sequences, which act as sequential blocks of execution that will execute each of their children in an order until a condition, selector, or child sequence fails to execute. Sequences will return true if all their children run successfully; if any one of their children returns false, the sequence immediately exits and returns false in turn:

SoldierLogic.lua:

```
local function CreateSequence()
    return BehaviorTreeNode.new(
        "sequence", BehaviorTreeNode.Type.SEQUENCE);
end
```

Creating a behavior tree object

Creating a behavior tree object is simple, as it primarily consists of a root node, evaluation function, and update function:

BehaviorTree.lua:

```
require "BehaviorTreeNode"

BehaviorTree = {};

local _EvaluateSelector;
local _EvaluateSequence;

function BehaviorTree.SetNode(self, node)
    tree.node_ = node;
end

function BehaviorTree.new()
    local tree = {};

    -- The BehaviorTree's data members.
    tree.currentNode_ = nil;
    tree.node_ = nil;

    return tree;
end
```

Behavior tree helper functions

Four primary evaluators are used to process the behavior tree structure: selector evaluation, sequence evaluation, actual node evaluation, and finally, a continue evaluation function that continues where a sequence's child finishes:

BehaviorTree.lua:

```
local EvaluateSelector;
local EvaluateSequence;
```

Selector evaluation

As selectors only return false if all child nodes have executed without returning true, we can iterate over all children and return the first positive result we get back. We need to return two values, the evaluation result as well as an action node if one is found. To do this, we'll return a table containing both values.

As our behavior tree can be of any arbitrary depth, we will recursively evaluate both selectors and sequences till we have a return result:

BehaviorTree.lua:

```
_EvaluateSelector = function(self, node, deltaTimeInMillis)
    -- Try and evaluate all children.  Returns the first child
    -- that can execute.  If no child can successfully execute the
    -- selector fails.

    for index = 1, #node.children_ do
        local child = node:GetChild(index);

        if (child.type_ == BehaviorTreeNode.Type.ACTION) then
            -- Execute all Actions, since Actions cannot fail.
            return { node = child, result = true};
        elseif (child.type_ ==
            BehaviorTreeNode.Type.CONDITION) then

            -- Conditions are only valid within sequences, if one
            -- is encountered in a selector the tree is malformed.
            assert(false);
            return { result = false };
        elseif (child.type_ ==
            BehaviorTreeNode.Type.SELECTOR) then

            -- Recursively evaluate child selectors.
            local result = _EvaluateSelector(
```

```
                self, child, deltaTimeInMillis);

        if (result.result) then
            return result;
        end
    elseif (child.type_ ==
        BehaviorTreeNode.Type.SEQUENCE) then

        -- Evaluate a sequence, if it returns successfully
        -- then return the result.
        -- The result of a sequence may not contain a node to
        -- execute.
        local result = _EvaluateSequence(
            self, child, deltaTimeInMillis);

        if (result.result) then
            return result;
        end
    end
end

return { result = false };
end
```

Sequence evaluation

A sequence is nearly the opposite of a selector where the first failure will result in the sequence returning a failure. As sequences can execute multiple actions sequentially, we can take in an index number that represents the current child from which we should start our evaluation. This allows the behavior tree to continue the evaluation from where it left off:

BehaviorTree.lua:

```
_EvaluateSequence = function(self, node, deltaTimeInMillis, index)
    -- Try and evaluate all children.  Returns a false result if a
    -- child is unable to execute, such as a condition failing or
    -- child sequence/selector being unable to find a valid Action
    -- to run.
    index = index or 1;

    for count=index, #node.children_ do
        local child = node:GetChild(count);

        if (child.type_ == BehaviorTreeNode.Type.ACTION) then
            -- Execute all Actions, since Actions cannot fail.
```

```
            return { node = child, result = true};
    elseif (child.type_ ==
        BehaviorTreeNode.Type.CONDITION) then

            local result = child.evaluator_(self.userData_);

            -- Break out of execution if a condition fails.
            if (not child.evaluator_(self.userData_)) then
                return { result = false };
            end
    elseif (child.type_ ==
        BehaviorTreeNode.Type.SELECTOR) then

            local result = _EvaluateSelector(
                self, child, deltaTimeInMillis);

            -- Unable to find an Action to run, return failure.
            if (not result.result) then
                return { result = false };
            elseif (result.result and result.node ~= nil) then
                -- Found an Action to execute, pass the result
                -- back to the caller.
                return result;
            end

            -- A selector must return an Action to be considered
            -- successful, if no Action was found, then the
            -- selector failed.
    elseif (child.type_ ==
        BehaviorTreeNode.Type.SEQUENCE) then

            local result = _EvaluateSequence(
                self, child, deltaTimeInMillis);

            -- Sequence reported failure, propagate failure to the
            -- caller.
            if (not result.result) then
                return { result = false };
            elseif (result.result and result.node ~= nil) then
                -- Found an Action to execute, pass the result
                -- back to the caller.
                return result;
            end

            -- There is a third possible case, the sequence
            -- completed successfully and has no additional
```

```
            -- children to execute. In that case let the sequence
            -- continue executing additional children.
        end

        -- Move to the next child to execute.
        count = count + 1;
    end

    -- Returns success without an Action to run if all children
    -- executed successfully.
    return { result = true };
end
```

Node evaluation

Basic node evaluation is only used to begin the recursive tree evaluation of the root node and handles all four possible root node type evaluations. If the root node is a condition, an assert is called to indicate a malformed tree:

BehaviorTree.lua:

```
local function _EvaluateNode(self, node, deltaTimeInMillis)
    if (node.type_ == BehaviorTreeNode.Type.ACTION) then
        -- No further evaluation is necessary if an Action is
        -- found.
        return node;
    elseif (node.type_ == BehaviorTreeNode.Type.CONDITION) then
        -- Conditions should be evaluated immediately, if the
        -- behavior tree is trying to evaluate this node, there is
        -- something structurally wrong in the behavior tree.
        assert(false);  -- invalid structure
    elseif (node.type_ == BehaviorTreeNode.Type.SELECTOR) then
        -- Treat the node like a selector and find the first valid
        -- child action.
        local result = _EvaluateSelector(
            self, node, deltaTimeInMillis);

        if (result.result) then
            return result.node;
        end
    elseif (node.type_ == BehaviorTreeNode.Type.SEQUENCE) then
        -- Treat the node like a sequence and find the first valid
        -- child action.
        local result = _EvaluateSequence(
            self, node, deltaTimeInMillis);
```

```
            if (result.result) then
                return result.node;
            end
        end
    end
```

Continue behavior tree evaluation

Continuing evaluation of the behavior tree is required whenever an action is completed, as the action's parentage could contain a sequence that the behavior tree must continue evaluating. In order to continue every possible sequence, we can use the currently executing node's parent to determine whether it's part of a sequence. We will continue moving through parents until the root node is processed and only continue sequence evaluation if one of the encountered parents is a sequence:

BehaviorTree.lua:

```lua
local function _ContinueEvaluation(self, node, deltaTimeInMillis)
    local parentNode = node:GetParent();
    local childNode = node;

    -- Navigates upward within the tree to find any sequences that
    -- require continued evaluation.
    while (parentNode ~= nil) do
        if (parentNode.type_ ==
            BehaviorTreeNode.Type.SEQUENCE) then

            -- Found a sequence, continue evaluating from the
            -- current executing node within the sequence.
            local childIndex = parentNode:ChildIndex(childNode);

            -- So long as the executing child was not the last
            -- node within the sequence, evaluate the sequence
            -- starting on the next child node.
            if (childIndex <
                parentNode:GetNumberOfChildren()) then

                return _EvaluateSequence(
                    self,
                    parentNode,
                    deltaTimeInMillis,
                    childIndex + 1);
            end
```

```
            end

        -- Move one parent up in the tree.
        childNode = parentNode;
        parentNode = childNode:GetParent();
    end
end
```

The behavior tree update loop

The main behavior tree update loop is responsible for both picking the current action that should be executing as well as initializing, updating, and terminating any running action:

BehaviorTree.lua:

```
function BehaviorTree.Update(self, deltaTimeInMillis)
    if (self.currentNode_ == nil) then
        -- Find the first valid Action to execute.
        self.currentNode_ = _EvaluateNode(
            self, self.node_, deltaTimeInMillis);
    end

    if (self.currentNode_ ~= nil) then
        local status = self.currentNode_.action_.status_;

        if (status == Action.Status.UNINITIALIZED) then
            self.currentNode_.action_:Initialize();
        elseif (status == Action.Status.TERMINATED) then
            self.currentNode_.action_:CleanUp();

            -- Continue evaluation in case the Action's parent was
            -- a sequence.  _ContinueEvaluation can return nil, in
            -- case the tree needs to be reevaluated.
            self.currentNode_ = _ContinueEvaluation(
                self, self.currentNode_, deltaTimeInMillis);
        elseif (status == Action.Status.RUNNING) then
            self.currentNode_.action_:Update(deltaTimeInMillis);
        end
    end
end
```

Updating the behavior tree

Now that the internals of our behavior tree are fleshed out, we can update the behavior tree class with the Update and SetNode functions:

BehaviorTree.lua:

```lua
function BehaviorTree.new(userData)
    local tree = {};

    -- The BehaviorTree's data members.
    tree.currentNode_ = nil;
    tree.node_ = nil;
    tree.userData_ = userData;

    -- The BehaviorTree's accessor functions.
    tree.SetNode = BehaviorTree.SetNode;
    tree.Update = BehaviorTree.Update;

    return tree;
end
```

Building a behavior tree

Building a behavior tree is very similar to building a decision tree, except for the addition of selectors and sequence node types.

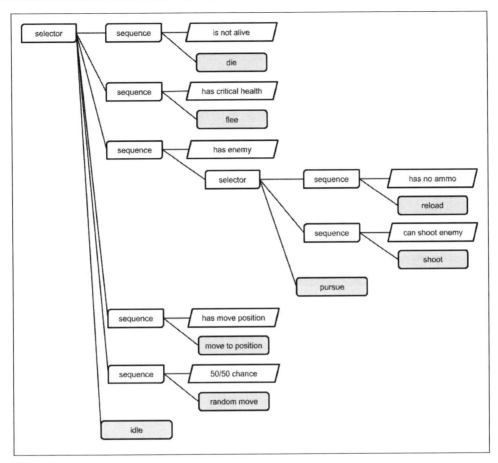

The soldier's behavior tree

We can start creating a behavior tree using a similarly wrapped function that instantiates a behavior tree and creates the first selector node for the tree:

SoldierLogic.lua:

```
function SoldierLogic_BehaviorTree(userData)
    local tree = BehaviorTree.new(userData);

    local node;
    local child;

    node = CreateSelector();
    tree:SetNode(node);

    return tree;
end
```

The death behavior

To add the first action, which is death, we add the required sequence, condition, and action nodes. As the behavior tree will completely re-evaluate once an action completes, we don't have to worry about other actions knowing about death. As prioritizing actions is based on how early in the tree they appear, we add death first, because it has the highest priority:

SoldierLogic.lua:

```
    function SoldierLogic_BehaviorTree(userData)

        . . .

        -- die action
        child = CreateSequence();
        node:AddChild(child);
        node = child;

        child = CreateCondition(
            "is not alive", SoldierEvaluators_IsNotAlive);
        node:AddChild(child);
        node = child;

        node = child:GetParent();
        child = CreateAction("die", DieAction(userData));
        node:AddChild(child);
        node = child;

        return tree;
    end
```

The flee behavior

Fleeing is another important behavior that extends the agent's lifespan. As fleeing is less important than death, the flee action has a lower priority in the behavior tree than the death behavior:

SoldierLogic.lua:

```
    function SoldierLogic_BehaviorTree(userData)

        . . .

        -- flee action
        node = node:GetParent();
```

```
    node = node:GetParent();
    child = CreateSequence();
    node:AddChild(child);
    node = child;

    child = CreateCondition(
        "has critical health",
        SoldierEvaluators_HasCriticalHealth);
    node:AddChild(child);
    node = child;

    node = node:GetParent();
    child = CreateAction("flee", FleeAction(userData));
    node:AddChild(child);
    node = child;

    return tree;
end
```

Combat behaviors

Combat behaviors encompass reloading, shooting, and pursuit; all have a common `SoldierEvaluators_HasEnemy` condition that must be true for any of these actions to execute. The strength of a behavior tree allows you to group common behaviors under common conditionals to reduce costly evaluations.

As our agent must choose a combat behavior if they have an enemy, the fallback action, pursuit requires no additional conditions before executing. If the behavior isn't able to process reloading or shooting, the pursuit action will be chosen automatically:

`SoldierLogic.lua`:

```
function SoldierLogic_BehaviorTree(userData)

    ...

    -- reload/shoot/pursue actions
    node = node:GetParent();
    node = node:GetParent();
    child = CreateSequence();
```

```
node:AddChild(child);
node = child;

child = CreateCondition(
    "has enemy", SoldierEvaluators_HasEnemy);
node:AddChild(child);
node = child;

node = node:GetParent();
child = CreateSelector();
node:AddChild(child);
node = child;
```

The reload behavior

Creating a reload behavior consists of a sequence with a single conditional and the
main reload action:

```
SoldierLogic.lua:

function SoldierLogic_BehaviorTree(userData)

    ...

    -- reload action
    child = CreateSequence();
    node:AddChild(child);
    node = child;

    child = CreateCondition(
        "has no ammo", SoldierEvaluators_HasNoAmmo);
    node:AddChild(child);
    node = child;

    node = node:GetParent();
    child = CreateAction("reload", ReloadAction(userData));
    node:AddChild(child);
    node = child;
```

The shoot behavior

The shoot behavior is identical to reloading, except that we must traverse back to the parent selector node to add the shoot sequence:

SoldierLogic.lua:

```
function SoldierLogic_BehaviorTree(userData)

    . . .

    -- shoot action
    node = node:GetParent();
    node = node:GetParent();
    child = CreateSequence();
    node:AddChild(child);
    node = child;

    child = CreateCondition(
        "can shoot enemy", SoldierEvaluators_CanShootAgent);
    node:AddChild(child);
    node = child;

    node = node:GetParent();
    child = CreateAction("shoot", ShootAction(userData));
    node:AddChild(child);
    node = child;
```

The pursue behavior

As pursuit is the action our agents can perform if they have an enemy, no condition is necessary:

SoldierLogic.lua:

```
function SoldierLogic_BehaviorTree(userData)

    . . .

    -- pursue action
    node = node:GetParent();
    node = node:GetParent();
```

```
        child = CreateAction("pursue", PursueAction(userData));
        node:AddChild(child);
        node = child;


        return tree;
    end
```

The move behavior

If our agent is unable to pursue an enemy and isn't fleeing, a general move behavior should operate on any target position our agent is currently moving toward. As target positions are only set by random move actions, the move behavior must have higher priority than a random move action; otherwise our agent will never be able to act on its target position:

SoldierLogic.lua:

```
    function SoldierLogic_BehaviorTree(userData)


        . . .


        -- move action
        node = node:GetParent();
        node = node:GetParent();
        node = node:GetParent();
        child = CreateSequence();
        node:AddChild(child);
        node = child;


        child = CreateCondition(
            "has move position", SoldierEvaluators_HasMovePosition);
        node:AddChild(child);
        node = child;


        node = node:GetParent();
        child = CreateAction(
            "move to position", MoveAction(userData));
        node:AddChild(child);
        node = child;


        return tree;
    end
```

The random move behavior

Randomly moving is one of the least prioritized behaviors and is a tossup between randomly choosing a spot to move to and just idling at a place:

```
function SoldierLogic_BehaviorTree(userData)

    ...

    -- random action
    node = node:GetParent();
    node = node:GetParent();
    child = CreateSequence();
    node:AddChild(child);
    node = child;

    child = CreateCondition(
        "50/50 chance", SoldierEvaluators_Random);
    node:AddChild(child);
    node = child;

    node = node:GetParent();
    child = CreateAction(
        "random move", RandomMoveAction(userData));
    node:AddChild(child);
    node = child;

    return tree;
end
```

The idle behavior

Just in case every other action has failed, the last action in a behavior tree should be something that can always execute. Behavior trees must find an action to execute regardless of the state of the agent. In our case, we simply allow the agent in order to idle at a place:

```
function SoldierLogic_BehaviorTree(userData)

    ...

    -- idle action
    node = node:GetParent();
    node = node:GetParent();
    child = CreateAction("idle", IdleAction(userData));
    node:AddChild(child);
    node = child;

    return tree;
end
```

Creating a behavior tree agent

To use our behavior tree, we can replace the finite state machine and perform the same update loop on our behavior tree instead. Regardless, if our agent is using a decision tree, state machine, or behavior tree, its actions will be nearly identical, as the logic is merely translated from one decision structure to another:

IndirectSoldierAgent.lua:

```
local soldier;
local soldierController;
local soldierBT;
local soldierUserData;

function Agent_Initialize(agent)

    ...

    soldierBT = SoldierLogic_BehaviorTree(
```

```
            soldierUserData);
    end

    function Agent_Update(agent, deltaTimeInMillis)
        if (soldierUserData.alive) then
            soldierBT:Update(deltaTimeInMillis);
        end

        soldierController:Update(agent, deltaTimeInMillis);
    end
```

Strengths of behavior trees

Compared to decision trees, behavior tree actions know very little about actions other than the priority they show up in the tree. This allows for actions to be modular in nature and can reduce the need to rebalance a complex tree when more actions are added.

Pitfalls of behavior trees

With reactive actions, behavior trees have shortcomings; they represent stateful logic very poorly. If statefulness needs to be preserved within a behavior tree, typically high-level conditions will dictate which branch is currently active. For instance, the noncombat and combat state of our agent isolates a lot of the behaviors that are available at any point in time.

Summary

With some rudimentary actions and decision-making logic controlling our agents, we can now begin to enhance how our agents see the world, as well as how they store information about the world.

In the next chapter, we'll create a data structure that can store knowledge as well as create senses for our agents to actually see and hear.

7
Knowledge Representation

In this chapter, we will cover the following topics:

- Creating knowledge sources
- Creating a blackboard architecture
- Using a blackboard for decision evaluators and actions

So far, our soldier has been using basic inputs from many different sources and in many different places. For instance, having conditional evaluators calculate the best enemy to attack is a very poor place to put decision selection, which mutates our soldier's knowledge of the sandbox. Going forward, knowledge can be consolidated in a central data structure that is available to all of our agent systems.

Knowledge sources

For our current soldier agents, we have two main sources of knowledge: the `userData` structure and logic evaluators that calculate results on the fly. While both of these techniques work, they quickly become unscalable, as no central system controls the rate at which they're updated, modified, or accessed from.

We can encapsulate our knowledge sources that require complex calculations into a data structure of their own. Once we've abstracted these sources, we can regulate their update frequency, cache calculations, and centralize access.

Creating a knowledge source

Knowledge sources have a few main characteristics: cached evaluation of the resulting calculation, the confidence of the evaluation, and the update frequency.

The cached evaluation is merely the result of the evaluator function the KnowledgeSource instance stores internally. The confidence measure is a value between 0 and 1, which our knowledge data structure can use to determine the best piece of knowledge to be used at any given time.

The update frequency is used to determine whether the knowledge source needs to re-evaluate the evaluator function when evaluation is invoked. Typically, this value can be used to throttle constant re-evaluations when the same knowledge source is used in multiple places within a logic structure:

KnowledgeSource.lua:

```
KnowledgeSource = {};

function KnowledgeSource.new(evaluator, updateFrequency)
    local source = {};

    -- The KnowledgeSource's data members.
    source.confidence_   = 0;
    source.evaluation_   = nil;
    source.evaluator_    = evaluator;
    source.lastUpdateTime_ = 0;
    source.updateFrequency_ = updateFrequency or 0;

    -- The KnowledgeSource's accessor functions.
    source.Evaluate = KnowledgeSource.Evaluate;

    return source;
end
```

Knowledge source evaluation

To evaluate a knowledge source, we first determine whether enough time has passed since the last time the source was evaluated. If this is the case, we can evaluate the source based on the passed-in function and store the confidence and evaluation within the source:

KnowledgeSource.lua:

```
function KnowledgeSource.Evaluate(self, userData)
    local time = Sandbox.GetTimeInMillis(userData.agent:GetSandbox());
```

```
      local nextUpdateTime = time + self.updateFrequency_;

      -- Wait till enough time has passed to re-evaluate the
      -- knowledge source.
      if (nextUpdateTime > self.lastUpdateTime_) then
          self.lastUpdateTime_ = time;

          local result = self.evaluator_(userData);
          self.confidence_ = result.confidence;
          self.evaluation_ = result.evaluation;
      end

      return { evaluation = self.evaluation_, confidence = self.
  confidence_ };
  end
```

Blackboards

To easily access and store arbitrary knowledge that agents use, we can implement a well-known data structure called a blackboard. In essence, a blackboard is a centralized place that allows the reading and writing of any arbitrary data that our agent's systems can use. Sources of the blackboard's knowledge can be sent directly to the blackboard, or it can be provided by encapsulated knowledge sources added to the blackboard. For an in-depth overview of blackboard systems, see the paper *Blackboard Systems* by Daniel Corkill.

Creating a blackboard

Creating a blackboard is relatively simple, as the blackboard can be represented almost entirely by an associated array index by knowledge attribute names. One small caveat to simply storing attributes, though, is the use of knowledge sources that create read-only attributes within the blackboard:

Blackboard.lua:

```
  Blackboard = {};

  function Blackboard.new(userData)
      local blackboard = {};

      -- The Blackboard's data members.
      blackboard.attributes_ = {};
      blackboard.sources_ = {};
      blackboard.userData_ = userData;

      return blackboard;
  end
```

Adding and removing knowledge sources

To add a knowledge source to the blackboard, we can store an array of knowledge sources indexed by the blackboard attribute they represent. Removal is the exact opposite of inserting, and simply iterates through each of the attributes' knowledge sources and removes the corresponding source, if found:

Blackboard.lua:

```
function Blackboard.AddSource(self, attribute, source)
    if (not self.sources_[attribute]) then
        self.sources_[attribute] = {};
    end

    table.insert(self.sources_[attribute], source);
end

function Blackboard.RemoveSource(self, attribute, source)
    -- Since there can be multiple sources for the same attribute,
    -- iterate over all sources to find the correct one to remove.
    if (self.sources_[attribute]) then
        for index = 1, #self.sources_[attribute] do
            if (self.sources_[attribute][index] == source) then
                table.remove(self.sources_[attribute], index);
                break;
            end
        end
    end
end
```

Evaluating knowledge sources

To evaluate a blackboard attribute, we iterate over each knowledge source and return the result with the highest confidence. As confidence indicates the best result, each blackboard attribute can have any number of knowledge sources providing resulting calculations.

 Even though the blackboard structure supports multiple attribute providers, balancing confidence values can quickly hit a dimensionality problem where balancing each confidence becomes unmaintainable.

To implement source evaluation, we'll evaluate all knowledge sources and return the result that has the highest confidence.

Blackboard.lua:

```lua
local function EvaluateSources(self, sources)
    local bestConfidence = 0;
    local bestResult = nil;

    -- Since there can be multiple data source for a single
    -- blackboard attribute, return the best result based on the
    -- confidence of the knowledge source.
    for index = 1, #sources do
        local eval = sources[index]:Evaluate(self.userData_);

        if (eval.confidence > bestConfidence) then
            bestConfidence = eval.confidence;
            bestResult = eval.evaluation;
        end
    end

    return bestResult;
end
```

Setting and retrieving blackboard attributes

Blackboard attributes aren't limited to knowledge sources that provide calculated results. Simple attributes that require no calculations can be stored and read using simple setters and getters. As our blackboard uses a Lua table to store attribute values, setting an attribute to a nil value will remove the attribute from the blackboard:

Blackboard.lua:

```lua
function Blackboard.Get(self, attribute)
    -- Return the evaluated information from a knowledge source.
    if (self.sources_[attribute]) then
        return EvaluateSources(self, self.sources_[attribute]);
    end

    -- Return stored data if there are no knowledge sources to
    -- evaluate.
    return self.attributes_[attribute];
end

function Blackboard.Set(self, attribute, value)
    self.attributes_[attribute] = value;
end
```

Blackboard member functions

With the basic functionality of the blackboard flushed out, we can modify the class in order to add the accessor functions:

Blackboard.lua:

```
function Blackboard.new(userData)

    ...

    -- object functions
    blackboard.AddSource = Blackboard.AddSource;
    blackboard.Get = Blackboard.Get;
    blackboard.RemoveSource = Blackboard.RemoveSource;
    blackboard.Set = Blackboard.Set;

    return blackboard;
end
```

Creating soldier knowledge sources

So far, our soldier's two main knowledge calculations are within enemy selection and flee position selection. With a proper KnowledgeSource instance implementation, we can refactor our original evaluator's internals to a standalone function that returns a result and confidence value in the format expected by our KnowledgeSource instance implementation.

Enemy selection

Converting the logic from the SoldierEvaluators_HasEnemy function only requires modifications that return both a confidence value and the final result. Since only one source will determine enemy selection, we will return a confidence of 1, as well as the selected enemy.

SoldierKnowledge.lua:

```
function SoldierKnowledge_ChooseBestEnemy(userData)
    local sandbox = userData.agent:GetSandbox();
    local position = Agent.GetPosition(userData.agent);
    local agents = Sandbox.GetAgents(userData.agent:GetSandbox());

    local closestEnemy;
    local distanceToEnemy;

    for index=1, #agents do
```

```
        local agent = agents[index];

        -- Only check against living agents.
        if (Agent.GetId(agent) ~= Agent.GetId(userData.agent) and
            Agent.GetHealth(agent) > 0) then

            local distanceToAgent =
                Vector.DistanceSquared(
                    position, agent:GetPosition());

            if (closestEnemy == nil or
                distanceToAgent < distanceToEnemy) then

                local path = Sandbox.FindPath(
                    sandbox,
                    "default",
                    position,
                    agent:GetPosition());

                -- Make sure the enemy is pathable.
                if (#path ~= 0) then
                    closestEnemy = agent;
                    distanceToEnemy = distanceToAgent;
                end
            end
        end
    end

    return { confidence = 1, evaluation = closestEnemy };
end
```

Flee position selection

Extracting the flee position calculation from SoldierActions_FleeInitialize
takes a bit more work but is just as easy. As the previous flee position calculations
were using additional information on the userData structure, we can convert the
use of userData values into values provided by the blackboard directly.

SoldierKnowledge.lua:

```
function SoldierKnowledge_ChooseBestFleePosition(userData)
    local sandbox = userData.agent:GetSandbox();
    local enemy = userData.blackboard:Get("enemy");

    local bestPosition;

    if (enemy) then
        local position;
```

```
            local bestDistance = 0;
            local enemyPosition = enemy:GetPosition();

            -- Try 32 points, and pick the furthest point away from
            -- the current enemy.
            for index=1, 32 do
                position = Sandbox.RandomPoint(sandbox, "default");

                local distanceToAgent =
                    Vector.DistanceSquared(position, enemyPosition);

                if (bestDistance < distanceToAgent) then
                    bestDistance = distanceToAgent;
                    bestPosition = position;
                end
            end
        else
            -- Any position will work if the agent doesn't have an
            -- enemy.
            bestPosition = Soldier_PathToRandomPoint(userData.agent);
        end

        return { confidence = 1, evaluation = bestPosition };
    end
```

Constructing a soldier blackboard

Previously, we stored any data from evaluators and actions on the userData structure. We can now move all this data to our blackboard. The following is the list of attribute values we'll be storing within the blackboard:

Blackboard attributes	Description
alive	Whether the agent is considered alive or dead
ammo	The current amount of ammunition the soldier's rifle has left
maxAmmo	The clip size of the soldier's rifle
maxHealth	The starting health of the agent
enemy	The best enemy agent that can be attacked
bestFleePosition	The best strategic position to avoid enemy agents

Constructing a blackboard requires you to set the initial attribute values we previously stored on the `soldierUserData` table directly. At this point, we can create `KnowledgeSource` instance implementations for enemy selection and flee position calculations. To allow access of the blackboard to all our agent systems, we can store the blackboard itself on `soldierUserData`. While there is fundamentally little difference between storing data on the `soldierUserData` directly and using the blackboard for basic attributes, having a common data structure that manages attributes allows for extensibility and easier debugging:

`IndirectSoldierAgent.lua`:

```lua
require "Blackboard"
require "DebugUtilities"
require "KnowledgeSource"
require "SandboxUtilities"
require "Soldier"
require "SoldierController"
require "SoldierKnowledge"
require "SoldierLogic"

function Agent_Initialize(agent)
    Soldier_InitializeAgent(agent);
    soldier = Soldier_CreateSoldier(agent);
    weapon = Soldier_CreateWeapon(agent);

    soldierController = SoldierController.new(
        agent, soldier, weapon);

    Soldier_AttachWeapon(soldier, weapon);
    weapon = nil;

    soldierUserData = {};
    soldierUserData.agent = agent;
    soldierUserData.controller = soldierController;
    soldierUserData.blackboard =
        Blackboard.new(soldierUserData);
    soldierUserData.blackboard:Set("alive", true);
    soldierUserData.blackboard:Set("ammo", 10);
    soldierUserData.blackboard:Set("maxAmmo", 10);
    soldierUserData.blackboard:Set(
        "maxHealth", Agent.GetHealth(agent));
    soldierUserData.blackboard:AddSource(
        "enemy",
        KnowledgeSource.new(SoldierKnowledge_ChooseBestEnemy));
    soldierUserData.blackboard:AddSource(
        "bestFleePosition",
        KnowledgeSource.new(
            SoldierKnowledge_ChooseBestFleePosition),
```

```
            5000);

        soldierLogic = SoldierLogic_BehaviorTree(soldierUserData);
    end
```

Updating decision evaluators

With a centralized data structure in place, we can refactor the decision evaluators in order to reference the blackboard directly. Removing the enemy evaluation from the SoldierEvaluators_CanShootAgent function solves a critical flaw in our previous implementation, which is the fact that no conditional evaluation should modify the agent. Logic evaluators should only make true or false calculations in a passive manner and never mutate the state of an agent:

SoldierEvaluators.lua:

```
    function SoldierEvaluators_CanShootAgent(userData)
        local enemy = userData.blackboard:Get("enemy");

        if (enemy ~= nil and
            Agent.GetHealth(enemy) > 0 and
            Vector.Distance(
                userData.agent:GetPosition(),
                enemy:GetPosition()) < 3) then

            return true;
        end;
        return false;
    end

    function SoldierEvaluators_HasAmmo(userData)
        local ammo = userData.blackboard:Get("ammo");

        return ammo ~= nil and ammo > 0;
    end

    function SoldierEvaluators_HasCriticalHealth(userData)
        local maxHealth = userData.blackboard:Get("maxHealth");

        return Agent.GetHealth(userData.agent) < (maxHealth * 0.2);
    end

    function SoldierEvaluators_HasEnemy(userData)
        return userData.blackboard:Get("enemy") ~= nil;
    end

    function SoldierEvaluators_HasMovePosition(userData)
```

```
local movePosition = userData.agent:GetTarget();

return movePosition ~= nil and
    (Vector.Distance(
        userData.agent:GetPosition(), movePosition) > 1.5);
end
```

Updating behavior actions

The only remaining work while using the blackboard is to refactor the data manipulation that occurs within a number of soldier behaviors.

The die action

Updating the die action requires us to set the blackboard's `alive` attribute instead of using `userData` directly:

`SoldierActions.lua`:

```
function SoldierActions_DieUpdate(deltaTimeInMillis, userData)
    userData.blackboard:Set("alive", false);
    return Action.Status.TERMINATED;
end
```

The flee action

With a `bestFleePosition` data source, our flee action no longer needs to perform any calculations and simply finds a path directly to the blackboard's stored position. With a flee position update frequency of 5 seconds, the `bestFleePosition` data source will get updated in a timely manner without any intervention from our flee behavior:

`SoldierActions.lua`:

```
function SoldierActions_FleeInitialize(userData)
    local sandbox = userData.agent:GetSandbox();
    local fleePosition =
        userData.blackboard:Get("bestFleePosition");
    local path = Sandbox.FindPath(
        sandbox,
        "default",
        userData.agent:GetPosition(),
        fleePosition);

    userData.agent:SetPath(path);
```

```
    userData.agent:SetTarget(fleePosition);

    userData.controller:QueueCommand(
        userData.agent,
        SoldierController.Commands.MOVE);

    return Action.Status.RUNNING;
end
```

The idle action

The blackboard can also be used for temporary data, such as the idle action's `idleEndTime` data. Once the idle action terminates, we merely set the blackboard attribute to `nil` in order to remove it from the blackboard:

SoldierActions.lua:

```
function SoldierActions_IdleInitialize(userData)
    userData.controller:QueueCommand(
        userData.agent,
        SoldierController.Commands.IDLE);

    local sandboxTimeInMillis =
        Sandbox.GetTimeInMillis(userData.agent:GetSandbox());
    userData.blackboard:Set(
        "idleEndTime",
        sandboxTimeInMillis + 2000);
end

function SoldierActions_IdleUpdate(deltaTimeInMillis, userData)
    local sandboxTimeInMillis =
        Sandbox.GetTimeInMillis(userData.agent:GetSandbox());
    if (sandboxTimeInMillis >=
        userData.blackboard:Get("idleEndTime")) then

        userData.blackboard:Set("idleEndTime", nil);
        return Action.Status.TERMINATED;
    end
    return Action.Status.RUNNING;
end
```

The move action

The move action is nearly identical to the idle action and uses the blackboard as a temporary data storage location for action-specific knowledge, and then removes the data once the action terminates by setting the `moveEndTime` attribute to `nil`:

SoldierActions.lua:

```
function SoldierActions_MoveToCleanUp(userData)
    userData.blackboard:Set("moveEndTime", nil);
end

function SoldierActions_MoveToInitialize(userData)
    userData.controller:QueueCommand(
        userData.agent,
        SoldierController.Commands.MOVE);

    local sandboxTimeInMillis =
        Sandbox.GetTimeInMillis(userData.agent:GetSandbox());
    userData.blackboard:Set(
        "moveEndTime", sandboxTimeInMillis + 500);

    return Action.Status.RUNNING;
end

function SoldierActions_MoveToUpdate(
    deltaTimeInMillis, userData)

    local sandboxTimeInMillis =
        Sandbox.GetTimeInMillis(userData.agent:GetSandbox());
    if (sandboxTimeInMillis >=
        userData.blackboard:Get("moveEndTime")) then

        userData.blackboard:Set("moveEndTime", nil);
        return Action.Status.TERMINATED;
    end

    ...

end
```

The pursue action

Previously, pursuit was using enemy calculations that were performed in the enemy evaluator. With a knowledge source now providing these calculations, the pursuit action merely fetches the enemy blackboard attribute to determine the best agent to be attacked:

SoldierActions.lua:

```
function SoldierActions_PursueInitialize(userData)
    local sandbox = userData.agent:GetSandbox();
    local enemy = userData.blackboard:Get("enemy");

    local endPoint = enemy:GetPosition();
    local path = Sandbox.FindPath(
        sandbox,
        "default",
        userData.agent:GetPosition(),
        endPoint);

    . . .

end

function SoldierActions_PursueUpdate(deltaTimeInMillis, userData)
    if (Agent.GetHealth(userData.agent) <= 0) then
        return Action.Status.TERMINATED;
    end

    local sandbox = userData.agent:GetSandbox();
    local enemy = userData.blackboard:Get("enemy");
    local endPoint = enemy:GetPosition();
    local path = Sandbox.FindPath(
        sandbox,
        "default",
        userData.agent:GetPosition(),
        endPoint);

    . . .

end
```

The reload action

As reloading modifies the amount of ammunition our soldier has, we can refactor the previous implementation in order to update the blackboard ammo attribute instead:

SoldierActions.lua:

```
function SoldierActions_ReloadUpdate(
    deltaTimeInMillis, userData)

    if (userData.controller:QueueLength() > 0) then
        return Action.Status.RUNNING;
    end

    userData.blackboard:Set(
        "ammo", userData.blackboard:Get("maxAmmo"));
    return Action.Status.TERMINATED;
end
```

The shoot action

Shooting requires the same modification to the ammunition and merely decrements the blackboard's ammo attribute instead of a userData value:

SoldierActions.lua:

```
function SoldierActions_ShootUpdate(deltaTimeInMillis, userData)

    ...

        userData.blackboard:Set(
            "ammo", userData.blackboard:Get("ammo") - 1);
    end

    return Action.Status.TERMINATED;
end
```

Summary

With a central data structure that stores knowledge, we can begin to flush out how our agents actually acquire their knowledge and perception about the world. In the next chapter, we'll provide you with additional sources of data that our agents can use for sight, sound, touch, as well as a means of agent communication.

8
Perception

In this chapter, we will cover the following topics:

- Creating, sending, and receiving events
- Giving sight and sound senses to agents
- Creating teams of competing agents
- Updating behaviors with event messaging
- Managing agent communications through messaging

Currently, our agents have a near-omnipotent view of the sandbox. Through the use of direct enemy position selection, our agents respond so quickly and precisely that players might call this cheating. To create more believable agent interactions and responses, we need to implement perception. Essentially, this means giving our agents the ability to see, hear, and communicate with each other.

Events

So far, each of our agents run within their own virtual machine and communicating between them is not easy. To alleviate this, we can create a data structure called an event, which can be passed between agents or the sandbox itself.

Attributes

Creating an event is as simple as creating a table within Lua with a few restrictions. As events are serialized by the sandbox and passed to each virtual machine, only simple table attributes can be added to the event.

Each supported attribute is listed as follows:

Event attribute type	Description
boolean	A true or false Lua value
number	Any Lua number internally represented as a float value
object	A code object, the sandbox, sandbox object, or an agent
string	Any Lua string value
vector	Any vector created from Vector.new

 Events might not have nested tables within them; any unsupported attribute type will be discarded during the serialization. Currently, this is a limitation of event serialization of the C++ side of the sandbox.

Sending events

Once we've created an event, we're ready to send the event off to the sandbox. As all objects are owned by the sandbox instance, the responsibility for dispatching events is handled internally by the sandbox itself. When sending an event, an additional event type string is required to help receivers specify how they should interpret the event data:

```
Sandbox.AddEvent(sandbox, eventType, event);
```

Receiving events

Receiving events requires you to create a callback function and then register that callback with the sandbox. The callback function itself receives the sandbox, the sandbox object that registered with the callback, the event type, and the event as parameters that are passed into the callback each time an event is processed:

```
Callback_Function(sandbox, sandboxObject, eventType, event);
```

Registering a callback simply requires you to pass the object that owns the callback as well as the callback function. The reason behind the callback ownership is that in cases where the owner is destroyed, the sandbox will also destroy any callbacks associated with the owner:

```
Sandbox.AddEventCallback(
    sandbox, sandboxObject, Callback_Function);
```

Managing events

As the sandbox broadcasts events to every sandbox object that registers a callback function, we'll create an agent communication system that provides commonly used functionalities such as event type registration and event filtering.

Assigning agent teams

So far, our agents fend for themselves in a free-for-all style; now, we'll assign teams to utilize team-based communication as well as the beginnings of cooperative strategy. By changing the initialization of the agent, we can assign the agent to either `team1` or `team2` and assign a different character model accordingly:

`IndirectSoldierAgent.lua`:

```
function Agent_Initialize(agent)
    Soldier_InitializeAgent(agent);
    agent:SetTeam("team" .. (agent:GetId() % 2 + 1));

    soldierUserData = {};

    if (agent:GetTeam() == "team1") then
        soldierUserData.soldier = Soldier_CreateSoldier(agent);
    else
        soldierUserData.soldier =
            Soldier_CreateLightSoldier(agent);
    end

    ...

end
```

Even with a team assigned to each agent, it will still behave in a free-for-all manner, as enemy selection is solely based on the distance. Going forward, we'll change our agent's behaviors to take these new team assignments into account.

Two distinct agent teams

Handling agent communications

Typically, agent communications will rely heavily on team-only events as well as specific callbacks based on the event type. First, we'll create internal event handling, which will pass back our userData table to the handler as well as filter team-specific events. By adding a teamOnly field to our event, we can filter messages that are only meant for the sending agent's team.

As we also want to filter out events that our agents don't want to handle, we'll manage an individual event callback per event type. This can be easily accomplished with an associative array indexed by our agent's ID:

AgentCommunications.lua:

```
local agentUserData = {};
```

```
local agentCallbacks = {};

local function AgentCommunications_HandleEvent(
    sandbox, agent, eventType, event)

    local callbacks = agentCallbacks[agent:GetId()];

    if (callbacks == nil or
        callbacks[eventType] == nil or
        type(callbacks[eventType]) ~= "function") then

        return;
    end

    if (not event["teamOnly"] or
        (event["teamOnly"] and agent:GetTeam() ==
        event["team"])) then

        callbacks[eventType](
            agentUserData[agent:GetId()], eventType, event);
    end
end
```

We can create an external function that will allow agents to register callbacks per event type. The callback we'll pass to this function will receive the userData table, event type, and event whenever a corresponding event is received:

AgentCommunications.lua:

```
function AgentCommunications_AddEventCallback(
    userData, eventType, callback)

    local agentId = userData.agent:GetId();

    if (agentCallbacks[agentId] == nil) then
        agentCallbacks[agentId] = {};
        agentUserData[agentId] = userData;

        Sandbox.AddEventCallback(
            userData.agent:GetSandbox(),
            userData.agent,
            AgentCommunications_HandleEvent);
    end

    agentCallbacks[agentId][eventType] = callback;
end
```

Two helper functions will be used to wrap the sandbox's `AddEvent` functionality. One variation will send the event without any modification and the other function will flag the message as a `teamOnly` message:

`AgentCommunications.lua`:

```
function AgentCommunications_SendMessage(
    sandbox, messageType, message)

    Sandbox.AddEvent(sandbox, messageType, message);
end

function AgentCommunications_SendTeamMessage(
    sandbox, agent, messageType, message)

    message["team"] = agent:GetTeam();
    message["teamOnly"] = true;

    Sandbox.AddEvent(sandbox, messageType, message);
end
```

Event types

To help centralize the event types that we want to support, we can create a global array within the `AgentCommunications` table of every `EventType` string we'll support. Going forward, we'll add new event types to this table, so it is guaranteed that every instance within our scripts will use the same event type string internally:

`AgentCommunications.lua`:

```
AgentCommunications = {};
AgentCommunications.EventType = {};
```

Creating agent senses

With basic agent communication out of the way, we can give our agents the ability to determine visibility with other agents.

Initializing senses

Initializing our agent's senses will follow a functional paradigm that is very similar to what we've used previously. Passing our `userData` table inside our initialization function will provide any custom per agent data we'll need going forward:

AgentSenses.lua:

```
function AgentSenses_InitializeSenses(userData)
end
```

Updating senses

Updating agent senses is nearly identical to initialization, except that we pass in the sandbox and a `deltaTimeInMillis` time difference, so we throttle the update rate of individual senses:

AgentSenses.lua:

```
function AgentSenses_UpdateSenses(
    sandbox, userData, deltaTimeInMillis)
end
```

Agent visibility

Implementing agent visibility begins with casting a number of raycasts into the sandbox to see whether the agent can visibly detect another agent without objects blocking our agent's sight. To cast a ray, the only requirements are a starting and ending point within the sandbox. The results of the raycast are returned as a Lua table that contains a result attribute indicating whether anything was hit; it also contains an optional object attribute of the sandbox object that the ray intersected with, if the raycast successfully intersected with an object.

 When casting rays, take care about selecting a starting position that isn't already intersecting with an object, otherwise the results returned might not be the expected outcome.

To case a ray we'll use the `RayCastToObject` function provided by the sandbox.

```
local raycastResult = Sandbox.RayCastToObject(
    sandbox, startPoint, endPoint);
```

In the following screenshot, you can see various rays that represent agent visibility patterns:

Detecting other visible agents

Detecting other visible agents can essentially be broken down into three sequential parts. To determine the starting position of our raycasts, we use the b_Head1 bone of our agent. This gives us a relative approximation for our agent's eye position and orientation.

Next, we determine whether the ray we want to cast to another agent's position falls within a 45 degree cone from the soldier model's b_Head1 bone position and orientation. This is easily accomplished with a dot product check between our possible ray used for ray casting and a vector to the other agent.

If the agent is within our viewing range, we can directly cast a ray to the centroid (which is the center of mass) of the other agent to determine whether our agent can actually see the other agent. There are a few possibilities: the ray penetrates an object that isn't the agent we want to see, the ray penetrates the agent we are trying to view, or the ray penetrates nothing. While the last case doesn't seem like it should happen, it can happen if the agent's body isn't where our centroid is expecting it to be; usually, this means that the agent is already dead and the body is lower on the floor than we're expecting:

AgentSenses.lua:

```
require "DebugUtilities"

function AgentSenses_CanSeeAgent(userData, agent, debug)
    local sandbox = userData.agent:GetSandbox();
    local position = Animation.GetBonePosition(
        userData.soldier, "b_Head1");
    local rotation = Animation.GetBoneRotation(
        userData.soldier, "b_Head1");

    -- The negative forward vector is used here, but is model
    -- specific.
    local forward = Vector.Rotate(Vector.new(0, 0, -1), rotation);
    local rayCastPosition = position + forward / 2;
    local sandboxTime = Sandbox.GetTimeInMillis(sandbox);

    local centroid = agent:GetPosition();
    local rayVector = Vector.Normalize(
        centroid - rayCastPosition);
    local dotProduct = Vector.DotProduct(rayVector, forward);

    -- Only check visibility within a 45 degree tolerance
    local cos45Degrees = 0.707;

    if (dotProduct >= cos45Degrees) then
        local raycast = Sandbox.RayCastToObject(
            sandbox, rayCastPosition, centroid);

        -- Check if the ray hit the intended agent.
        if ((raycast.result and
            Agent.IsAgent(raycast.object) and
            raycast.object:GetId() == agent:GetId()) or
            not raycast.result) then

            if (debug) then
                Core.DrawLine(
                    rayCastPosition,
```

```
                centroid,
                DebugUtilities.Green);
        end

        local visibleAgent = {};
        visibleAgent["agent"] = agent;
        visibleAgent["seenAt"] = centroid;
        visibleAgent["lastSeen"] = sandboxTime;

        return visibleAgent;
    else
        if (debug) then
            Core.DrawLine(
                rayCastPosition,
                centroid,
                DebugUtilities.Red);
        end
    end
  end

  return false;
end
```

We can draw debug lines to help us visibly understand what is happening; in this case, red lines represent rays that intersected with something other than an agent, and green lines represent rays that intersected with another agent.

Agent sighting events

Now that we can detect when another agent is visible, we can create specific messages about an agent sighting, a dead enemy, or even a dead friend that can be sent to teammates. By extending our EventType table, we can create the three new event types for which we'll be sending out events:

```
AgentCommunications.lua
AgentCommunications.EventType.DeadEnemySighted =
    "DeadEnemySighted";
AgentCommunications.EventType.DeadFriendlySighted =
    "DeadFriendlySighted";
AgentCommunications.EventType.EnemySighted = "EnemySighted";
```

New enemy sighted event

To send out a new enemy sighted event, we can create a wrapper that handles all the event-specific information such as the sighted agent, where it was sighted, as well as the time at which it was sighted. The last information about when they were sighted will come in handy when dealing with stale information:

AgentSenses.lua:

```
function SendNewEnemyEvent(
    sandbox, agent, enemy, seenAt, lastSeen)

    local event = {
        agent = enemy,
        seenAt = seenAt,
        lastSeen = lastSeen};

    AgentCommunications_SendTeamMessage(
        sandbox,
        agent,
        AgentCommunications.EventType.EnemySighted,
        event);
end
```

New dead enemy body sighted event

Just like an enemy sighted event, seeing a dead enemy sends out the same information but flags the event as a different type. While we haven't started using this information yet, it can be useful to store locations of dead bodies in order to mark potentially dangerous areas:

AgentSenses.lua:

```
function SendNewDeadEnemyEvent(
    sandbox, agent, enemy, seenAt, lastSeen)

    local event = {
        agent = enemy,
        seenAt = seenAt,
        lastSeen = lastSeen};

    AgentCommunications_SendTeamMessage(
        sandbox,
        agent,
        AgentCommunications.EventType.DeadEnemySighted,
        event);
end
```

New dead teammate body sighted event

To prevent omnipotent agents, we'll also send out friendly dead body locations when they are sighted, as our agents won't be communicating to their teammates about their own death positions when they die:

AgentSenses.lua:

```
function SendNewDeadFriendlyEvent(
    sandbox, agent, friendly, seenAt, lastSeen)

    local event = {
        agent = friendly,
        seenAt = seenAt,
        lastSeen = lastSeen};

    AgentCommunications_SendTeamMessage(
        sandbox,
        agent,
        AgentCommunications.EventType.DeadFriendlySighted,
        event);
end
```

Handling new agent sightings

As visibility can be updated very often, we only want to send out events for new agent sightings. We can create a helper function that will take a list of known agents indexed by their agent ID numbers and a list of currently visible agents. By storing the lastSeen time of a sighting, we can determine whether an event should be sent out.

Throttling events in this fashion prevents an abundance of redundant events from being propagated. As events are sent to every registered object, this can have an impact on performance when massive amounts of events are being sent:

AgentSenses.lua:

```
local function HandleNewAgentSightings(
    userData, knownAgents, spottedAgents)

    local newAgentSightings = {};

    for key, value in pairs(spottedAgents) do
        local agentId = value.agent:GetId();
        local lastSeen =
            value.lastSeen - knownAgents[agentId].lastSeen;

        if (knownAgents[agentId] == nil or lastSeen > 500) then
```

```
                newAgentSightings[agentId] = value;
        end
    end

    local sandbox = userData.agent:GetSandbox();

    for key, value in pairs(newAgentSightings) do
        if (userData.agent:GetTeam() ~=
            value.agent:GetTeam()) then

            if (value.agent:GetHealth() > 0) then
                SendNewEnemyEvent(
                    sandbox, userData.agent,
                    value.agent,
                    value.seenAt,
                    value.lastSeen);
            else
                SendNewDeadEnemyEvent(
                    sandbox,
                    userData.agent,
                    value.agent,
                    value.seenAt,
                    value.lastSeen);
            end
        elseif (value.agent:GetHealth() <= 0) then
            SendNewDeadFriendlyEvent(
                sandbox,
                userData.agent,
                value.agent,
                value.seenAt,
                value.lastSeen);
        end
    end
end
```

Intermittent agent sightings

Now that we can handle sending out agent sighting events, we need a way to keep track of the agents we currently know about. We can use the agent's blackboard as a place to store all the visible agents the agent has ever seen and use that information to determine whether new events should be sent out:

AgentSenses.lua:

```
local function UpdateVisibility(userData)
    local agents = Sandbox.GetAgents(
        userData.agent:GetSandbox());
```

```
            local visibleAgents = {};

            for index = 1, #agents do
                if (agents[index] ~= userData.agent) then
                    canSeeAgentInfo = AgentSenses_CanSeeAgent(
                        userData, agents[index], true);

                    if (canSeeAgentInfo) then
                        visibleAgents[agents[index]:GetId()] =
                            canSeeAgentInfo;
                    end
                end
            end

            local knownAgents =
                userData.blackboard:Get("visibleAgents") or {};
            HandleNewAgentSightings(
                userData, knownAgents, visibleAgents);

            for key, value in pairs(visibleAgents) do
                knownAgents[key] = value;
            end

            userData.blackboard:Set("visibleAgents", knownAgents);
        end
```

Throttling agent visibility updates

As we've throttled how often sight events are sent out to teammates, we should also throttle how often our agent will cast rays into the environment, as raycasts can quickly become expensive. All that's required to update our agent's visibility is to determine the last update time and see whether at least half a second has gone by in order to determine whether the visibility should be updated:

AgentSenses.lua:

```
    local lastUpdate = 0;

    function AgentSenses_UpdateSenses(
        sandbox, userData, deltaTimeInMillis)

        local updateInterval = 500;

        lastUpdate = lastUpdate + deltaTimeInMillis;

        if (lastUpdate > updateInterval) then
            UpdateVisibility(userData);
```

```
            lastUpdate = lastUpdate % updateInterval;
        end
    end
```

Creating event handlers

Now that agents on the same team are sending out sight events, we need to start processing them so that agents will share the same information. When a new enemy is sighted, we can update the blackboard and overwrite any stale information we already have about known enemies:

AgentSenses.lua:

```
    local function HandleEnemySightedEvent(
        userData, eventType, event)

        local blackboard = userData.blackboard;
        local knownAgents =
            userData.blackboard:Get("visibleAgents") or {};

        knownAgents[event.agent:GetId()] = event;
        userData.blackboard:Set("visibleAgents", knownAgents);
    end
```

If a dead body is found, we'll erase the current information from the visibleAgents blackboard entry so that visibleAgents will only contain known living enemies, and any known dead enemies are added to the deadEnemies blackboard entry:

AgentSenses.lua:

```
    local function HandleDeadEnemySightedEvent(
        userData, eventType, event)

        local blackboard = userData.blackboard;
        local knownAgents =
            userData.blackboard:Get("visibleAgents") or {};
        local knownBodies =
            userData.blackboard:Get("deadEnemies") or {};

        knownAgents[event.agent:GetId()] = nil;
        knownBodies[event.agent:GetId()] = event;

        userData.blackboard:Set("visibleAgents", knownAgents);
        userData.blackboard:Set("deadEnemies", knownBodies);
    end
```

We'll keep track of any friendly dead bodies as well so that we can have agents avoid areas that might be potentially dangerous:

AgentSenses.lua:

```
local function HandleDeadFriendlySightedEvent(
    userData, eventType, event)

    local blackboard = userData.blackboard;
    local knownBodies =
        userData.blackboard:Get("deadFriendlies") or {};

    knownBodies[event.agent:GetId()] = event;
    userData.blackboard:Set("deadFriendlies", knownBodies);
end
```

Adding event handlers

We can now register our event callbacks with the AgentCommunications system based on the event types we want to handle. After this, no other update is necessary, as the AgentCommunications system itself will handle event processing and dispatching:

AgentSenses.lua:

```
function AgentSenses_InitializeSenses(userData)
    local eventCallbacks = {};

    eventCallbacks[
        AgentCommunications.EventType.EnemySighted] =
            HandleEnemySightedEvent;

    eventCallbacks[
        AgentCommunications.EventType.DeadEnemySighted] =
            HandleDeadEnemySightedEvent;

    eventCallbacks[
        AgentCommunications.EventType.DeadFriendlySighted] =
            HandleDeadFriendlySightedEvent;

    for eventType, callback in pairs(eventCallbacks) do
        AgentCommunications_AddEventCallback(
            userData, eventType, callback);
    end
end
```

Agent auditory senses

As agents have no way of hearing something, we can simulate what information they can receive by sending events when auditory actions occur, such as a bullet shot or bullet impact.

Auditory events

Auditory events are created from the sandbox itself and are sent to all agents. It's up to the agent to determine what to do with the information, such as disregarding the event based on the distance.

The BulletShot event

To send an event when bullets are shot, we can update the ShootBullet function to send out an event based on the bullet's shot position:

AgentCommunications.lua:

```
AgentCommunications.EventType.BulletShot = "BulletShot";
```

Soldier.lua:

```
local function SendShootEvent(sandbox, shootPosition)
    local event = { position = shootPosition };

    AgentCommunications_SendMessage(
        sandbox,
        AgentCommunications.EventType.BulletShot,
        event);
end

local function ShootBullet(sandbox, position, rotation)

    . . .

    SendShootEvent(sandbox, position);
end
```

The BulletImpact event

An event similar to the `BulletShot` event can be sent out when a bullet impacts a location:

`AgentCommunications.lua:`

```
AgentCommunications.EventType.BulletImpact = "BulletImpact";
```

`Soldier.lua:`

```
local function SendImpactEvent(sandbox, hitPosition)
    local event = { position = hitPosition };

    AgentCommunications_SendMessage(
        sandbox,
        AgentCommunications.EventType.BulletImpact,
        event);
end

local function ParticleImpact(sandbox, collision)

    ...

    SendImpactEvent(sandbox, collision.pointA);
end
```

Handling auditory events

Handling auditory events requires you to add additional time-to-live information to each stored event. As a large number of bullet shots and impacts events are emitted, the time-to-live information will be used to prune out old events:

`AgentSenses.lua:`

```
local function HandleBulletImpactEvent(
    userData, eventType, event)

    local blackboard = userData.blackboard;
    local bulletImpacts = blackboard:Get("bulletImpacts") or {};

    table.insert(
        bulletImpacts,
        { position = event.position, ttl = 1000 });
    blackboard:Set("bulletImpacts", bulletImpacts);
end

local function HandleBulletShotEvent(userData, eventType, event)
    local blackboard = userData.blackboard;
```

```
      local bulletShots = blackboard:Get("bulletShots") or {};

      table.insert(
          bulletShots,
          { position = event.position, ttl = 1000 });
      blackboard:Set("bulletShots", bulletShots);
   end
```

We can now add our auditory event handlers during the `AgentSenses` initialization:

AgentSenses.lua:

```
   function AgentSenses_InitializeSenses(userData)
      local eventCallbacks = {};

      eventCallbacks[AgentCommunications.EventType.BulletImpact] =
          HandleBulletImpactEvent;
      eventCallbacks[AgentCommunications.EventType.BulletShot] =
          HandleBulletShotEvent;

      ...

      end
   end
```

Decaying blackboard events

When we update our agent senses, we can use the `deltaTimeInMillis` to decrement the time-to-live value of each stored event. If the time-to-live drops below 0, we'll remove the stored event:

AgentSenses.lua:

```
   local function PruneEvents(events, deltaTimeInMillis)
      local validEvents = {};

      for index = 1, #events do
          local event = events[index];
          event.ttl = event.ttl - deltaTimeInMillis;

          if (event.ttl > 0) then
              table.insert(validEvents, event);
          end
      end

      return validEvents;
   end
```

Providing a helper function to wrap pruning events is useful, as most auditory events will require being pruned during the normal agent's update loop:

AgentSenses.lua:

```
local function PruneBlackboardEvents(
    blackboard, attribute, deltaTimeInMillis)

    local attributeValue = blackboard:Get(attribute);

    if (attributeValue) then
        blackboard:Set(
            attribute,
            PruneEvents(attributeValue, deltaTimeInMillis));
    end
end
```

Decaying auditory events

Now, we can update our AgentSenses update loop to prune both the bulletImpacts as well as bulletShots entries that are being stored on the blackboard. Pruning out old events prevents Lua from consuming large amounts of data, as both of these event types occur frequently:

AgentSenses.lua:

```
function AgentSenses_UpdateSenses(
    sandbox, userData, deltaTimeInMillis)

    PruneBlackboardEvents(
        userData.blackboard,
        "bulletImpacts",
        deltaTimeInMillis);

    PruneBlackboardEvents(
        userData.blackboard,
        "bulletShots",
        deltaTimeInMillis);

    ...

end
```

Team communications

So far, team communication has revolved around agent visibility; we can now extend these communications to include behavioral logic selections such as new enemy selection, position updates, and retreat positions.

The EnemySelection event

To coordinate attacks, our agents need to notify their teammates when they've selected a new enemy. Sending out an event when a new enemy is being pursued requires you to add a new EventType string. With a specific EventType, we can create a wrapper function that will message the team about the enemy:

AgentCommunications.lua:

```
AgentCommunications.EventType.EnemySelection = "EnemySelection";
```

SoldierActions.lua:

```
local function SendEnemySelection(sandbox, agent, enemy)
    AgentCommunications_SendTeamMessage(
        sandbox,
        agent,
        AgentCommunications.EventType.EnemySelection,
        { agent = agent });
end

function SoldierActions_PursueInitialize(userData)

        ...

        userData.controller:QueueCommand(
            userData.agent,
            SoldierController.Commands.MOVE);

        SendEnemySelection(
            userData.agent:GetSandbox(),
            userData.agent,
            enemy);
    end

    return Action.Status.RUNNING;
end
```

The PositionUpdate event

Instead of directly looking up a teammate's position within the sandbox, we can message out periodic updates as teammates move around the environment. As our move behavior only executes every half second, we can update teammates on the agent's position once the behavior has terminated:

AgentCommunications.lua:

```
AgentCommunications.EventType.PositionUpdate = "PositionUpdate";
```

SoldierActions.lua:

```
local function SendPositionUpdate(sandbox, agent, position)
    AgentCommunications_SendTeamMessage(
        sandbox,
        agent,
        AgentCommunications.EventType.PositionUpdate,
        { agent = agent, position = position });
end

function SoldierActions_PursueCleanUp(userData)
    SendPositionUpdate(
        userData.agent:GetSandbox(),
        userData.agent,
        userData.agent:GetPosition());
end
```

The RetreatPosition event

To communicate where our agents retreat to, we can send a similar position event when a flee position is chosen and our agent has decided to flee:

AgentCommunications.lua:

```
AgentCommunications.EventType.RetreatPosition = "RetreatPosition";
```

SoldierActions.lua:

```
local function SendRetreatPosition(sandbox, agent, position)
    AgentCommunications_SendTeamMessage(
        sandbox,
        agent,
        AgentCommunications.EventType.RetreatPosition,
        { agent = agent, position = position });
```

```
end

function SoldierActions_FleeInitialize(userData)

    ...

    userData.controller:QueueCommand(
        userData.agent,
        SoldierController.Commands.MOVE);

    SendRetreatPosition(
        userData.agent:GetSandbox(),
        userData.agent,
        userData.agent:GetPosition());

    return Action.Status.RUNNING;
end
```

Updating agent behaviors

Now that we have a number of different senses, team-based communications, and knowledge about the environment, we can update our agent's blackboard selections to account for the additional information.

Enemy selection

With additional visibility information, we can update our enemy selection to take into account only agents that aren't teammates as well as ones that have been visible within the last second. As teammates send out enemy sightings and essentially share their visibility about the environment, the response time for our agents to pursue a newly spotted enemy is rather quick.

 Currently, our agents share immediate knowledge with each other. With only a small amount of work, you can delay knowledge propagation or even preference agents in order to select enemies they've seen firsthand.

Creating a new function for choosing the best enemy will now only process known visible agents that are stored on the blackboard.

SoldierKnowledge.lua:

```
function SoldierKnowledge_ChooseBestVisibleEnemy(userData)
    local sandbox = userData.agent:GetSandbox();
    local sandboxTime = Sandbox.GetTimeInMillis(sandbox);
    local position = Agent.GetPosition(userData.agent);
    local team = userData.agent:GetTeam();
```

```
        local visibleEnemies = userData.blackboard:Get(
            "visibleAgents") or {};

    local closestEnemy;
    local distanceToEnemy;

    for key, value in pairs(visibleEnemies) do
        if ((sandboxTime - value.lastSeen) <= 1000) then
            local agent = value.agent;

            if (agent:GetId() ~= userData.agent:GetId() and
                Agent.GetHealth(agent) > 0 and
                agent:GetTeam() ~= team) then
                local distanceToAgent = Vector.DistanceSquared(
                    position, Agent.GetPosition(agent));
                if (closestEnemy == nil or
                    distanceToAgent < distanceToEnemy) then

                    local path = Sandbox.FindPath(
                        sandbox,
                        "default",
                        position,
                        agent:GetPosition());

                    if (#path ~= 0) then
                        closestEnemy = agent;
                        distanceToEnemy = distanceToAgent;
                    end
                end
            end
        end
    end

    return { confidence = 1, evaluation = closestEnemy };
end
```

As we've created a completely new way of selecting enemies, we can swap the knowledge source within our agent's blackboard in order to provide easy A/B testing on the new behavioral selection:

IndirectSoldierAgent.lua:

```
function Agent_Initialize(agent)

    ...

    soldierUserData.blackboard:AddSource(
        "enemy",
```

```
KnowledgeSource.new(
    SoldierKnowledge_ChooseBestVisibleEnemy));

    ...

end
```

Scoring dangerous positions

We can also update how retreat positions are selected within the sandbox using a number of different sources of information. A utility pattern comes in handy when individually weighing the importance of each piece of information, as it pertains to our randomly selected retreat positions.

Score danger from bullet impacts

First, we can score our sandbox retreat positions based on known bullet impacts positions. If a bullet impact happened within 10 meters of a position, we can reduce the score by a small value. As a large number of bullet impacts typically happen within the same area, this will quickly avoid positions where combat is taking place readily:

`SoldierKnowledge.lua:`

```
local function ScoreDangerFromBulletImpacts(
    positions, impacts, scores)

    local safeDistanceFromBulletImpactSquared = 10 * 10;

    for index=1, #positions do
        for key, impact in pairs(impacts) do
            local distanceToImpact = Vector.DistanceSquared(
                positions[index], impact.position);

            if (distanceToImpact <
                safeDistanceFromBulletImpactSquared) then

                scores[index] = scores[index] - 0.5;
            end
        end
    end
end
```

Score danger from bullet shots

Scoring dangerous shots is almost identical to scoring bullet impacts, except that we can try out an even wider radius while simultaneously reducing the score contribution:

SoldierKnowledge.lua:

```
local function ScoreDangerFromBulletShots(
    positions, shots, scores)

    local safeDistanceFromBulletShotSquared = 20 * 20;

    for index=1, #positions do
        for key, shot in pairs(shots) do
            local distanceToShot = Vector.DistanceSquared(
                positions[index], shot.position);

            if (distanceToShot <
                safeDistanceFromBulletShotSquared) then

                scores[index] = scores[index] - 0.25;
            end
        end
    end
end
```

Score danger from enemies

Enemies, on the other hand, are the most dangerous to consider when selecting retreat positions. Extending the safe distance radius and increasing the scoring penalty further pushes our agents away from known and potentially dangerous positions. Using known enemy information instead of the sandbox's exact agent position allows enemies to surprise and ambush agents as they retreat:

SoldierKnowledge.lua:

```
local function ScoreDangerFromEnemies(
    positions, enemies, scores)

    local safeDistanceFromEnemySquared = 30 * 30;

    for index=1, #positions do
```

```
            for key, value in pairs(enemies) do
                local enemyInfo = value;

                local distanceToAgent = Vector.DistanceSquared(
                    positions[index], enemyInfo.seenAt);

                if (distanceToAgent <
                    safeDistanceFromEnemySquared) then

                    scores[index] = scores[index] - 1;
                end
            end
        end
    end
```

Score danger from dead bodies

To add an additional dimension to our agents, we can also negatively weigh positions that are close to dead bodies. This helps our agents stay away from positions that can essentially be deadly choke points:

SoldierKnowledge.lua:

```
    local function ScoreDangerFromDeadBodies(
        positions, bodies, scores)
        local safeDistanceFromDeadBody = 20 * 20;

        for index=1, #positions do
            for key, body in pairs(bodies) do
                local distanceToBody = Vector.DistanceSquared(
                    positions[index], body.seenAt);

                if (distanceToBody < safeDistanceFromDeadBody) then
                    scores[index] = scores[index] - 1;
                end
            end
        end
    end
```

Calculating the best flee position

To take all these scoring functions into account, we can update how we choose the best flee position by processing each of the random points we've selected on the navigation mesh. After each point is scored, we'll return the best possible position and have our agent immediately flee to that location.

 Using scoring functions is an easy way to evaluate a large number of factors that need to be considered. Each new factor to be scored against increases the dimensionality of the problem and can quickly lead to problems with balancing.

Updating the `ChooseBestFleePosition` function will start with fetching all relevant blackboard information and then process the 32 random navmesh points based on our scoring functions.

SoldierKnowledge.lua:

```lua
function SoldierKnowledge_ChooseBestFleePosition(userData)
    local sandbox = userData.agent:GetSandbox();
    local bestPosition;

    local bulletImpacts =
        userData.blackboard:Get("bulletImpacts") or {};
    local bulletShots =
        userData.blackboard:Get("bulletShots") or {};
    local visibleEnemies =
        userData.blackboard:Get("visibleAgents") or {};
    local deadEnemies =
        userData.blackboard:Get("deadEnemies") or {};
    local deadFriendlies =
        userData.blackboard:Get("deadFriendlies") or {};

    if (#visibleEnemies) then
        local positions = {};
        local scores = {};
        local bestScore = 0;

        for index=1, 32 do
            table.insert(
                positions,
                Sandbox.RandomPoint(sandbox, "default"));
            scores[index] = 0;
        end

        ScoreDangerFromBulletImpacts(
            positions, bulletImpacts, scores);
```

```
ScoreDangerFromBulletShots(
    positions, bulletShots, scores);
ScoreDangerFromDeadBodies(
    positions, deadFriendlies, scores);
ScoreDangerFromDeadBodies(
    positions, deadEnemies, scores);
ScoreDangerFromEnemies(
    positions, visibleEnemies, scores);

-- find the best position
bestScore = scores[1];
bestPosition = positions[1];

for index=2, #positions do
    if (bestScore < scores[index]) then
        bestScore = scores[index];
        bestPosition = positions[index];
    end
end
    else
        bestPosition = Sandbox.RandomPoint(sandbox, "default");
    end

    return { confidence = 1, evaluation = bestPosition };
end
```

Summary

Now that we've grounded our agents within their environment, limiting what they
can see and hear, and adding a layer of team-based communication, we can start
building up more believable and strategic choices for them. Going forward, we can
start building up tactics and influencing how our agents choose to move throughout
the environment and not just their destinations and closest enemies. In the next
chapter, we'll introduce a new spatial data structure that provides tactical
information about the sandbox.

9
Tactics

In this chapter, we will cover the following topics:

- Generating layer-based influence maps
- Drawing individual influence map layers
- Learning about influence map modifiers
- Manipulating and spreading influence values
- Creating an influence map for agent occupancy
- Creating a tactical influence map for potentially dangerous regions

So far, our agents have a limited number of data sources that allow for spatial reasoning about their surroundings. Navigation meshes allow agents to determine all walkable positions, and perception gives our agents the ability to see and hear; the lack of a fine-grained quantized view of the sandbox prevents our agents from reasoning about other possible places of interest within the sandbox.

Influence maps

Influence maps help alleviate the understanding of the environment from a high level. This type of spatial data can come in many different forms, but all essentially break down the environment into quantifiable regions where additional data can be stored and evaluated. In particular, we'll be using a three-dimensional grid-based representation for our influence maps. Each cell of the influence grid represents a three-dimensional cube of space. The sandbox uses an internal three-dimensional array structure that stores influence map data, and therefore, grows quickly in size based on the dimensions of each grid cell.

With influence maps, we can easily perform tasks such as spacing out agent positions or moving agents toward friendly regions and away from dangerous regions within the sandbox. Previously, we would use a utility-based approach that would become performance-intensive as more agents were introduced into the sandbox. With a central data structure shared by all agents, the performance cost is kept to a minimum.

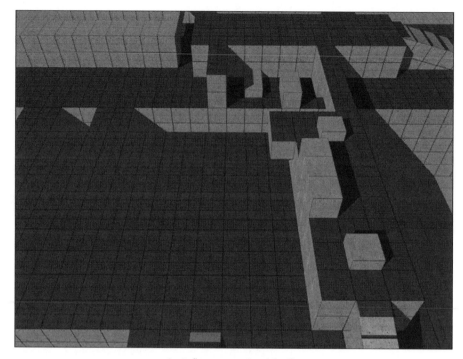

An influence map's grid cells

The cell height

As our influence grid represents a three-dimensional area instead of just a two-dimensional surface, a cell height is required in order to quantize geometry at varying heights. The following screenshot is an example of an influence map using a cell height of half a meter. Notice that each cell used for debugging purposes is displayed as a plane oriented along the x axis but actually represents a cube that is one meter tall.

A cell height of 0.5 meters

The following is the same geometry but with an influence map configured for quarter meter tall grid cells. While there isn't much difference in either configuration, setting a taller cell height dramatically reduces the amount of memory the influence map costs, as the number of total cells within the influence map will be reduced by half, in this case.

Here, the memory use of the influence map is double in comparison to the half-meter tall version. Additionally, any operations that have to evaluate or manipulate large number of grid cells will perform slower.

A cell height of 0.25 meters

Try to configure your influence maps with the largest cell height without losing too much spatial information. This can be an easy performance optimization if your influence map is particularly large.

The cell width

The cell width essentially determines the resolution of spatial information the influence map can contain. While the cell height can dramatically reduce the memory footprint without losing much spatial information, the same cannot be said about the cell width.

Here, an influence map is generated with a cell width of two meters with specific influences set, shown by the blue and red regions:

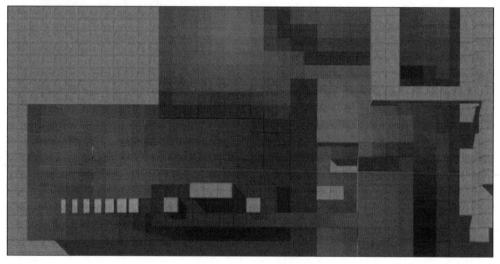

A cell width of 2.0 meters

The same influence map is generated in the following screenshot with a cell width of one meter. Even though the positions of influences remain the same in both examples, the resulting influence maps are not equivalent. The low resolution influence map lost information as multiple influence points happened to fall within the same cell, essentially contributing no additional influence.

 Grid cells have a maximum and minimum amount of influence they can contain; any values above or below these influences are truncated.

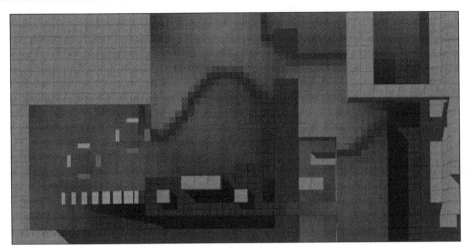

A cell width of 1.0 meter

Constructing an influence map

Constructing an influence map requires configuration parameters as well as a navigation mesh on which we can base the influence map. Instead of analyzing all geometry in the sandbox, an optimization is done by constructing grid cells along the navigation mesh itself. As all walkable areas are represented by the navigation mesh, the influence map will be able to store spatial data for all regions that agents can path to.

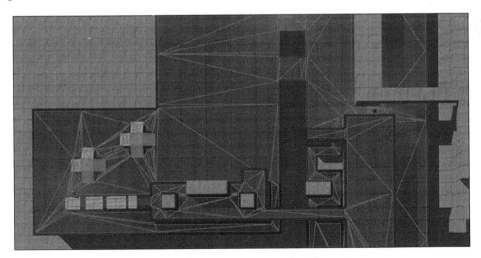

A navigation mesh used to construct the influence map

While information about all possible areas might be useful for certain tactical analysis, in practice, the additional memory and performance constraints are a higher priority.

 As the influence map is based on the underlying navigation mesh, try changing the configuration of the navigation map to generate different influence map representations.

Configuration

Configuring the influence map boils down to specifying a cell width, cell height, and any boundary offsets. Even though the maximum size of the influence map is calculated automatically based on the size of the navigation mesh, the boundary offset can be used to extend or contract the automatic calculation:

```
local influenceMapConfig = {
    CellHeight = 0.5,
    CellWidth = 1.0,
    BoundaryMinOffset = minVectorOffset,
    BoundaryMaxOffset = maxVectorOffset
};
```

Voxelizing a navigation mesh

Internally, the influence map is created by iterating over all possible influence map cells, also known as voxels, and determining which grid cells intersect with the navigation mesh. Only cells that intersect with the navigation mesh are marked for use within influence map calculations, but empty cells still add to the total memory footprint of the influence map. As navigation meshes are able to overlap themselves, the influence map allows for the same ability.

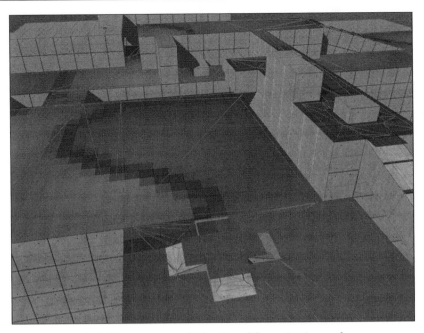

An influence map overlaid on top of the navigation mesh

In theory, you can dramatically reduce the memory footprint of the influence map by only allowing a single layer of grid cells to represent the entire navigation mesh as long as the navigation mesh never overlaps itself. Better yet, you can modify the influence map to contain only a collection of used cells ignoring height completely. These optimizations would be excellent extensions that can support much larger navigation meshes and are left to the user to extend.

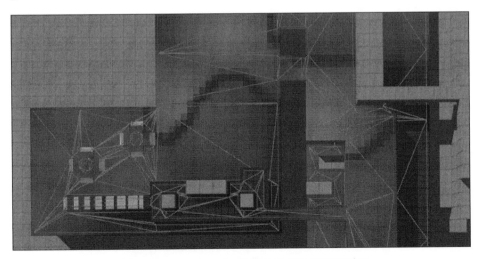

A top-down overlay of an influence map construction

To create an influence map, simply pass in the navigation mesh to base the influence map on as well as a configuration of how to create the map. Currently, only one influence map is supported, as the sandbox contains a single instance of the influence map data structure. Additional influence maps can be added to the sandbox C++ code and will require you to create multiple instances and modify the Lua accessor functions to specify which influence map should be accessed:

```
Sandbox.CreateInfluenceMap(
    sandbox, navMeshName, influenceMapConfig);
```

Drawing influence maps

To display the current state of the influence map, you can call `Sandbox.DrawInfluenceMap`. The `influenceMapLayer` function that is passed in determines which of the 10 possible layers are to be drawn. As our influence maps support both positive and negative influences, three different colors are used to draw the resulting map:

```
Sandbox.DrawInfluenceMap(
    sandbox,
    influenceMapLayer,
    positiveInfluenceColor,
    neutralInfluenceColor,
    negativeInfluenceColor);
```

Each color passed to `DrawInfluenceMap` is a Lua table that represents the red, green, blue, and alpha properties of the color in the range of 0 to 1. In the earlier cases, the influence map was drawn with these settings:

```
Sandbox.DrawInfluenceMap(
    sandbox,
    0,
    { 0, 0, 1, 0.9 },
    { 0, 0, 0, 0.75 },
    { 1, 0, 0, 0.9 });
```

 Drawing the influence map only shows what the influence map looks like at that exact moment. The debug drawing of the influence map will not get updated on its own. Adding a keyboard shortcut to manually refresh the debug influence map can be helpful in debugging issues.

In order to hide or show the drawn influence map, you can call `SetInfluenceMap`, passing in whether to hide or show the previously drawn influence map. By default, drawing the influence map is enabled:

```
Sandbox.SetInfluenceMap(sandbox, enabled);
```

Accessing influences

Grid cells are accessed by their world position. Typically, you can use an agent's own position to determine which cell it's in, or you can generate random points on the navigation mesh to pick a random grid cell. Once a cell has been selected, you can manually change the influence or retrieve the current influence.

Setting influences

To set an influence value, you can call `Sandbox.SetInfluence`, passing in the layer of the map to be affected, the vector position to be affected, as well as the value. The influence map automatically truncates values outside the supported range from negative to positive:

```
Sandbox.SetInfluence(
    sandbox,
    influenceMapLayer,
    position,
    influenceValue);
```

The following screenshot illustrates what happens when you set a value directly on the influence map:

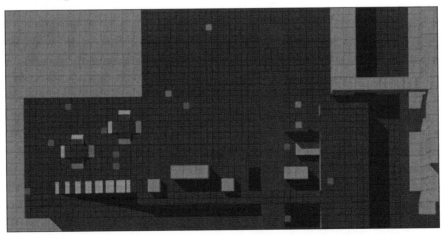

An influence map showing the positions of influence for all previous examples

Getting influences

Retrieving values from the influence map is just as simple as calling `Sandbox.`
`GetInfluence` at the specific position. As the influence map is built from the
navigation mesh, any valid point on the navigation mesh is also a valid grid cell
on the influence map. You can always use `Sandbox.RandomPoint` or the agent's
position to generate random points that can be influenced:

```
Sandbox.GetInfluence(
    sandbox, influenceMapLayer, position);
```

Clearing influences

To remove all current influences on a specific layer of the map, you can call
`Sandbox.ClearInfluenceMap`. Influences on the map will not decay with time;
so typically, you must clear the influence map before calculating a new spread
of influences:

```
Sandbox.ClearInfluenceMap(sandbox, influenceMapLayer);
```

Visualizing what occurs when clearing the influence map; any cells set to any
value other than zero will be set back to zero.

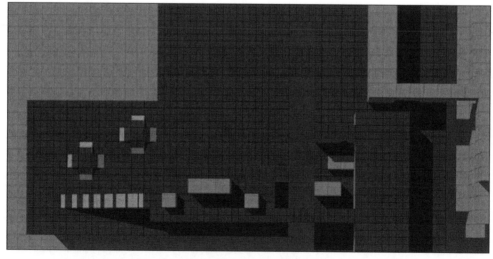

A cleared influence map

Spreading influences

To actually spread the current influences to their maximum possible regions, you can call `Sandbox.SpreadInfluenceMap`. Based on how influences are configured to fall off over distances, the spreading of influences will be calculated automatically. The reason behind spreading influences allows for a quantization of areas where multiple systems can access spatial data with no overhead cost of calculating values:

```
Sandbox.SpreadInfluenceMap(sandbox, influenceMapLayer);
```

The overall algorithm used to calculate influence has a maximum of 20 iterations in case the set falloff of influence is so low that it could propagate past 20 cells in any direction. Additionally, if the propagation of influence drops below the minimum of one percent, the algorithm will terminate early:

```
iterationMax = 20
minPropagation = 0.01
currentPropagation = 1 - falloff

for (iteration; iteration < iterationMax; ++iteration) {
    UpdateInfluenceGrid(grid, layer, inertia, falloff)

    currentPropagation = currentPropagation * (1 - falloff)

    if ( currentPropagation <= minPropagation ) {
        break
    }
}
```

The following screenshot illustrates what happens when you spread existing influences through the influence map:

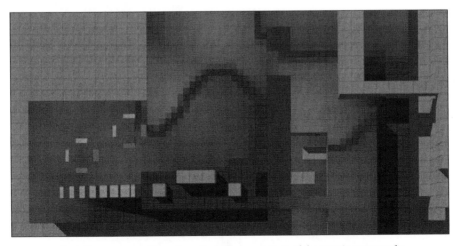

An influence spread based on the influence points of the previous example

Cell inertia

One of the key attributes that determine how influence spreads throughout the influence map is based on the inertia of the current value of each cell, which is essentially the resistance of the cell to not change from its current value. Cell inertia is a means of linearly controlling the amount of influence propagation.

The use of inertia in an influence map is one of many controls used to specify how influences will dissipate within an area. As the use of influence maps varies depending on the type of application, different knobs are useful in order to tune expected outcomes based on how your agents will use the influence map data:

```
Sandbox.SetInertia(sandbox, influenceMapLayer, inertiaValue);
```

Setting the inertia to 1 or 100 percent prevents any influence from propagating to surrounding cells.

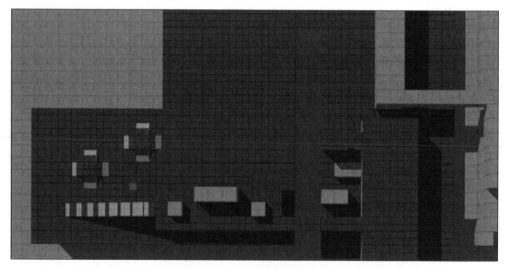

Cell inertia of 1.0, 100 percent inertia

An influence of 0.8 out of 1.0 will allow 20 percent of a cell's influence to propagate while spreading. The inertia of each cell determines the linear drop-off of the cell influence.

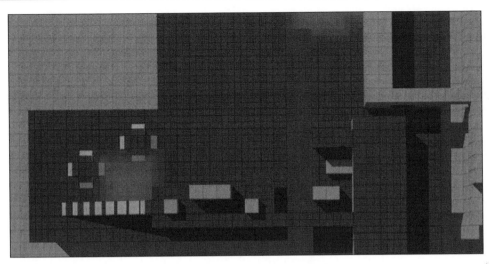

Cell inertia of 0.8 — 80 percent inertia

A Valid inertias range from 0 to 1, representing 0 percent contribution to 100 percent contribution.

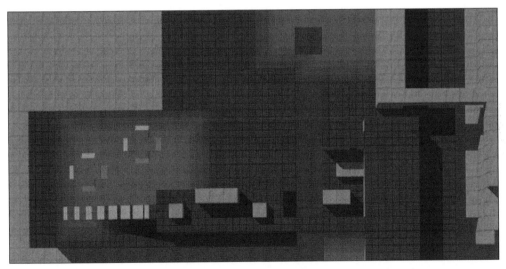

Cell inertia of 0.5 — 50 percent inertia

An inertia of 0 will not consider the current value of the cell when propagating influence, while an inertia of 1 will only consider the current value of the cell. You can think of inertia as the amount of interpolation that is used to calculate the final cell's value.

Tactics

 As influence spreads in iterations, the inertia determines how a single iteration will spread the influence to the next iteration.

Cell falloff

The influence falloff is the second attribute that determines how influence will spread and has the same value range from 0 to 1. When calculating how much influence a given cell should have, the 26 surrounding cells are considered using an exponential falloff based on their distance to the current cell.

Internally, each of the 26 cells is evaluated based on the following function:

```
cellInfluence = powf((1.0f - falloff), distanceToCell) * falloff;
```

The maximum and minimum evaluations of the 26 cells are then summed together to create the final influence that will be used to interpolate toward the cell's current influence based on the inertia:

```
Sandbox.SetFalloff(sandbox, influenceMapLayer, falloffValue);
```

Setting a falloff of 50 percent results in the following type of influence spread, as shown:

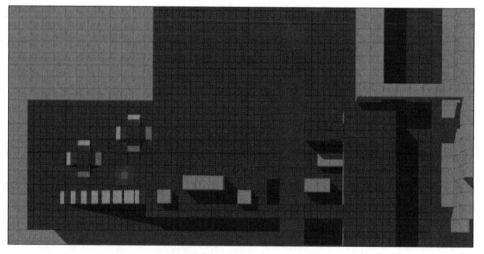

Falloff of 0.5 — 50 percent falloff

With a falloff of only 30 percent, the following is the result of the influence spread:

[302]

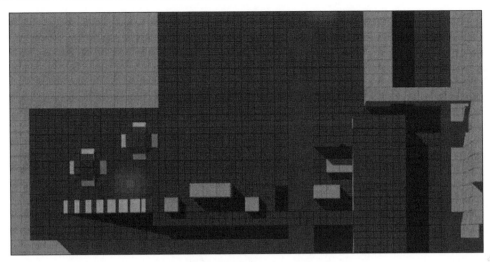

Falloff of 0.3 − 30 percent falloff

As falloff affects influence exponentially while considering all surrounding grid cells, the influence from a single cell forms a circle of influence. Falloff provides us with a nonlinear way of controlling the spread of influence, while inertia is used to control a linear spread of influence.

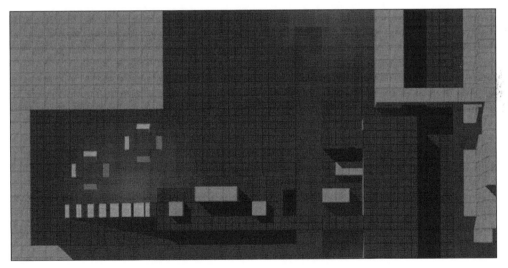

Falloff of 0.1 − 10 percent falloff

Influence map layers

So far, we've talked about different layers of the influence map without showing you how they can be useful. Currently, the red influences used on the influence map are negative values, while the blue influences are positive values. When combined together on a single influence map layer, the boundary where blue meets red becomes the neutral influence of 0. While this can be very useful, we might want to see the total influence of either the negative influences or positive influences.

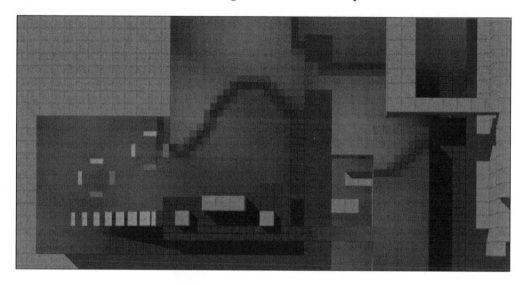

Combined negative and positive influences

Using a separate layer on the influence map, we can see the full negative influence unaffected by positive influences.

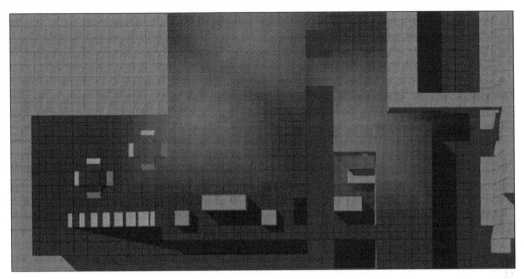

Only negative influences spread to their maximum

We can also do this for the positive influences and use an additional layer that maps only positive values.

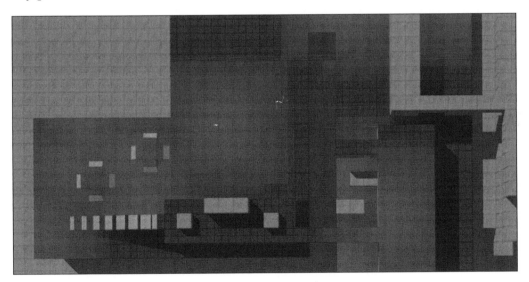

Only positive influences spread to their maximum

Updating the influence map

So far, we've seen how to configure and spread influences in isolation. The actual update loop for the influence map combines each of these steps together. Remember that clearing the influence map is necessary in between spreading influences; otherwise the resulting influences will be oversaturated:

```
function Sandbox_Update(sandbox, deltaTimeInMillis)
    Sandbox.ClearInfluenceMap(sandbox, 0);

    for i=1, 15 do
        Sandbox.SetInfluence(
            sandbox,
            0,
            Sandbox.RandomPoint(sandbox, "default"),
            1);
    end

    Sandbox.SpreadInfluenceMap(sandbox, 0);
end
```

While this simple update scheme will work, it is incredibly CPU-intensive to calculate the entire influence map every sandbox update. Typically, a slightly out of date influence map will not adversely affect tactical decision making based on influence map data. As the sandbox internally updates at a frequency independent of frame rate, we can use an updateInterval time to space out each update of the influence map and keep a deterministic simulation:

```
local lastUpdate = 0;
local updateFrequency = 200;

function Sandbox_Update(sandbox, deltaTimeInMillis)
    lastUpdate = lastUpdate + deltaTimeInMillis;

    if (lastUpdate > updateFrequency) then
        Sandbox.ClearInfluenceMap(sandbox, 0);

        for i=1, 15 do
            Sandbox.SetInfluence(
                sandbox,
                0,
                Sandbox.RandomPoint(sandbox, "default"),
```

```
                    1);
          end

       Sandbox.SpreadInfluenceMap(sandbox, 0);

       lastUpdate = 0;
    end
  end
```

Soldier tactics

In order to manage multiple influence maps, we can create common initialize and update functions that wrap the update interval of different influence maps as well as the initial setup. As the SoldierTactics initialize function will be responsible for the influence map's configuration and construction, we can move the previous initialization code from Sandbox.lua:

SoldierTactics.lua:

```
  SoldierTactics = {};
  SoldierTactics.InfluenceMap = {};

  function SoldierTactics_InitializeTactics(sandbox)
      -- Override the default influence map configuration.
      local influenceMapConfig = {
          CellHeight = 1,
          CellWidth = 2,
          BoundaryMinOffset = Vector.new(0.18, 0, 0.35) };

      -- Create the sandbox influence map.
      Sandbox.CreateInfluenceMap(
          sandbox, "default", influenceMapConfig);

      -- Initialize each layer of the influence map that has
      -- an initialization function.
      for key, value in pairs(SoldierTactics.InfluenceMap) do
          value.initializeFunction(sandbox, value.layer);
      end
  end
```

Updating each influence map layer can be wrapped within the update function that the sandbox will eventually call. Here, we can store layer-specific influence map update intervals as well as the time since the last update:

SoldierTactics.lua:

```
function SoldierTactics_UpdateTactics(sandbox, deltaTimeInMillis)
    -- Update each influence map layer if enough time has passed,
    -- specified by the layer.
    for key, value in pairs(SoldierTactics.InfluenceMap) do
        value.lastUpdate = value.lastUpdate + deltaTimeInMillis;

        if (value.lastUpdate > value.updateFrequency) then
            value.updateFunction(
                sandbox, value.layer, deltaTimeInMillis);
            value.lastUpdate = 0;
        end
    end
end
```

For debugging purposes, we can also encapsulate drawing the influence map with specific color values provided by the SoldierTactics implementation:

SoldierTactics.lua:

```
function SoldierTactics_DrawInfluenceMap(sandbox, layer)
    Sandbox.DrawInfluenceMap(
        sandbox,
        layer,
        { 0, 0, 1, 0.9 },
        { 0, 0, 0, 0.75 },
        { 1, 0, 0, 0.9 });
end
```

Initializing and updating tactics

Once we have a basic initialization and update scheme, we can update our sandbox to incorporate the new systems. From here, any other Lua file can easily access different layers of influence maps for strategic information without worrying about update rates or how each influence layer is populated:

Sandbox.lua:

```
function Sandbox_Initialize(sandbox)

    ...

    SoldierTactics_InitializeTactics(sandbox);
end

function Sandbox_Update(sandbox, deltaTimeInMillis)
    SoldierTactics_UpdateTactics(
        sandbox, deltaTimeInMillis);

    ...

end
```

Scoring team influences

Now, we can create an influence map that represents each of the agent teams that are moving around the sandbox. From the sandbox's point of view, we will be using perfect knowledge of the situation to acquire the locations of each agent; this means that the system will access the immediate location of every agent compared to the perception system that uses last seen locations. While this data is certainly useful for decision making, be aware that this is a form of cheating that agents use to query this influence layer.

Initializing team influences

Initializing a team influence layer consists of setting the desired falloff and inertia of the influence layer. A 20 percent falloff as well as a 50 percent inertia works well based on a cell width of 2 meters for the default sandbox layout.

Finding useful ranges for falloff and inertia requires experimentation and is very application-specific. A 20 percent falloff and 50 percent inertia works well with the default sandbox layout, but different sandbox layouts and influence map configurations will require other values.

> If your cell widths are smaller or larger, you will need to change these values to create similar results.

We'll create a helper function, `InitializeTeamAreas`, to use on each of our team-based influence layers.

`SoldierTactics.lua`:

```lua
local function InitializeTeamAreas(sandbox, layer)
    Sandbox.SetFalloff(sandbox, layer, 0.2);
    Sandbox.SetInertia(sandbox, layer, 0.5);
end
```

Updating team influences

When setting influences based on the agent's position, we need to modify these positions to correctly influence the cell the agent is occupying. As an agent's position is its midpoint, we can clamp that position to the closest point on the navigation mesh in order to affect a valid influence cell.

As the influence map is composed of three-dimensional cells, there are many more empty cells compared to cells that intersect with the navigation mesh. Empty cells don't contribute toward spreading actual influence, so it is important that setting an influence value affect a cell that is overlapping with the navmesh.

> Accidentally setting the influence of an empty cell is a common error when influences might disappear momentarily and reappear as the agent moves around the sandbox. Always clamp positions to the navigation mesh before using them for influence locations.

To update each team layer, we'll influence grid cells based on the closest position on the navmesh our agents are standing on. `team1` will influence the layer negatively, while `team2` will influence the layer positively.

SoldierTactics.lua:

```
local function UpdateTeamAreas(sandbox, layer, deltaTimeInMillis)
    -- Updates influences for both team1 and team2.

    -- Remove all current influences, otherwise influences
    -- compound.
    Sandbox.ClearInfluenceMap(sandbox, layer);

    local agents = Sandbox.GetAgents(sandbox);

    for index = 1, #agents do
        local agent = agents[index];
        if (agent:GetHealth() > 0) then
            -- Clamp each position to the navmesh.
            local position = Sandbox.FindClosestPoint(
                sandbox, "default", agent:GetPosition());

            if (agent:GetTeam() == "team1") then
                -- Team1 marks the influence map with negatives.
                Sandbox.SetInfluence(
                    sandbox, layer, position, -1);
            else
                -- Team2 marks the influence map with positives.
                Sandbox.SetInfluence(sandbox, layer, position, 1);
            end
        end
    end

    Sandbox.SpreadInfluenceMap(sandbox, layer);

    SoldierTactics_DrawInfluenceMap(sandbox, layer);
end
```

Configuring team influences

Now that we have both a team area initialization function as well as the update function, we can configure the rest of the layer's parameters and allow the tactics system to manage everything else. Here, we update this particular layer two times a second, which provides a fast enough refresh to still be relevant:

```
SoldierTactics.InfluenceMap.TeamAreas = {
    initializeFunction = InitializeTeamAreas,
    layer = 0,
```

```
lastUpdate = 0,
-- Update in milliseconds.
updateFrequency = 500,
updateFunction = UpdateTeamAreas };
```

Currently, this influence map shows you how much of the sandbox is controlled by any team at any point in time if we consider the spread of influence based solely on each agent's position. While no decisions are made based on this data yet, it can be used to help maintain strategy areas in the future.

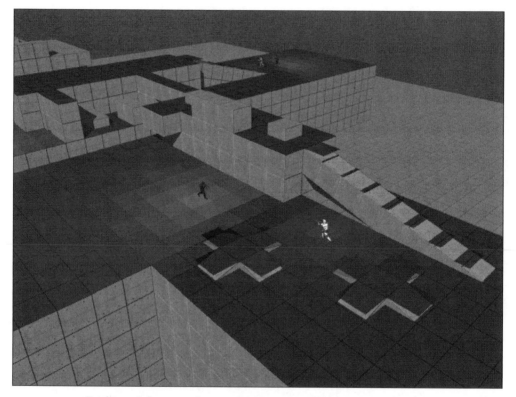

Total team influence, red representing team2, and blue representing team1

Scoring dangerous areas

The next influence map we'll create is scoring dangerous areas from a team-specific perspective. Using the events that the agents are currently sending out for communication, we can set influence values on the information the team rightfully knows about without resorting to scoring calculations:

SoldierTactics.lua:

```
require "AgentSenses"

local eventHandlers = {};
local bulletImpacts = {};
local bulletShots = {};
local deadFriendlies = {};
local seenEnemies = {};
```

Tapping into agent events

Without modifying the existing event system, we can create simple event handlers to store, process, and prune any number of events the agents are already sending. As events are processed differently for the influence map, we store local copies of each event and manage the lifetime of events separately from how agents process them:

SoldierTactics.lua:

```
local function HandleBulletImpactEvent(sandbox, eventType, event)
    table.insert(
        bulletImpacts, { position = event.position, ttl = 1500 });
end

local function HandleBulletShotEvent(sandbox, eventType, event)
    table.insert(
        bulletShots, { position = event.position, ttl = 1500 });
end

local function HandleDeadFriendlySightedEvent(
    sandbox, eventType, event)

    deadFriendlies[event.agent:GetId()] = event;
end

local function HandleEnemySightedEvents(sandbox, eventType, event)
    seenEnemies[event.agent:GetId()] = event;
end

local function HandleEvent(sandbox, sandbox, eventType, event)
    if (eventHandlers[eventType]) then
        eventHandlers[eventType](sandbox, eventType, event);
    end
```

```
    end

    local function PruneEvents(events, deltaTimeInMillis)
        local validEvents = {};

        -- Remove all events when their time-to-live becomes negative.
        for index = 1, #events do
            local event = events[index];
            event.ttl = event.ttl - deltaTimeInMillis;

            if (event.ttl > 0) then
                table.insert(validEvents, event);
            end
        end

        return validEvents;
    end
```

Adding event handlers

As event management isn't specific to a particular influence map layer, we can add
a general way of adding event handlers. We can change the initialization function
to account for registering the sandbox for event callbacks:

SoldierTactics.lua:

```
    function SoldierTactics_InitializeTactics(sandbox)
        -- Create a lookup table of event types to function handlers.
        eventHandlers[AgentCommunications.EventType.BulletImpact] =
            HandleBulletImpactEvent;
        eventHandlers[AgentCommunications.EventType.BulletShot] =
            HandleBulletShotEvent;
        eventHandlers[
            AgentCommunications.EventType.DeadFriendlySighted] =
                HandleDeadFriendlySightedEvent;
        eventHandlers[AgentCommunications.EventType.EnemySighted] =
            HandleEnemySightedEvents;

        -- Register the soldier tactic's system for event callbacks.
        Sandbox.AddEventCallback(sandbox, sandbox, HandleEvent);

        ...

    end
```

Initializing dangerous influences

Initializing the actual influence layer for dangerous areas is identical to the team's influence map layer. A value of 20 percent falloff and 50 percent inertia produces desirable results:

SoldierTactics.lua:

```lua
local function InitializeDangerousAreas(sandbox, layer)
    Sandbox.SetFalloff(sandbox, layer, 0.2);
    Sandbox.SetInertia(sandbox, layer, 0.5);
end
```

Updating dangerous influences

Updating dangerous influences requires processing each of the stored events similar to how agent positions were calculated previously. Always remember to clamp the event location to the navigation mesh regardless of whether the event actually took place at a position that was slightly higher than the influence map cell.

For instance, a bullet impact can take place in an empty influence map cell as the agent's shot might go high and hit a wall. Clamping the location to the navigation mesh will allow these impacts to influence dangerous areas; otherwise they would be discarded from contribution:

SoldierTactics.lua:

```lua
local function UpdateDangerousAreas(
    sandbox, layer, deltaTimeInMillis)

    -- Updates dangerous areas from team2's perspective.

    -- Remove all current influences, otherwise influences
    -- compound.
    Sandbox.ClearInfluenceMap(sandbox, layer);

    -- Remove bullet impact events that are too old.
    bulletImpacts = PruneEvents(bulletImpacts, deltaTimeInMillis);

    -- Add influences for all bullet impact positions.
    for key, value in pairs(bulletImpacts) do
        -- Clamp each event position to the navmesh.
        local position = Sandbox.FindClosestPoint(
            sandbox, "default", value.position);

        Sandbox.SetInfluence(sandbox, layer, position, -1);
```

```
    end

    -- Remove bullet shot events that are too old.
    bulletShots = PruneEvents(bulletShots, deltaTimeInMillis);

    -- Add influences for all bullet shot positions.
    for key, value in pairs(bulletShots) do
        -- Clamp each event position to the navmesh.
        local position = Sandbox.FindClosestPoint(
            sandbox, "default", value.position);

        Sandbox.SetInfluence(sandbox, layer, position, -1);
    end

    -- Add influences for each known dead friendly position.
    for key, value in pairs(deadFriendlies) do
        -- Clamp each position to the navmesh.
        local position = Sandbox.FindClosestPoint(
            sandbox, "default", value.agent:GetPosition());

        -- Add influences for positions belonging to team2.
        if (value.agent:GetTeam() == "team2") then
            Sandbox.SetInfluence(sandbox, layer, position, -1);
        end
    end

    -- Add influences for last seen enemy position.
    for key, value in pairs(seenEnemies) do
        -- Clamp each position to the navmesh.
        local position = Sandbox.FindClosestPoint(
            sandbox, "default", value.seenAt);

        -- Add influences for any positions not belonging to
        -- team2.
        if (value.agent:GetTeam() ~= "team2") then
            Sandbox.SetInfluence(sandbox, layer, position, -1);
        end
    end

    -- Spread each influence point position.
    Sandbox.SpreadInfluenceMap(sandbox, layer);

    -- SoldierTactics_DrawInfluenceMap(sandbox, layer);
end
```

Configuring team influences

With our initialization and updating implemented, we can configure the influence layer for the tactics systems. For this particular influence map, we'll use layer 1 to store information. While no implementation showing danger from the perspective of `team1` is presented, creating an additional influence map layer to store that information simply requires you to create a new `UpdateDangerousAreas` function that replaces the usage of `team2` with `team1`:

`SoldierTactics.lua`:

```
SoldierTactics.InfluenceMap.DangerousAreas = {
    initializeFunction = InitializeDangerousAreas,
    layer = 1,
    lastUpdate = 0,
    updateFrequency = 500,
    updateFunction = UpdateDangerousAreas };
```

The following is the influence map layer showing dangerous areas from the perspective of `team2`:

Danger-influenced areas seen from team2's perspective

Summary

New data sources for spatial analysis open many new opportunities to create interesting behaviors that allow agents to evaluate more than just a fixed perspective of the world. So far, we've created just a few types of influence maps and haven't even begun to access their data that affects the decision making. Even though changing our current agent's logic is left to you, going forward, the examples shown so far already allow for many interesting scenarios to play out.

Looking back, though, we've progressed quite far from the simple moving capsules we created in the earlier chapters. After adding system upon system to the sandbox, we can now manage AI animations, steering-based movements, agent behaviors, decision making, pathfinding, and a myriad of other AI facets. Even though we've only touched on each of the topics lightly, the sandbox is now yours to mold and expand, as you see fit. Every library the sandbox uses, as well as the sandbox itself, is open source. I eagerly look forward to seeing what you're able to create from here. Cheers and best wishes!

Index

target radius 51
knowledge sources
  about 243
  adding, to blackboard 246
  creating 244
  evaluating 244
  evaluating, in blackboard 246
  logic evaluators 243, 244
  removing, from blackboard 246

L

layers, influence map 304, 305
linear blending, animation 87
location, agent
  about 49
  position 49
looping animations 84
Lua
  function binding process 24, 25
Lua, calling C functions 24, 25
Lua, calling C++ functions 24, 25
Lua primitives
  Boolean 21
  function 21
  nil 21
  number 21
  string 21
  table 21
  thread 21
  userdata 21
Lua scripts
  debugging 15
Lua stack 20, 21
Lua virtual machine 20

M

member functions
  assigning 146
meshes
  about 74
  adding, to sandbox 42
  animated mesh, loading 74
  attaching, to bones 75
  weapons, attaching to soldier 76

mesh skeletons 74
metamethod 22
metatable 21
mind body control, approaches
  direct animation control 126
move action
  about 184, 185
  updating 255
move behavior 238
move command 143
movement state 214
moving state 130, 131

N

navigation mesh (navmesh)
  building 163
  configuring 157
  creating 156, 171
  drawing 163
  minimum region area 162, 163
  pathfinding 164
  walkable climb height 160
  walkable height 157, 158
  walkable radius 158, 159
  walkable slope angle 161
new dead enemy body sighted event 269
new dead teammate body sighted event 270
new enemy sighted event 269
non-looping animation
  about 84
  playing 85
normalized time, animation 84

O

Object-Oriented Input System (OIS)
  library 29
obstacle course
  creating 113
  direct control agent, creating 150, 151
  indirect control agent, controlling 152
  indirect control agent, creating 151
  indirect control agent initialization 151
  indirect control agents, spawning 153
  indirect control agent, updating 152

Thank you for buying
Learning Game AI Programming with Lua

About Packt Publishing

Packt, pronounced 'packed', published its first book "*Mastering phpMyAdmin for Effective MySQL Management*" in April 2004 and subsequently continued to specialize in publishing highly focused books on specific technologies and solutions.

Our books and publications share the experiences of your fellow IT professionals in adapting and customizing today's systems, applications, and frameworks. Our solution based books give you the knowledge and power to customize the software and technologies you're using to get the job done. Packt books are more specific and less general than the IT books you have seen in the past. Our unique business model allows us to bring you more focused information, giving you more of what you need to know, and less of what you don't.

Packt is a modern, yet unique publishing company, which focuses on producing quality, cutting-edge books for communities of developers, administrators, and newbies alike. For more information, please visit our website: www.packtpub.com.

About Packt Open Source

In 2010, Packt launched two new brands, Packt Open Source and Packt Enterprise, in order to continue its focus on specialization. This book is part of the Packt Open Source brand, home to books published on software built around Open Source licenses, and offering information to anybody from advanced developers to budding web designers. The Open Source brand also runs Packt's Open Source Royalty Scheme, by which Packt gives a royalty to each Open Source project about whose software a book is sold.

Writing for Packt

We welcome all inquiries from people who are interested in authoring. Book proposals should be sent to author@packtpub.com. If your book idea is still at an early stage and you would like to discuss it first before writing a formal book proposal, contact us; one of our commissioning editors will get in touch with you.

We're not just looking for published authors; if you have strong technical skills but no writing experience, our experienced editors can help you develop a writing career, or simply get some additional reward for your expertise.

LÖVE for Lua Game Programming

ISBN: 978-1-78216-160-8   Paperback: 106 pages

Master the Lua programming language and build exciting strategy-based games in 2D using the LÖVE framework

1. Discover the LÖVE framework and build games easily and efficiently.

2. Learn how to utilize the LÖVE framework's tools to create a 2D game world.

3. A step-by-step approach to learn game development.

CryENGINE Game Programming with C++, C#, and Lua

ISBN: 978-1-84969-590-9   Paperback: 276 pages

Get to grips with the essential tools for developing games with the awesome and powerful CryENGINE

1. Dive into the various CryENGINE subsystems to quickly learn how to master the engine.

2. Create your very own game using C++, C#, or Lua in CryENGINE.

3. Understand the structure and design of the engine.

Please check **www.PacktPub.com** for information on our titles

CryENGINE 3 Game Development Beginner's Guide

ISBN: 978-1-84969-200-7   Paperback: 354 pages

Discover how to use the CryENGINE 3 free SDK, the next-generation, real-time game development tool

1. Begin developing your own games of any scale by learning how to harness the power of the award winning CryENGINE 3 game engine.

2. Build your game worlds in real time with CryENGINE 3 Sandbox as we share insights into some of the tools and features usable right out of the box.

3. Harness your imagination by learning how to create customized content for use within your own custom games through the detailed asset creation examples within the book.

Gideros Mobile Game Development

ISBN: 978-1-84969-670-8   Paperback: 154 pages

A practical guide to develop exciting cross-platform mobile games with Gideros

1. Develop engaging iOS and Android mobile games quickly and efficiently.

2. Build your very first game following practical and easy-to-understand instructions.

3. Full of code examples and descriptions to help you master the basics of mobile game development.

Please check **www.PacktPub.com** for information on our titles

Printed in Great Britain
by Amazon